P9-CLP-961

The New Age Movement in American Culture

Richard Kyle

University Press of America, Inc.
Lanham • New York • London

Copyright © 1995 by
University Press of America,® Inc.
4720 Boston Way
Lanham, Maryland 20706

3 Henrietta Street
London, WC2E 8LU England

Library of Congress Cataloging-in-Publication Data

Kyle, Richard G.
The New Age movement in American culture / Richard Kyle.
p.   cm.
Includes bibliographical references and index.
1. New Age movement--United States--History. 2. United States--
Religion--1960.   I. Title.
BP605.N48K95   1995   299'.93'0973--dc20   95-9574 CIP

ISBN 0-7618-0010-7 (cloth: alk ppr.)
ISBN 0-7618-0011-5 (pbk: alk ppr.)

⊖™ The paper used in this publication meets the minimum
requirements of American National Standard for Information
Sciences—Permanence of Paper for Printed Library Materials,
ANSI Z39.48—1984

In Memory of My Mother, Evelyn M. Kyle

CONTENTS

PREFACE

In recent years there has been an avalanche of publications on the New Age movement and related subjects. Most of these books and articles have come from two sources: New Age writers and evangelical Christians. Moreover, most of these publications, especially those by evangelical Christians, are directed to a popular audience.

These many publications notwithstanding, several important gaps still exist in respect to the coverage of the New Age movement. Because the bulk of these publications are on a popular level, there is a need for serious studies of the New Age, analyzing it as a cultural movement rather than as an evil plot. Moreover, the study of the New Age movement has been largely the domain of theology and the social sciences. The movement has deep historical roots and it has existed long enough to merit an historical approach. While they have not written a history of the New Age, by the early 1990s only the works by Gordon Melton and his colleagues have incorporated considerable historical information.

With the present volume I hope to partially alleviate this need. I make no claims to comprehensiveness. The New Age is too multifaceted and diffuse to be covered in its entirety by this volume. So I have selected what I regard as the most important aspects of the New Age movement and related these to their historical context. Four chapters directly address the roots of New Age. Six chapters emphasize the more contemporary New Age developments. But even in these chapters, the current expressions of the New Age movement are closely linked to their historical roots. Considerable care is given to relating the New Age to the historical and cultural context from which it has developed.

A historical approach to the New Age movement must wrestle with several problems. A work on the New Age often involves a study of phenomena--that is, exceptional and unusual persons, things, or occurrences. History measures and evaluates events in the human or natural dimension, not the supernatural. Thus, any historical study of such phenomena must answer the questions of cause and effect in human or natural terms. The historian, whatever his or her religious convictions may be, does not have license to attribute cause and effect to supernatural forces, whether divine or demonic. Thus this study considers the occult phenomena associated with the New Age as a product of their historical and cultural contexts.

Another problem has to do with value judgments. While no historian is free of personal biases, all of us must resist the temptation to polemicize a work of history. This problem arises in any serious endeavor to write history. But the difficulty is compounded in any attempt to write a history of the New Age. In recent years this movement has evoked much emotion and controversy. For eleven chapters I have taken a more or less detached approach to the New Age. However, because the New Age is a "heated" subject, I believe some evaluation is necessary. Thus, in chapter twelve I have shed my historian's garb and have not only evaluated the New Age but also attempted to predict something about the future of the movement.

The fact that the New Age is a contemporary movement presents another set of problems. Time and distance help to promote a more objective approach to any subject. Also, as with any contemporary subject, one has to decide when to end the coverage. I have selected the early 1990s to end this study. In part, this decision was made because the movement appears to be in a decline--a subject addressed in chapter twelve. At any rate, I have not attempted to record the new developments that this changing movement has taken since the early 1990s.

I hope that this study demonstrates that the New Age movement has its roots in the past and that it is a product of the culture that has spawned it. On one hand, it is a current expression of the old occult tradition. It is an old movement in new clothes. On the other hand, it is the occult blended with two post-World War II developments: the emerging Eastern spirituality in America and new developments in psychology that have a religious expression. Like most alternative religions, the New Age reflects its culture--at times by exaggerating current trends, at times by rejecting these trends and taking an opposite path. At any rate, the New Age movement provides insights into modern American culture.

This story of the New Age movement follows a pattern. There are twelve chapters in this volume. Chapter one introduces the subject--it defines the New Age and describes it. The next four chapters provide the historical background for the New Age movement. Chapter two relates the New Age to the Western occult tradition. The next chapter focuses on precursors of the New Age in America, e.g., Transcendentalism, Spiritualism, New Thought, and Theosophy. Chapter four connects the New Age with modern American culture, demonstrating that it is an outgrowth of individualism, religious pluralism, the counterculture, and the occult revival. The next chapter describes how the New Age expanded in the post-World War II years.

Chapters six to eleven focus on contemporary expressions of the New Age, discussing current topics while relating these subjects to their historical roots. Chapter six sets forth the religious and philosophical assumptions that provide the basis for most New Age beliefs and practices. Building on this worldview, chapters seven and eight focus on issues through which the New Age hopes to transform society, namely, science, education, politics, and economics. Chapters nine and ten pertain more to individual needs--salvation through psychology and health and healing. The next chapter describes the occult practices that have gained popular attention. Chapter twelve evaluates the New Age and attempts to ascertain where the movement is going.

In the formal sense, this book began as a research project during my 1993 sabbatical from Tabor College. Informally, however, this book began several years earlier. My previous book, *The Religious Fringe*, contains one chapter on the New Age movement. Having my interest aroused, I pursued a more extensive study of the New Age movement.

No one writes a book alone. In the time that this book has been in gestation, I have accumulated debts to several individuals and institutions. I hope that my memory is not short in this regard and that I do not inadvertently omit any thanks that are due. Particular thanks must go to Bruce Entz and the library staff at Tabor College for arranging for the acquisition of many books and articles through interlibrary loan. Without these sources, my work would not have been possible. Appreciation must be offered to Tabor College for my 1993 sabbatical, the time when this book was largely written.

In a modified form, some material in this book can be found in one of my previous publications. My book *The Religious Fringe: A History of Alternative Religions in America*, published by InterVarsity Press, is a larger work on the cults and occult. As noted, the New Age movement is rooted in the Western occult tradition and certain developments in contemporary American culture. Thus, in chapters two, three, and four of the present study--which provide the background for the New Age--I have drawn material from my earlier work, *The Religious Fringe*.

Many debts also have been incurred in the production of this book. I especially thank Marcella Mohn for typing the various drafts and for getting the manuscript camera ready. Thanks must go to Beth Impson for editing the manuscript. Appreciation must go to Jody Anderson for her help in setting up the computer formats necessary for producing a camera manuscript. Academic publishing entails many problems. Therefore, thanks must go to the staff of the University Press of America for publishing this book--especially to acquisitions editor Michelle Harris, and production editor Helen Hudson.

My gratitude goes also to some who were involved only indirectly with the writing and publishing process. In particular, I am grateful to my wife, Joyce, and two sons, Bryan and Brent, for sharing me with this project. Without their support and patience, this book would not have been possible.

Chapter 1

THE NEW AGE HAS ARRIVED

During the 1980s the New Age penetrated American culture. For the first time, many Americans were introduced to crystals and channeling. Reincarnation staged a comeback. Shamanism and Native American spirituality captured the imagination of many. People turned from traditional medicine and embraced holistic health practices. Television commercials borrowed New Age concepts and slogans. Cable stations instructed people to dial a 900 number for a psychic reading; Master Card's pitch to "Master the Possibilities" was copied from Werner Erhard's est; and the U.S. Army told recruits to "Be All You Can Be."[1]

The New Age has become a commercial success. The sales of health foods and herbal medicines has increased. Bookstores have reported a billion-dollar business in books that incorporate New Age ideas. The spectrum ranges from self-improvement psychology books such as Scott Peck's *The Road Less Traveled* to overtly occult publications like the *Urantia Book*, allegedly channeled from an extraterrestrial being.[2]

A variety of practices and services are now offered to the public. A few examples include tarot, psychic readings, acupuncture, hypnotherapy, spiritual healing, prayer power, and New Age travel packages. If you want a date with your "soul mate," a New Age dating service can arrange one. If your nerves are on edge, New Age music can soothe you. There are even New Age accountants and attorneys.[3] The New Age has reached the public through a number of products and gadgets. On a short list are the following: Pyramids, esoteric vitamins, singing Tibetan bowls, crystal color wands, charms, talismans, "rebirthing tanks," astrology charts, and fortune-telling devices.[4]

The business and political worlds have embraced New Age ideas and practices. Major corporations employ New Age consultants for management training seminars and employee motivational sessions--all for the purpose of improving productivity. Certain political action groups and think tanks, especially those with an environmental agenda, have been penetrated by New Age beliefs.[5]

Movies and television have made the New Age worldview commonplace. Saturday morning TV cartoons introduce children to magic and the occult. NBC-TV's "ALF" and the movie E.T. have popularized extraterrestrial beings. The Star Wars epics have many occult dimensions, especially the energy field known as the Force. Other films such as *Rosemary's Baby, The Exorcist, Clockwork Orange, Dr. Strangelove, 2001,* and *Cocoon* convey occult and New Age themes.[6]

The New Age has grabbed the attention of the news media. Actress Shirley MacLaine's 1983 book, *Out on a Limb,* captured the headlines, and the 1987 television version of this book was seen by millions. The same year saw thousands of people gather throughout the nation for the Harmonic Convergence, an event that intensified interest in the New Age. As a result of this convergence, in December 1987, *Time* published "New Age Harmonies," the most significant article on the New Age to appear in a news magazine.[7] In 1988 the nation discovered that Nancy Reagan regularly consulted an astrologer and advised her husband to make political decisions at favorable moments. Elizabeth Clare Prophet's prediction about a 1990 nuclear holocaust, which would usher in the New Age, gained global attention.[8]

Much of what I have described to this point is New Age "pop" culture--the faddish element. By the early 1990s some critics say that the New Age is fading. It was a "bleep" on the radar screen closely associated with the consumer culture of the 1980s. These critics are partially correct--many of the popular aspects of the New Age either have leveled off or declined. Moreover, some of the more serious elements have been proven wrong by several academic disciplines.

Also, the New Age has come under serious attack by the evangelical community.

But the New Age must not be shrugged off as the latest religious fashion. The New Agers are probably inaccurate in predicting the advent of the Age of Aquarius. Yet we are currently living on the "hinge of history"--a major turning point in how people live, think, and earn their living, to say nothing about the major changes in global affairs such as the decline of Communism and the collapse of the Soviet Union. Moreover, New Age ideas (which will be addressed later) have penetrated many aspects of society-- environmental science, health care, mental health, religion, psychology, education, business enterprises, plus a vast number of self-help groups. While it may not be called "New Age" in the future, it is this aspect of the New Age that will influence society. Thus, all segments of the American religious community--evangelicals, mainstream Protestants, Catholics, and Eastern orthodoxy--will benefit from acquiring a proper understanding of the New Age movement.

The New Age is Hard to Define

Despite the New Age's visibility and popularity, it is difficult to define. Is it a passing fad? In some ways, yes, but aspects of the New Age have deep roots and will probably be around for quite a while. Is it a religious cult? No, but some cults teach New Age beliefs and might be classified as New Age groups. Is it a conspiracy? Despite what some fundamentalists allege, the New Age is not organized well enough for this. Is it a political movement? No, but it has global political objectives. Is it a business? No, but many entrepreneurs have sold New Age products for billions of dollars.[9] Is it New? Definitely not. The New Age has roots that go way back. Indeed, it may not even be a movement.

The Problem of Boundaries

Why is the New Age so difficult to describe? The New Age movement does not have distinct boundaries. When studying such a shapeless movement, one almost always has difficulties deciding where the phenomenon "begins and ends," writes New Age analyst James Lewis. Unlike a group with distinct boundaries such as the

Hare Krishna movement, one cannot always draw a line between what is New Age and what is not.[10]

In part the problem of boundaries relates to the relationship of the New Age to its predecessor movements. The New Age grew out of a long-standing occult-metaphysical subculture. The New Age borrowed many elements from movements such as Theosophy, Spiritualism, and New Thought, but it did not absorb them. These movements still exist and, while sharing much with the New Age, they have a life of their own. Thus, the New Age is not always distinguished from the movements that preceded it.[11]

The New Age also has a boundary problem with several contemporary Eastern religions and occult-metaphysical movements. While the New Age did not emerge from these groups, it shares much with them. For example, the New Age and feminist spirituality have much in common. Yet they are not identical movements. The same can be said for neopagan witchcraft, feminist astrology, and many Eastern religious groups--they overlap with the New Age but are distinct movements.[12]

Other Identity Problems

Confusion over what the New Age is and what it is not exists because, as Lewis notes, the term has at least two meanings. New Age can be used in the narrow sense, usually in reference to the "phenomena, personalities, and events given prominence by the media (e.g., channeling, Shirley MacLaine, and the Harmonic Convergence)." This is the faddish element of the New Age, a recent development that is downplayed by its serious advocates. The New Age also has a broad meaning, referring to a more serious adherence to the occult-metaphysical tradition and an attempt to transform society.[13]

The fact that many New Agers no longer use the term *New Age* also complicates the identity problem. Before the news media made the New Age a fad, the term was claimed by many people in the occult-metaphysical subculture. Since the media began to focus on the New Age "pop" culture, many serious individuals in this spiritual subculture shy away from the New Age label. In fact, even before all of this media attention, prominent New Age spokesperson David Spangler said that "the phrase an *emerging planetary culture* is replacing the phrase *an emerging new age.* . . ."[14]

In part, this situation helps to explain why a 1991 *New York Times* survey indicated that only 28,000 Americans identified themselves as New Agers. At its narrowest, New Age membership could be limited to those who subscribe to New Age periodicals and list themselves in New Age directories or who attend certain key New Age events. A broad interpretation of interest in the New Age would encompass anyone participating in New Age activities. Surveys indicate that about twenty-five percent of Americans believe in reincarnation. While such a belief is not synonymous with the New Age, it does point to an interest in New Age activities. Gordon Melton, a researcher of fringe religions, estimates that about twenty-five percent of the American population have been involved in some aspect of the New Age movement.[15]

The movement's lack of organization is an obvious obstacle to a clear identity. The New Age is a shadowy cultural and religious movement. It has little structure and institutionalization. It is not a church, a denomination, or any other readily definable religion. As a result, the New Age lacks the framework for a clear identity.

Above all, the New Age is hard to define because it is highly eclectic, including a whole range of fads, rituals, and beliefs. Some individuals endorse some parts, some accept other aspects. Because of this diversity, statements made by representatives of the New Age may not hold for all those associated with it. Furthermore, the New Age movement exalts change and evolution; thus, many of its ideas and practices are constantly changing.

What is the New Age?

David Spangler speaks of four levels of the New Age movement. There is the commercial--a superficial level where the label New Age is used to market products (e.g., New Age toothpaste, New Age shoes, New Age restaurants). Second is the level of glamour and popular culture--the object of much media attention. Spangler describes this level as being "populated with strange and exotic beings, masters, adepts, extraterrestrials; it is a place of psychic powers and occult mysteries, of conspiracies and hidden teachings."[16]

In the third level, Spangler characterizes the New Age as "an image of change." Here he is concerned with the idea of transformation, which is usually expressed as a paradigm shift. Originally referring to a scientific hypothesis, a paradigm has come to mean "the assumptions and values--or worldview--at the heart of a particular culture." The fourth level, which Spangler regards as the essence of the New Age, contains the birth of the sacred and a resacralizing of life on earth.   At this level, transformation is a spiritual process and the "new age is fundamentally a spiritual event."[17] This study will define the New Age as it primarily relates to the serious dimensions of the movement--approximating Spangler's third and fourth levels.

Jonathan Adolph, editor of the *New Age Journal*, also divides the New Age into its serious and fringe dimensions. He places crystals and channeling on the fringe of the movement.   He criticizes the media for focusing on this aspect of the it, insisting that these practices are a side show distracting people from the "down-to-earth matters that lie at the center of new age thinking." As for the serious New Age, Adolph speaks of environmental issues, holistic medicine, natural farming, health foods, the Green movement, biofeedback, relaxation training, and "ethical purchasing"--"buying stock or products on the basis of the company's positive contribution to society. . . ."[18]

A Cultural Shift

The New Age can be seen as a cultural shift with social and religions dimensions. The word *movement* has several meanings. If it is regarded as a series of organized activities working toward an objective, the term *movement* may be too strong a term. The New Age is not this institutionalized and organized. As sociologist Eileen Barker points out, the New Age is "not so much a movement as a number of groups and individuals that have a number of beliefs and orientations that have what philosopher Ludwig Wittgenstein has called a 'family resemblance.'"[19]

If a movement is defined as a tendency or trend, the New Age can be called a movement. Actually, the New Age can best be described as a network, or as New Age critic Elliot Miller puts it, "a metanetwork (network of networks)."[20] New Agers themselves describe their movement as a network. Marilyn Ferguson calls it "a leaderless but powerful network." Jessica Lipnack and Jeffrey Stamps regard the New Age as a series of networks, which they define as informal, loosely knit organizations "spontaneously created by people to address problems and offer possibilities primarily outside of established institutions. "[21] These networks address different issues, some focusing on ecology, peace, holistic health, human potential, or social justice.

The New Age is but the most visible aspect of a larger cultural shift. Gordon Melton regards it as "a social, religious, political and cultural convergence between the new Eastern and mystical religions and the religious disenchantment of many Westerners."[22] The New Age is a meeting of three cultural forces: the Judeo-Christian tradition, Western occult-mysticism, and Eastern religions.

The Western world is currently undergoing a shift in worldview. Ferguson argues that we are in the midst of "the most rapid cultural realignment in history." This great shift is not a "new political, religious, or philosophical system. It is a new mind--the ascendence of a startling worldview . . . ." She sees this historic change as part of a global "paradigm shift"--"a distinctly new way of thinking about old problems."[23] Other New Age sources say that society is now in the midst of a transformation, "a change potentially as sweeping as the Renaissance or the Protestant Reformation."[24]

Critics of the New Age also agree that Western society is experiencing a change in ideology. Over the past few decades, Professor Norman Geisler has observed a "shift from secular humanism to New Age pantheism."[25] The New Age is something of a third way, offering an alternative to atheism or Christian theism. Editor and writer Robert Burrows says that "the world view of the New Age movement has emerged as a viable contender to the secular humanism on one hand, and the Judeo-Christian tradition on the other."[26]

Scholars neither promoting nor criticizing the New Age also see a major shift underway. Intellectually, Christianity has been on the defensive for centuries. But now the assumptions of the modern world are being challenged. Professor Diogenes Allen believes that a massive intellectual revolution is in progress, one "as great as that which marked off the modern world from the Middle Ages." He believes that the intellectual foundations of the modern world forged from the Age of Reason (c. 1600-1780) are "collapsing, and we are entering a postmodern world." Author Os Guinness sees similar trends, but he would prefer to call it "anti-modern" rather than post-modern because nothing definite has replaced modernity.[27]

Viewing the New Age as part of a larger cultural and ideological change fits into historian William McLoughlin's interpretation of

American religion. McLoughlin sees five great periods of ideological transformation in American religion. The old religious consensus, Liberal Protestantism, has declined, and the newest one will emerge perhaps by the 1990s.[28] In an age of religious pluralism, it would seem that the occult-mystical tradition will have some place in any new consensus.

An Eclectic Movement

The convergence of Eastern and Western ideas, a shift in worldview, and a loose network structure have all combined to produce a highly eclectic movement. According to theologian Ted Peters, in simplest terms the New Age movement is a "diversified stream of coalitions, organizations, and individuals all striving to induce a new age of enlightenment and harmony in our society." What unites these groups, says Peters, is their desire to promote a new worldview and to revitalize humanity on the basis of a combination of Eastern religions, humanistic ethics, the human potential movement, and holistic health ideas.[29]

This element of transformation, according to Melton, defines the New Age movement. New Agers have either experienced or are seeking a profound personal transformation from an unacceptable old life to an exciting future. When this personal transformation is experienced, New Agers hold out as their goal the transformation of culture and humanity itself.[30]

The New Age must be seen as an updating of the Western occult tradition. The New Age mind-set, this way of perceiving reality, writes author and New Age critic Brooks Alexander, is "the worldview of occult mysticism, articulated in secular terms." Thus, the New Age movement is an "ancient wisdom, expressed with a modern vocabulary."[31] Alternative religions expert Robert Ellwood regards the New Age as "a contemporary manifestation of a western alternative spirituality (occult-mystical) tradition going back to at least the Greco-Roman world."[32]

A Millennial Movement

The New Age also can be regarded as a millennial movement. As Alexander also notes, "the heart of the New Age message is the conviction that humanity is poised between two epochs, or ages"--the

Piscean Age and the Age of Aquarius. New Agers believe that humanity is "at a crossroads, that the human condition is in a desperate state." But they are not without hope. They believe that humanity is about to make changes that will "transform our society, our behavior, and even our nature." The coming new age is believed to be a new stage in the evolution of humankind, not physically, but psychologically, spiritually, and socially.[33]

In 1967 *Hair* burst like a fireworks display on the American cultural scene. This popular musical production revealed to the "straight" world something largely forgotten for centuries except by the astrologers: one age in world history is ending and another is about to begin. The generation now living will witness the fading of the Piscean Age--mystically, the era of Christianity--and the first glimmerings of the Age of Aquarius.[34]

Astrologers say that about every 2,000 years the sun's spring equinox (day and night of equal lengths) shifts by one Zodiac sign and a new age begins. During the Piscean age, Christianity dominated and occult knowledge was undervalued. But this is changing. The occult worldview holds that science, religion, and art will become one and usher in the Age of Aquarius, a new golden era of peace, brotherhood, and progress--an age where the occult will have a prominent place.[35]

A Quasi Religion

The New Age can be seen as a quasi religion, a cultural trend with religious dimensions. While it may not meet all the criteria for a full fledged religion, it does have a spiritual focus. Journalist Otto Friedrich says that the New Age can be regarded as "a cloudy sort of religion," a quasi religion, "claiming vague connections with both Christianity and the major faiths of the East, . . . plus an occasional dab of pantheism and sorcery." The objectives and methods of the New Age resemble those of other religions, namely, the attempt to answer the believer's spiritual concerns with the hope of an afterlife, or in the case of the New Age, an improved life on earth. Moreover, the New Age requires its followers to believe in things that cannot be proven scientifically--channeling, for example.[36]

Yet the "underlying faith (of the New Age) is a lack of faith" in the orthodoxies of Christianity, rationalism, high technology, routine living, and the political establishment. Somehow, the New Agers believe that there must be "some secret and mysterious shortcut or alternative path to happiness and health."[37]

Two tendencies are evident in the relationships between religion and the world. One inclination is to endeavor to change society and to even compromise with society. The second tendency, a minority opinion, separates from the world and rejects compromise with the dominant culture. Sociologist Roy Wallis places all new religions on a continuum marked by two poles: world-rejecting and world-affirming movements. The first category, the culture rejecting groups, are usually called sects or cults. The New Age should be regarded as a world-affirming movement.[38] While New Agers insist that society has serious problems, they believe that humanity contains within itself "enormous potential power," and optimistically believe that the world can be improved.

Who Joins the New Age?

The New Age is an international phenomenon. It is strong in North America, northern Europe, and Australia. The movement is also visible in southern Europe, Japan, and several countries in Africa. Yet its greatest strength is in North America, especially the United States.[39]

Within the United States, New Age representation varies according to geographical areas. The findings of sociologists Rodney Stark and William Sims Bainbridge indicate that cults are strong in certain regions and weaker in others.[40] While the New Age is not a cult, New Agers apparently gravitate to the same spiritual environment and thus have a similar population distribution. New Age adherents are more likely to live on the Pacific coast, the Rocky Mountain region, and the South Atlantic area, especially Florida. In order to develop networks which facilitate the formation of communities of like-minded people, New Agers tend to live in clusters.[41]

Marilyn Ferguson contends that New Agers come from "all levels of income and education, from the humblest to the highest," and from all ranks of employment.[42] Authorities outside the movement offer a different perspective. The counterculture cults of the 1960s attracted youth who were rebelling against their middle-class parents. On the other hand, as Professor Ruth Tucker points out, the New Age movement "attracts middle-aged people--primarily women" who are in most cases financially able to maintain a comfortable lifestyle and afford New Age activities at the same time. The New Age is a movement in which "respectable people can participate and solicit their friends without embarrassment." New Agers usually possess a better-than-average education and are urban, middle class, upwardly mobile, and not particularly alienated from society.[43]

New Age religion was a response to the social situation of the counterculture. It also has a special relationship with the generation born and reared during this era--the babyboomers (those born between 1946 and 1964). The New Age has drawn its followers heavily from the aging segment of this generation, which has incubated and transmitted New Age religion to other parts of American society.[44]

More women (about 70 percent) than men identify with the New Age movement. Considering that women outnumber men in some other fringe religions (witchcraft, spiritualism, astrology), this comes as no surprise. Why are women more attracted to such fringe religions, in particular the New Age? Sociologist Shoshanah Feher says that the theories addressing this question focus on two themes. First, unlike the mainline religions, the New Age "gives women a voice and in doing so allows them to move out of their traditional roles." Second, New Age ideology "particularly appeals to women." According to this argument, women are attracted to the intuitive, holistic, global, and nurturing aspects of the New Age.[45]

Chapter 2

THE NEW AGE AND THE OCCULT
TRADITION

J. Gordon Melton says that "the New Age Movement can best be dated from 1971." By that time, several components had come together and a self-conscious movement became visible to the public. The New Age now had a periodical, the *East-West Journal*, and several directories and organizational forms to connect its widely dispersed elements. But even in the 1960s, small groups began to call themselves "New Age" and adopt some of the components that would characterize the movement in the 1970s.[1]

But the New Age is not new. It has had many precursors. The modern New Age movement is a current manifestation of the longstanding Western occult-metaphysical tradition. To this tradition the New Age has added two modern components--changes in science, especially psychology; and an infusion of Eastern spirituality.[2]

The roots of the New Age can be seen in previous attempts to find points of convergence between East and West. As philosopher and New Age critic Douglas Groothuis notes, New Age thought is not necessarily "reducible to the classical Eastern religions . . . . " Instead, the injection of neo-pagan, occult and Eastern ideas into traditional "Western religious thought has produced a hybrid spirituality. It takes the essence of Eastern religions but retains some elements of the Western, Judeo-Christian worldview. What results is a mutation."[3]

The oldest aspect of the New Age resides in its relationship to the occult-metaphysical tradition. This tradition has, as Robert Ellwood indicates, flowed "like an underground river through the Christian centuries, breaking into high visibility in the Renaissance occultism of the so-called 'Rosicrucian Enlightenment,' eighteenth-century Freemasonry, and nineteenth-century Spiritualism and Theosophy."[4]

The terms *occult* and *metaphysical* will be used frequently in this study, at times separately and at times in conjunction with each other. Therefore, some definitions are appropriate. Modern definitions of the occult contain several ideas. First, the occult is mysterious, beyond the range of ordinary knowledge. Second, it is secret and disclosed or communicated only to the initiated or select few. Third, the occult pertains to magic, astrology, and other alleged sciences claiming the use or knowledge of the secret, mysterious, or supernatural.[5]

When defined in the context of metaphysical movements, the term *metaphysics* has a different meaning than it does as a division of philosophy. As a movement, it stands for the deeper realities of the universe, the practical application of that absolute Truth of Being in daily affairs. It is a practical type of philosophy considered to be both scientific and religious.[6]

Any direct links between the modern New Age and the occult-metaphysical tradition had to wait until the nineteenth century. Prior to this time, the relationship between the New Age and earlier occult activities was one of a "type"or forerunner, not a direct lineage. But at all times, the larger occult-metaphysical tradition responds and reacts to, and is shaped by, its cultural context. In response to conditions in the modern world, the occult has taken the shape of the New Age movement.

Views of Reality

The New Age represents a shift in worldviews, a convergence of East and West. In very general terms, despite much religious diversity, Western spiritual life can be placed into three categories. These traditions began in the ancient world and represent three views of reality or three worldviews. Many ancient Hebrews and Homeric Greeks assumed that human beings were separate entities, living in the flow of world history above nature, over which they were dominant. Though Christianity contains components from several worldviews, it built on this Hebrew and Greek view of reality. Christian theism, which held center stage in the West from the early Middle Ages, insists that God is personal, infinite and transcendent-- that is, beyond humankind and creation. Theism also contends that humanity was created in God's image and is thus over nature. Science also borrows from this Hebrew and Greek view of reality. Rather than only attaining a mystical unity with nature, humans are to analyze and exploit it.[7]

Western religion has also known two other views of reality, which have shaped the beliefs of many fringe religions, including the New Age movement. The most prominent of these two worldviews is usually called monism. It came to the West through early contacts with India and developed in Platonism and Neoplatonism. This view sees one all-inclusive reality out of which every particular emanates. Human beings are at one with the universe. They have a divine essence and are part of nature. A person's task is thus to attain an expansion of consciousness until he or she becomes mentally one with the whole cosmos.[8]

A smaller minority stream is religious or ethical dualism. Dualism conceives of two eternal realities, spirit and matter--the one good, the other evil. The cosmos becomes a battleground for these forces of good and evil. Dualism can be traced to the ancient Persian religion, Zoroastrianism, through Gnosticism, Manichaenism, and Catharism. Christianity accepts a modified dualism by recognizing a powerful and evil Satan. But this is not the usual dualism, for Satan is a created entity with only limited authority.[9]

Fringe religions can be traced to all three views of reality--even Christian theism. Yet, out of the two minority streams of monism and dualism have come the worldviews of many occult-metaphysical groups. These options have never been absent in Western history and represent alternative reality traditions. While dualism is not dead in the modern world, the fusion of Western occult monism with that of the `Eastern religions has produced a strong minority force in modern America--one that can contend with Christian theism.[10] Most New Agers embrace a monistic view of reality. Yet the New Age is an aspect of the "New Consciousness" that draws from several worldviews--monism, dualism, pantheism, and animism.

Two other worldviews directly relate to the New Age--pantheism and animism. Pantheism comes from the Greek words *pan* and *theos* and means "everything is God." Pantheism takes a monistic view of reality, and identifies God and nature with each other. It can be regarded as a variation of monism and underpins much of the New Age thinking on ecology. Animism is the notion that all things in the universe are endowed with a life force, mind or soul. It is the general outlook on life undergirding primitive religions. Animism commonly appears in the occult and spiritism, thus providing the basis for some New Age occult practices such as channeling.[11]

The New Age also has an indirect relationship to another view of reality--natural humanism. The roots of humanism in general go back to the Greco-Roman and Judeo-Christian traditions. The natural (sometimes called scientific or secular) aspect is a product of the eighteenth century Enlightenment. Natural humanism rejects the notion of a supernatural worldview and that God is the source of creation and the unfolding of human history. Instead, natural humanism looks to natural causes as the origin of all developments. Also, the focus of natural humanism is on humanity and human concerns--not God. The New Age rejects the secularism of the modern world, but not its humanism. Natural humanism has diminished the strength of Christian theism in the modern world-- leaving something of a spiritual void. The New Age can be seen as a spiritual force rushing in to fill the void left by the decline of Christian theism. Yet, it is humanistic in that it places human concerns at the center of its agenda.[12]

The Hellenistic Era

The Hellenistic world was characterized by the convergence of Eastern and Western culture--even more than the modern world. As a cultural movement, Hellenism ranges from about 300 B.C. to 200 A.D. Hellenistic culture grew out of the confrontation of Greek philosophy with Egyptian and Near Eastern life and represents a new culture, one that was syncretistic, mystical, and cosmopolitan. The culture of the Hellenistic period bore much resemblance to that of modern civilization. Like the Hellenistic civilization, the last half of the twentieth century is a period in which a struggle with the hectic pace of life and an increased cultural pluralism has thrown up a radical reaction in the form of new religious movements.[13]

During the Hellenistic era, interest in religion grew considerably. The eastern and central Mediterranean in the first and second centuries after Christ swarmed with an infinite multitude of religious ideas, all attempting to propagate themselves. Nearly every religious group was unstable and fissiparous, splitting up and reassembling in new forms.[14]

According to author Paul Johnson, Rome was "in some respects a liberal empire." In particular, Rome displayed tolerance "towards the two great philosophical and religious cultures which it confronted in the central and eastern Mediterranean: Hellenism and Judaism." Rome insisted on the observance of a marginal civic creed, but everyone could practice a second religion if they chose. This freedom plus the fermenting of ideas produced an atmosphere of religious pluralism, something that had to wait until the twentieth century to be duplicated in the West. By the time of Christ there existed hundreds of cults, perhaps even thousands of sub-cults. The range of choices was tremendous.[15]

This diversity helped to produce several entities that have had an indirect relationship to fringe religions in modern America, including the New Age movement. Neoplatonism has influenced occult-metaphysical groups throughout history. Plotinus (204-270 A.D.) and his followers offered a new interpretation of Platonic philosophy. According to Plotinus, the universe consists of a series of emanations from the One, and that humanity's goal is to return to the One by a mystical experience. In such an experience the individual is to transcend the confines established by matter and the intervening mental emanations, that is, the archetypes and the world soul.[16]

Another important religious phenomenon closely connected with the development of dynamic new religious movements through history is shamanism. Indeed, it is one of the leading fads in the modern New Age movement. Shamans are mediumistic persons, often of an unstable type, who are selected as religious leaders solely because of their peculiar gifts, especially curing or causing disease and communicating with the spirit world. In several ways, the brilliance of the primitive shaman is revived in those individuals called masters, magi, adepts, magicians, mediums, and other names, who have been so important to the occult-metaphysical tradition.[17]

Many of the New Age developments are a throwback to the wisdom and worldview of the ancient world. Connected with such a trend is Hermeticism, the name for much of the "ancient wisdom" type of teaching and magic. The name comes from the *Book of Hermes Trismegistus*, written in Alexandria in the third or fourth century after Christ. Hermeticism has often been used in both the ancient world and in the present day to broadly cover an ill-defined mass of Gnostic and Neoplatonic philosophy, astrology, and magic derived from the Hellenistic and Judaic milieu of Alexandria. Many contemporary occultists regard Hermeticism as the oldest accessible human wisdom.[18]

Also prominent in the ancient Near East was astrology, one of the oldest and most popular occult activities. It began in the dim recesses of history, by at least 3000 B.C. Astronomy is the study of the heavenly bodies, while astrology is the study of their influence on earth and on human beings.[19] Astrology is alive and well in the modern world and is a component of the New Age movement.

Gnosticism

Important in both the ancient and the modern worlds is Gnosticism. It presented a major threat to the early church. It has penetrated modern society in many ways and its alternative view of reality has parented several modern cults.[20] Though superficially Christian and often regarded as a Christian heresy, Gnosticism has origins independent of Christianity and at heart contains Judaism-Platonism combinations.[21]

Historian Edwin Yamauchi speaks of Gnosticism as a version of dualism, setting "a transcendent God over against an ignorant creator (who is often a caricature of the God of the Old Testament)." All Gnostics regarded the material world as evil. However, encapsuled in the bodies of certain 'spiritual' individuals destined for salvation are sparks of divinity. God therefore sends a "redeemer who brings them salvation in the form of secret knowledge (*gnosis*) of themselves, their origin and their destiny." After being awakened, "the 'spirituals' escape from the prison of their bodies at death" and are united with God.[22]

Many Gnostic ideas have lived on in modified forms, influencing important aspects of the occult-metaphysical tradition through history. In fact, more scholars have compared the New Age with Gnosticism than with any other religion of antiquity. Indeed, some individuals believe that the Gnostic type has permeated American religion and culture.

Professor Harold Bloom sees much of American religion, including the New Age, as a variation of Gnosticism. In his view, the emphasis on knowing God in a personal way has led many Americans to a belief in individual divinity and the idea that something inside of them is in contact with God.[23] Clergyman Philip Lee points to a number of Gnostic tendencies in American religion: the promise of salvation by knowledge, not faith; a stress upon the secret or hidden as against the open; elitism in respect to faith; religious syncretism; and a concentration upon radical individualism. But he does say that Gnosticism has no continuous line through history. Thus, the connection between ancient and modern Gnosticism is not historical but is something of a Gnostic "type."[24]

Historian Christopher Lasch regards aspects of modern science as Gnostic: "its equation of salvation with knowledge . . ., its belief that knowledge will enable men to triumph over the material world . . ., and above all in its assumption that saving knowledge must remain esoteric, accessible only to a spiritual or intellectual elite."[25] Professor Carl Raschke takes a similar approach, contending that "modern gnosticism encompasses not only . . . underground religious communities," but also those "taking a rear-guard action against the 'progress' of the modern industrial world. They are in revolt against the course of modern history and seek salvation within the sphere of the timeless."[26]

Sociologist Andrew Greeley detects the Gnostic theme of a new age running the gamut of history, from the fourteenth century mystic Joachim of Flora (the age of the Holy Spirit) to modern figures such as Auguste Comte (the age of sociology) and Karl Marx (the classless society). He concludes that modern occult groups abound with secret knowledge and are a form of Gnosticism.[27]

New Age critics draw parallels between the New Age and Gnosticism. Professor Peter Jones sees the New Age as a revival of ancient Gnosticism. He points to Gnostic elements in the following New Age tenets: pantheistic ecology, the female principle in salvation, the identification of ignorance as the basic human problem, and God as an impersonal and unknowable being.[28] In a less strident critique of Gnosticism, Ted Peters boils New Age beliefs down to eight basic tenets, which he regards as variants of Gnosticism. Gnosis, he argues, penetrates the New Age views on holism, the higher self, human potentiality, reincarnation, transformation, knowledge, and even Jesus Christ.[29]

Even individuals with New Age connections relate the New Age to a form of Neognosticism. Transformation, which is the New Age equivalent of salvation, comes through gnosis or knowledge. Jacob Needleman believes that the modern mind is asleep and needs to be awakened by a "salvational knowledge that actually brings about spiritual change in the midst of the material world . . . ."[30] Marilyn Ferguson also believes that an awakening is necessary and that it must come by a direct knowledge, which comes only through "a quasi-mystical experience."[31]

The Middle Ages

The Hellenistic era saw such religious diversity that no one religion could hope to prevail. During the Middle Ages, the opposite was true. The Catholic Church dominated--although not to the extent commonly believed.[32] Heretics, dissenters, and the sect and cult groups always existed, even flourished at times, and occasionally threatened to infest the church.

Cracks in religious uniformity existed throughout the entire Middle Ages, but for different reasons and in varying amounts. During the early Middle Ages (ca. 400-1050), the church did not have a firm hold on society. Divisions existed within the church, and paganism and Arianism persisted.[33] During the high Middle Ages (ca. 1050-1350), the church reached the peak of its strength, establishing something of a total Christian society where most people consented to the beliefs of the church. From this point on, dissent became open, developing in part as a protest to the power and corruptions of the church.[34]

Sect and cult groups often arise during periods of intense religious consciousness. The high Middle Ages was such a time: it experienced an outburst of religious vitality. The late Middle Ages (ca. 1350-1500) witnessed great religious dissatisfaction, prompting many to seek alternatives outside the church. The church had been humiliated by the secular powers and racked by schism and was thus in decline. The upheavals and horrors of the time--plagues, famines, and a sustained economic decline--created a climate suitable for new and strange religious movements.[35]

Gnostic elements can be seen in Catharism, called Albigensianism in southern France. This radical dissent movement that developed in the mid-twelfth century was a form of Eastern dualism. Like the

Zoroastrians, Gnostics, and Manicheans before them, the Catharists believed that all matter was created by an evil principle and that therefore the flesh should be thoroughly mortified. They claimed to be in possession of a new, secret understanding of Christianity.[36]

During the Middle Ages there appeared a number of dissenters who taught a combination of intellectual and mystical doctrines. Best known was Joachim of Flora (d. 1201), a millennarian whom some modern New Age adherents regard as one of their forerunners. His complicated metaphysics included the belief that there were three ages of the world: the age of God the Father, the age of the Son, in which Joachim lived, and the age of the Holy Spirit, which was shortly to begin. In the third age, humanity, filled with the Spirit, would create a kingdom of God on earth.[37]

An important mystical theorist whose views bore some resemblance to those of the contemporary occult tradition and Eastern spirituality was the German Dominican, Meister Eckhart (ca. 1260-1327). He taught that there existed a power or "spark," deep within every human soul, which was really the dwelling place of God. By renouncing all sense of selfhood, one could retreat into one's innermost being and then find divinity.[38]

A major fringe religion in the Middle Ages, one that exists today, was witchcraft. The European witchcraft phenomena relates to pagan survival and Christian heresy, which was persecuted as a form of diabolism.[39] While the New Age movement and modern witchcraft are not the same, they do have much in common. Modern witchcraft, called Neopaganism, relates to early pagan witchcraft, which focused on sorcery and folklore.

The Kabbalah, a mystical expression of Judaism, has maintained a presence in the occult tradition since the Middle Ages and contains elements found in the New Age. Kabbalah's distinctive is a complicated principle for finding hidden or spiritual meanings in the Hebrew Bible. Such a method allows for new interpretations, many with occult meanings. The Kabbalah pictures God as being above all existence. Through a series of emanations, the world was created. Good deeds by pious Jews supposedly affect the emanations, ultimately influencing God in behalf of humanity. Kabbalah also includes a belief in reincarnation and the notion that evil is only the negation of good.[40]

Renaissance and Reformation Europe

Together the Renaissance and Reformation movements (ca. 1400-1650) represent a period of transition from the Middle Ages to the modern world. In respect to religious toleration and diversity, these years are paradoxical. Extreme bigotry and intolerance existed well into seventeenth century, serving as a force to repress minority religions.[41]   Yet the fragmentation of Christendom by the Reformation, the bitter wars over religion, the overseas expansion, economic growth and stagnation, the change in world-order, new intellectual developments, and a changing worldview all worked together to further the development of religious toleration and the growth of fringe religions. During the Renaissance-Reformation period, the fringe religions included a confusing variety of Christian sect groups, religious bodies outside the norm of orthodoxy though marginally related to Christianity, a resurgence of the occult, and the peak of the witchcraft craze. Of these three categories, shades of the New Age can be detected in some of the occult bodies.

The Renaissance represents a rebirth of the culture and learning of antiquity, including many aspects of the occult. As the Renaissance dawned, occultism, alchemy, Neoplatonism, astrology, and the like flourished in Europe as never before or since. The individuals who took up these things were among the most independent and intelligent of the age. For them, occult activities were not mindless superstition, but a plunge into the unconscious in order to prepare humanity for a leap into the modern world.[42] For many occultists, Neoplatonism contained eternal laws upon which science is based: astrology became astronomy, chemistry can be traced to alchemy, and there is a possible connection between Kabbalah and psychoanalysis. To these occultists, such occult ideas were not outdated but represent a deeper wisdom that the world experiences only once every few centuries.[43] Some would claim that the late twentieth century is one of these times.

Most Renaissance occult movements were Hellenistic holdovers. Yet, one new occult movement did emerge on the scene. The obscure roots of Rosicrucianism can be traced back to at least the seventeenth century. Rosicrucianism is active in the twentieth century and by most standards can be regarded as cultic. It has much in common with Unity, Christian Science, Theosophy, and the Mighty I AM. Secret societies have existed in many ages and countries. But in Western culture, the modern idea of the secret society can be tracked to late sixteenth and early seventeenth century Rosicrucianism, which had a definite relationship with esoteric, Gnostic alchemy. Moreover, Rosicrucianism has close ties to Freemasonry, whose French and Scottish rites both give evidence of the Rose-Cross.[44]

The Early Modern World

The years from the end of the Thirty Years' War to the constitutional settlement in America and the French Revolution in Europe represent a lull in respect to the birth of new religions. Yet, this century and a half was by no means devoid of significant religious activity. In fact, these years saw several landmark developments that would change forever the face of religion in the West. These unfoldings would also provide a backdrop for the development of the modern occult-metaphysical tradition.

In respect to intellectual developments, by the middle of the seventeenth century, Europe stood at the gateway to the modern world. The years from 1650 to 1800 saw increased scientific developments, an intellectual revolution, and a gradual change in worldview from one that was predominantely medieval to one which is essentially modern. The supernatural, especially its magical components--astrology, healing, prophecies, alchemy, witchcraft, ghosts, omens, and aspects of church ritual--were regarded as practical. They met specific human needs. But various developments robbed the old magical systems of their capacity to satisfy the educated elite. As a consequence, the importance of the supernatural was greatly reduced. The adjustment of religion to this unfolding helped to produce new religious movements, including some that have provided a backdrop for the New Age movement.[45]

The early modern period represented a time of transition for the occult. During much of Western history, the occult was in touch with the major strands of European culture. But as Catherine Albanese notes, this was to change. After the Enlightenment, the new science radically revised "the way educated people viewed the world." As science grew in status, it not only challenged the worldview of traditional Christianity, but occultism became more and more "a secret knowledge," and even "a rejected knowledge."[46]

Traditionally, the occult had been "an assorted mixture of elements" taken from paganism and blended with "insights from Judaism and Christianity." Such a mixture now was regarded as superstition. Therefore, by the nineteenth century, to maintain such beliefs was to "run counter" to the main trend of Western culture. Occultists were often estranged people, alienated from the ordinary religion of the culture by their beliefs and practices.[47]

Albanese points out two types of the occult. First is the "natural and traditional occultism," the simple folk beliefs which supported individuals as they tried to cope with everyday tasks. A partial list would include planting crops by the zodiac, using anatomical charts, and observing rules about breaking mirrors and avoiding black cats. Second are the learned and scholarly aspects of occultism, often associated with serious astrology, alchemy, high magic, numerology, and even some witchcraft beliefs. These elements of the occult declined more rapidly and thoroughly than did the simple folk beliefs.[48]

On the other hand, a new occultism, with scholarly and educated elements, developed in the nineteenth century. This occultism was metaphysical and concerned more with spiritual than material things as sources of reality. This metaphysical occult had its roots in the eighteenth century and began to develop as the older, intellectual occult went into decline.[49]

In eighteenth-century Europe, there appeared entities connected with the occult-metaphysical tradition that have a clear continuity with contemporary American occultism and have helped to shape the New Age movement. Some examples of these groups or movements include Rosicrucianism, Freemasonry, Swedenborgianism, and Mesmerism. The eighteenth century was a time of increasing polarization between reason and fascination, belief and feeling. There was, therefore, a great interest in secret societies.[50]

One such society, Freemasonry, developed in eighteenth century England. This new endeavor bore the stamp of a combination of rational science, Rosicrucian occultism, and biblical literalism. Its lodges were penetrated by occultists, who instituted ceremonies based on occult symbolism, particularly that of alchemy and the Kabbalah.[51] English Masonry combined grades or levels. Eventually there arose the legend of the "Secret Chiefs." This story, which always lives behind occult Masonry, says that there are "Hidden Chiefs" or "Unknown Superiors" who held themselves aloof from the daily affairs of the fraternity, but were themselves in possession of ultimate secrets. Such a notion was to become common occult doctrine. For example, the Theosophical Masters were derived from the same theory.[52]

A clear lineage for the modern occult can be traced to Emanuel Swedenborg (1688-1772). In fact, Swedenborg has been regarded as perhaps the most influential eighteenth century individual in respect to the occult. He is considered as the major link between the old medieval alchemist or Rosicrucian secretive activity and the Spiritualist seance in America or the modern Theosophical lecture. After his death, his teachings produced the Church of the New Jerusalem, which has survived into the twentieth century, and a Swedenborgian Society. Except for direct Eastern imports, the modern occult and metaphysical movements owe perhaps their greatest debt to him.[53]

Swedenborg had a vision which he said had carried him into the spiritual world, where he had been able to see eternal truths. He began to write voluminously, even believing that his writings were the dawn of a new age in the history of the world and of religion. In fact, he asserted that what had occurred when he received his revelations was actually what the Bible meant in its references to the second coming of Christ. As expected, his ideas were not well received by most of his contempories.[54]

Yet, as a precursor of modern occult thought, he contributed much to future generations. He taught the Spiritualist notion of communication with persons on the other side, the Kabbalist and Gnostic belief in pre- and post-existence in a spiritual state, a Gnostic idea of important events occurring in an invisible world known only to those being inducted into an occult society, and a monistic concept of God. Most important, Swedenborg declared that the Second Coming of Christ happened spiritually in 1757. His focus on this invisible end of an age can be seen as a forerunner of the modern Aquarian Age and New Age ideas.[55]

Swedenborg received many of these ideas in ways that bore resemblance to early Gnostic techniques, writes Kay Alexander. He claimed to have discovered an inner esoteric meaning of the Bible through "direct revelations from the angels" and to have taken "out-of-body journeys to heaven and hell."[56]

Several other eighteenth-century figures pointed toward the modern occult. One of the better known was the Austrian doctor

Franz Antoine Mesmer (1733-1815). He engaged in what scientists label as pseudo-science. While the word *mesmerism* is derived from his name, Mesmer did not personally practice the induced trance. Rather, he claimed to have discovered a universal fluid which he called animal magnetism, supposedly a health-giving matter transported by iron rods from a tank to patients seated near by. What modern people call the power of suggestion was in operation. Background music created a hypnotic atmosphere. Patients often went into strange convulsions and finally lethargy. From further developments of such a process by Mesmer's followers, modern hypnotism was born.[57]

Chapter 3

PRECURSORS OF THE NEW AGE IN AMERICA

The contemporary New Age movement is the occult-metaphysical tradition modified by Eastern religions and modern psychology. As noted, the occult has a long history, flowing like an underground stream through western history. In America from about 1800 to 1950, some new ingredients were added to the occult tradition-- Eastern religions and psychology. The full infusion of these new components came after World War II, enabling the New Age to take off. Yet during the preceding century and a half, these three elements--the occult, Eastern religions, and psychology--began to come together, thus preparing the way for the New Age.

Nineteenth-Century America

The early predecessors of the New Age movement thrived in a context of religious change. Nineteenth century America, particularly during the decades of the 1830s and 1840s, witnessed an explosion of new religious movements not seen since the sixteenth century. The nineteenth century was one of extraordinary religious diversity that continued into the twentieth. Such pluralism began in the colonial period; it surged in the first half of the nineteenth century and increased during the last half of that century and the first half of the twentieth.[1]

Such tumultuous religious developments occurred in the context of rapid social and economic change. As major demographic shifts, westward expansion, rapid urbanization, unprecedented advances in transportation and communication, and industrial development transformed American society, the structure of most people's lives--residence, work place, family life, and religion--changed dramatically. Political developments, especially increased democratization and a pronounced nationalism, affected many individuals. A dramatic increase in immigration complicated the already diverse social and religious picture. Ideas drawn from sources as eclectic as the Enlightenment, Romanticism, science, revivalism, millennialism, perfectionism, fundamentalism, theological liberalism, and the new academic disciplines--geology, sociology, and psychology--often worked in diverse directions, but their total impact must be regarded as significant.[2]

The torrential flood of new religions that swept across America included groups of all types: Christian deviations, occult-metaphysical groups, communal bodies, Eastern religions, and Black religions. Of these religious types, only certain occult-metaphysical types had a direct connection with the New Age movement, namely, Transcendentalism, Spiritualism, Theosophy, New Thought, and Christian Science. In fact, the direct line of influence could be pushed back a step further to eighteenth century Europe and Swedenborgianism and Mesmerism. Until after World War II, the Eastern religions and psychology played only an indirect role in shaping the emerging New Age--that of penetrating the occult-metaphysical groups.

Transcendentalism

The New Age is a syncretistic movement, incorporating many elements, some from the early nineteenth century. Much of the inspiration for the American occult-metaphysical tradition was drawn from Europe. The occult philosophy that flourished in eighteenth and nineteenth century Europe--Swedenborgianism, Mesmerism, Neoplatonism, quasi-Gnosticism, Kabbalism, astrology, and Hermeticism--all contributed to the development of the occult in America. Another pillar of the occult originated in America--

Transcendentalism.[3]   Transcendentalism   with   its   facets   of
Neoplatonism, Swedenborgianism, and Eastern philosophy laid the
foundation for a broad range of metaphysical movements. The spirit
of freedom now abounding in nineteenth-century America expressed
itself in the individualism of the new religious movements, which
included the occult and metaphysical groups.[4]

Transcendentalism is difficult to define. Without a definite creed,
it was at once a faith, a mystical religion, a philosophy, and an ethical
way of life. In general, it emphasized the spiritual over the material.[5]
Its leader was Ralph Waldo Emerson (1803-1882), who, as Gordon
Melton   writes,   "successfully   integrated   the   Eastern   idealistic
metaphysics   with   more   popular   American   values   such   as
individualism, personal responsibility, and the drive to get ahead in
life." Transcendentalism was the first American religion with a
substantial infusion of Asiatic ideas. Yet this Eastern spirituality
came exclusively from literary sources, not direct contacts with
people from the Far East.[6]

Transcendentalism can also be seen as a form of pagan nature
mysticism. As historian Catherine Albanese notes, Emerson's book,
called *Nature*, gave "the Transcendental movement its gospel." The
Transcendentalists looked to nature to teach them spiritual truths.
By a study of nature they believed they could "uncover the secrets of
their inner selves and a corresponding knowledge of divine things."
From Transcendentalism came a strong sense of self-reliance and a
mystical self, both characteristics of the New Age.[7]

A question that concerned most Transcendentalists was the
meaning of the Oversoul. Their interest in the great World Soul of
the Neoplatonists, to which individuals were bound, took them in an
unusual direction. The Transcendentalists traveled down the road
toward saving knowledge, a journey in which each person must turn
within and develop the qualities necessary for harmony with self and
the   universe.[8]   In   developing   this   new   teaching,   the
Transcendentalists, like many with occult and metaphysical interests,
were eclectic. According to Albanese, "they mixed together elements
from Oriental sources, from Neoplatonic philosophy, from European
Romantic writers, and from the metaphysical system of Emanuel
Swedenborg."[9]

The influence of Transcendentalism on groups and individuals
outside the religious mainstream in America has been significant. It
paved the way for several nineteenth-century occult and metaphysical

movements such as New Thought and Christian Science. Less obvious but of significance, Transcendentalism represents the first serious attempt in American history to retain the spiritual experience of the Christian faith without the substance of its belief. Transcendentalism claimed a basic innocence for humankind, substituted a direct intuition of God or truth for any form of revelation, and foresaw a future of indefinite but certain glory for humanity--views embraced by the modern New Age. The Transcendentalists also encouraged the rise of many romantic notions that have become an essential part of the American experience over the last century and a half.[10]

Spiritualism

Aside from Theosophy, the modern New Age movement has probably drawn its greatest inspiration from Spiritualism. Channeling, the most distinctive practice of the New Age during the 1980s, can be seen as a type of Spiritualism. Spiritualism or spiritism refers to the practice in which the living attempt to communicate with the spirits of the dead or departed extra-human intelligences, usually through a human medium.[11]

Since ancient times people in many cultures have attempted to communicate with the dead. This practice has run the course of Western civilization. Over time, Spiritualism acquired a modern flavor, with the first seance--people sitting with a medium through whom the spirits reveal themselves--occurring by at least the eighteenth century.[12]

Much of the impulse for modern Spiritualism, including the prototype for the modern seance, can be traced to Franz Mesmer. At his seances people sat around a tub holding both the hand of the person next to them and a rod extending from the tub. They often went into trance states, resembling those in which contact with spirits was likely to occur.[13]

Another European source for Spiritualism came from Emanuel Swedenborg. Swedenborg claimed the ability to contact the spirits of dead humans. Also, many of the spirit messages found in American seances were based on Swedenborg's teachings concerning a hierarchical series of spiritual spheres surrounding the earth. In fact, Spiritualism "proved to be the single most important vehicle for the popularization of Swedenborgianism in America," writes historian R. Laurence Moore.[14]

In America Spiritualism had a number of forerunners. Spiritualism drew much from the Transcendentalists, including their attitude toward the supernatural.[15] Mesmerism influenced Andrew Jackson Davis (1826-1910), whose writings gave Spiritualism its theoretical basis. Davis believed that spirits existed on several planes, some closer and others farther from earth. To Davis, contact with spirits close to earth seemed a realistic possibility. Davis said he had contacts with the spirits of Swedenborg and Galen, a famous doctor from antiquity.[16] In their ecstatic dances, the Shakers claimed to have been visited by spirit beings from the world beyond time.[17]

Modern Spiritualism can be dated to the rappings heard by the Fox sisters in Hydesville, New York, in 1848. The 1850s witnessed a virtual explosion of interest in Spiritualism with hundreds of thousands of Americans dabbling in it in various ways. After a decline during the Civil War, the desire to communicate with those killed in the war fostered a new surge of Spiritualism, which lasted until the 1870s.[18] Another growth period occurred after World War I, also fueled by the desire to contact loved ones killed during the war.[19]

Robert Ellwood notes many parallels between nineteenth-century Spiritualism and the modern New Age movement. The contemporary explosion of spiritism goes by the name of channeling. While channeling and Spiritualism are not identical, both attempt to place the living in contact with the spirits of the deceased. Both early Spiritualism and the New Age relied on the mass media and the desire for spiritual experimentation to promote their movement. Nineteenth century Spiritualism and the New Age both regarded themselves as the "progressive" movements for their time. Spiritualism championed the abolition of slavery, temperance, women's rights, and more. The New Age advocates environmentalism, political reform, feminism, an overhaul of the health care system, and more.[20] As a result, both movements were optimistic. The Spiritualists had faith in the growing democracy of the time and believed social reform to be possible. The New Age maintains an optimistic eschatology, holding out hope for a better future.[21]

New Thought

The New Age movement also has its roots in New Thought. In this case the traffic runs both ways. Many New Thought ideas have been incorporated by the New Age movement. In the other direction, New Age beliefs are compatible with New Thought and have penetrated its various organizations.

New Thought is a late nineteenth-century development that Robert Ellwood says "is not so much a cult or a church in itself as a type of teaching which has influenced a number of groups." New Thought's beliefs have provided the foundation for several churches, including the Church of Divine Science, Unity, and the Church of Religious Science. Moreover, New Thought has given impetus to varieties of what are labeled as "metaphysical" activities and even the "positive thinking" tradition.[22]

Like Spiritualism, Theosophy, and the modern New Age, New Thought was diffuse and lacked boundaries. Thus, it took many forms and could not be confined to a specific religious body. New Thought's basic assumption is that mind is fundamental and causative. In its insistence that every event is an internal, nonmaterial idea, New Thought represents a modern Western adaptation of a concept that was common to Neoplatonism and Eastern religions.[23]

In concrete ways, New Thought teachers have sought to demonstrate how thoughts of wholeness, health, and success can create equivalent material realities. Given the assumption that the basis of the physical world resides in the mind, then altering one's thoughts should bring changes in the physical world. Even such mundane objectives, such as getting better employment, can become a reality if one's thoughts are focused on such a desired end. But much more important than such material benefits, the healing of mind and body have had an important place in the New Thought movement.[24]

New Thought's distant roots can be traced to German idealism and New England Transcendentalism. Yet the immediate impetus for New Thought came from the healing and teaching practice of Phineas P. Quimby (1802-1866). Quimby was a mental healer with the practical desire to heal people. But he also delved more deeply into the basis of inner healing. Quimby taught that human beings had a spiritual nature, and inhabited a world higher than earth. He also believed the soul to be in a direct relationship with the divine mind. Therefore, Quimby concluded that people received healing because of the divine spirit's work on a human soul. In this process, a person experienced an awakening by which he or she became aware of his or her inner spiritual nature.[25]

Next to Quimby in importance for New Thought is Warren Felt Evans (1814-1889), a former Methodist minister. Evans said that disease came from a loss of mental balance which in turn affected the body. Illness resulted from the translation into flesh of a wrong idea in the mind. Consequently, the way to restored health was correct thinking, which would restore the harmony between the divine and the human spirit.[26] But most important, Evans believed in the power of suggestion in healing. He emphasized the power of conscious affirmation, and his thinking on this subject turned New Thought toward such a practice. Such a development had a significant impact on later New Thought. Mind cure now meant that the sick individual must think positively, affirming health in deliberate internal statements.[27]

New Thought and the New Age have much in common. Both movements have been more individual than communal in their emphasis, a fact that has led their adherents to emphasize inwardness and private religious experience.[28] Healing by means of nonmedical practices has been central to New Thought. The New Age offers many mental and physical therapies that go outside the framework of Western medicine. Melton tells us that New Thought ideas on prosperity have penetrated much of American religious life "through the work of ministers such as Norman Vincent Peale and Robert Schuller and Pentecostal evangelists . . . ." New Agers have been attracted to such views on prosperity and success. But such ideas on prosperity run counter to the New Age's concern for the environment and "the need to live more simply."[29]

As Melton also notes, "the presence of New Thought . . . goes a long way to explaining the quickness with which the New Age movement spread . . . ." New Thought absorbed many New Age ideas and provided institutions to propagate such beliefs. In fact, the boundaries between New Thought and the New Age have become blurred--so much so that New Thought groups have moved against what they regard as New Age encroachments and distortions of their teachings.[30]

Theosophy

In several respects Theosophy was a forerunner of the New Age movement. Both theosophical teachings and organizational structures have a direct connection with the modern New Age. The New Age movement represents a convergence of Eastern and Western beliefs. At earlier times in American history, the East and the West have come together. Theosophy and its various offshoots were one of the clearest examples of such a convergence.

Theosophy has been called the "mother of the occult" in modern America, a "seedbed" from which many twentieth-century occult movements would emerge. More specifically, Theosophy was "the single most important avenue of Eastern teaching to the West," writes Melton.[31] Theosophy began in the nineteenth century. Its guiding spirit and principle founder was Helen Petrovna Blavatsky (1831-1891). She developed many ideas which in the late twentieth century became part of the New Age movement.[32]

Blavatsky was born in Russia and after traveling widely throughout the world she came to America in 1874. Here she met Colonel Henry Steel Olcott (1832-1907), who became a co-founder of the Theosophical Society. However, since its founding in 1875 the Theosophical Society has experienced many divisions. In the late twentieth century there are over forty Theosophical related bodies.[33]

Theosophical Teachings

Beyond the specific features of Theosophical teachings, there are several beliefs commonly identified with occultism and Eastern spirituality, including the New Age. Theosophy maintains an impersonal concept of God. God is the one Uncreated, Universal, Infinite and Everlasting Cause--the Absolute Principle. Moreover, Theosophy is profoundly pantheistic. Theosophists say that there is only one life, one consciousness, and one power--God's life which is immanent in all aspects of life.[34]

Another of Theosophy's central principles concerns the perfectibility of human nature. Human beings represent a phase of the general evolutionary process which is constantly going on in the universe. Theosophists regard humanity as a Spark of Divine Fire, an elementary substance belonging to the monadic world. An individual is but a fragment of the group soul, demonstrating its ego as spirit, intuition, and intelligence.[35]   As with most occult and eastern groups, reincarnation occupied an important place in Theosophy's teachings.   In fact, Blavatsky played a major role in standardizing the use of the term reincarnation.[36]

In addition to such common occult teachings, Theosophy introduced an idea central to the modern New Age--humanity is entering a new age. The Theosophists rewrote Darwinian evolution to suit their objectives.   Because of Blavatsky's contacts with the Mahatmas, or masters, Theosophists expected that one of these masters would come to earth as a savior for humanity. As Catherine Albanese notes, Blavatsky "borrowed from the Buddhist doctrine of Maitreya Buddha, the Buddha of the final age, to teach that the Lord Maitreya would come as world teacher to launch a new age in the human evolutionary cycle." The presence of such a master would usher in a new age.[37]

In fact, the issue of a coming master who would inaugurate a new age became very important to the Theosophists--so much so that they proclaimed his "existence in a young Indian boy, Jiddu Kishnamurti (1895-1986)." Theosophists promoted this notion until 1929 when Kishnamurti denied he was the world teacher and began his own religious work.[38]

Professor Mary Farrell Bednarowski tells us that modern "New Age thought is both a continuation and an expansion" of many religious concepts that "Theosophy pulled together." The New Age, she claims, "captures the spirit of Theosophy's three objects--to establish a Universal Brotherhood of Humanity; to encourage the study of comparative religion, philosophy and science; and to investigate   unexplained laws of nature and powers latent in man . . . ." Like Theosophy, the New Age attempts to bring religion and science together, largely by reforming the scientific method until it is appropriate for spiritual matters.[39]

Theosophical Organizations

Theosophy spawned many organizations, some of which have a close relationship to the New Age. Most important in helping to shape the contemporary New Age movement are the Arcane School and the I AM movement. Alice Bailey (1880-1949) of the Arcane School claimed that the Ascended Master Djwhal Khul (D. K.) was communicating to humankind through her. D. K.'s messages spoke of the coming of a world teacher near the end of a century and of a Great White Brotherhood who directed human events. Gary Ballard (1878-1939) of the I AM movement said that an Ascended Master named Saint-Germain contacted him, imparting to him wisdom from the ancient past. While the term emerged later, both Bailey and Ballard began to "channel" in the contemporary New Age sense. They wrote down the exact words delivered to them by the masters.[40]

Despite a close relationship between Theosophy and the New Age, the two movements are not identical. They are different movements with their own distinctives. Theosophy had a definite founder, Helen Blavatsky, and it is a more cohesive movement than the New Age. Moreover, while Theosophists sometimes speak of participating in the coming of a new age, the term is not usually applied to their movement.[41]

Eastern Religions

The contemporary New Age movement is a synthesis of several religious and cultural traditions. Eastern spirituality is one of these components. Eastern religions helped to forge the New Age movement after World War II. In fact, Asiatic religions experienced a tremendous surge of growth in post-war America. But this explosion of Eastern spirituality did not come out of no-where. Asiatic religions have had a long presence in America--a situation that provided the basis for their dynamic growth after World War II.[42]

As philosopher Andrea Diem and researcher James Lewis note, Asian religion "entered the United States in at least three distinct waves." The first wave, occurring in the late eighteenth century, was "almost purely literary." Hindu religious scriptures reached America by way of the British East India Company. These Hindu scriptures influenced nontraditional religious bodies in the nineteenth century-- the Transcendentalists, New Thought, and Theosophy. In turn these alternative religions became the primary vehicle for the entry of Asiatic religious teachings and paved the way for the New Age.[43]

The second wave involved personal contacts with a small number of Hindu teachers who came to America in the late nineteenth and early twentieth centuries. In 1893, at the World Parliament of Religions, representatives of all the major world religions gathered in Chicago for a sharing of their belief systems. Most important of the

Indian religious teachers reaching the United States during this early period were Swami Vivekananda and Swami Paramahansa Yogananda who inspired the founding of the Vedanta Society and the Self-Realization Fellowship respectively.[44]

However, this small stream of Easterners arriving in America came to a halt. A series of Oriental exclusion acts in the early twentieth century barred Asiatics from entering the United States.[45] According to Gordon Melton, these acts had the effect of limiting "the spread of Hinduism and Buddhism." Because Asian teachers no longer entered America, Eastern teachings were now transmitted (and often distorted) "through the writings of American occult teachers." As a result, during the first half of the twentieth century, the secret wisdom which Americans encountered was really a combination of Eastern spirituality and Western occult thought.[46] By the late twentieth century, such a synthesis would provide much of the basis for New Age teachings.

The restrictions barring Asiatics from entering the United States were lifted in 1965. This prompted the third wave of Eastern religions into the United States. During the sixties and seventies a new influx of Eastern gurus entered the country, preparing a spiritual subculture that, when combined with the other elements, would lead directly to the New Age movement.[47] This story, however, is the subject for a later chapter.

Psychology

Psychology developed in the late nineteenth century. Yet its impact on religion was not significant until after World War II. In fact, the blending of psychology with the occult tradition and Eastern spirituality have become the primary ingredients in the New Age movement, many psycho-religions, and many self-help groups that sprang up during the 1970s and 1980s. This development occurred in the post-war era and was associated with the rise of humanistic and transpersonal psychology. But the foundation for the fusion of religion and psychology came during the first half of the twentieth century.

In the early stages of its development, psychology was irreligious and even hostile to religion. In the early twentieth century, behaviorism and psychoanalysis became the two major schools in psychology. Behaviorism developed out of the work of the Russian

Ivan Pavlov (1849-1936) and attempted to study the human being as a purely physiological organism. It reduced all human behavior to a series of physical responses. The Austrian Sigmund Freud (1856-1939) founded psychoanalysis, a school in psychology that interprets human behavior mainly in terms of the subconscious or unconscious mind.[48]

However, the first half of the twentieth century also produced some psychological systems that opened avenues to alternative religions. Some of these systems drew from the occult and became legitimizing agents for some fringe religions and quasi-religions. An important example are the ideas of C. G. Jung (1875-1961). Jung studied the occult, and his concept of archetypes supported magic and modern Neopaganism.[49]

Parapsychology

The most important example of psychology with a quasi-religious dimension is parapsychology.   J. B. Rhine, a pioneer in parapsychology, defines it as a "science of psychic abilities." Parapsychology is the systematic inquiry into whether human minds receive information in ways that bypass the normal channels of sensory communication, or interact with matter in ways not yet understood by physical science.   The two primary categories of parapsychology are extrasensory perception (ESP) and psychokinesis (PK), with each having their subdivisions.[50]

Parapsychology has always had a close relationship with religion, especially the occult, and has been the seedbed from which many quasi-religious speculations have arisen.   Such a development came about when scientific advancements produced a skepticism regarding the supernatural aspects of religion. Naturalistic theories arose in an attempt to account for the miraculous. Early examples of this include Swedenborg's   spirit   communication,   Mesmerism,   hypnosis, Spiritualism, and Christian Science. Most important, parapsychology sprang from Spiritualism, for it was believed that mediums were gifted with telepathy.[51]

The work of J. B. Rhine beginning at Duke University in 1927 gave parapsychology some scientific legitimacy. The admission of the Parapsychological Association into the American Academy for the Advancement of Science furthered such a perception. Yet tensions exist as to whether parapsychology is a science or the occult.[52]

Whatever it may be, parapsychology clearly has religious and mystical dimensions.   Such a relationship between science, religion, and mysticism would be continued in humanistic and transpersonal psychology--two later developments that are necessary steps in the formulation of the New Age.

Chapter 4

AMERICAN SOCIETY
AND THE NEW AGE

While the New Age aspires to be an international movement, its greatest visibility is in the United States. Its roots run deep in American history. Yet, the New Age movement also must be regarded as a product of contemporary American society. The New Age is a cultural movement that has been shaped by the changes in modern American society. The New Age must be seen as but a part of a larger cultural shift that has taken place in America since the 1960s.

At the close of World War II, the moral and religious base of American society was still the Judeo-Christian tradition. In the post-war era, the dominance of Christianity as a cultural force was challenged by two sources--natural humanism and occult-Eastern mysticism. While the Judeo-Christian tradition is still a leading force, these challenges have substantially reduced its influence--so much so that in the late twentieth century American society has been described as post-Christian. The term *post-Christian* means that Christianity is no longer the definer of cultural values. Yet, secularism has not completely taken over. Its challenges to Christianity have helped to create a spiritual void that has in part been filled by the occult-Eastern tradition. In fact, the New Age movement is a revolt against the secularism of the modern world. As a result, the New Age arose out of a convergence of East and West in modern America and draws from all three traditions. But its worldview is that of occult-Eastern mysticism.

Religious Pluralism

A longstanding component of American culture--religious and cultural pluralism--has helped to give birth to the New Age movement. America has had a rich tradition of religious pluralism that can be traced back to the colonial period and the Constitutional settlement of 1789. Even when this tradition is taken into consideration, religious pluralism has taken a quantum leap since World War II. As sociologist Robert Wuthnow points out, "Few decades have given rise to as many religious movements as the late 1960s and early 1970s."[1] These years represent one of the greatest periods of religious experimentation in Western history, in some ways resembling the Hellenistic era, the Reformation period, and the 1830s and 1840s in antebellum America.[2]

Eastern Contacts

A very important factor in the growth of new religions in the 1960s and 1970s, and one which provided a catalyst for the New Age, was the expansion of cultural pluralism. This cultural expansion developed in several directions but came primarily by means of increased contacts with the East. The immigration laws of the early twentieth century reduced the flow of people from Asia to a trickle. But this would change dramatically after World War II. Wars against Japan, Korea, and Vietnam, plus all the contacts that global leadership entails, to say nothing of an increased secularism, would push American pluralism beyond the Judeo-Christian tradition.[3]

Gordon Melton writes about the specific events that prompted the flow of Eastern religions to the West. First, after World War II, religious freedom developed in Japan. As a result, hundreds of new religious groups emerged and many formerly suppressed ones spread, some to the United States. Second, India gained its independence in 1948 and became a member of the British Commonwealth. Indians, including swamis and gurus, now traveled more freely to the West. Third, in 1965 President Johnson "rescinded the Oriental Exclusion Act." The results were staggering. Johnson's action unleashed a massive human flood from Asia. Melton calls this "change in the limits of Asian immigration. . .the single most important factor in the rise of new religions in America."[4]

Influence on the New Age

This explosion of religious pluralism has shaped the New Age movement in several ways. First, Eastern religions are a significant component in the New Age synthesis. Eastern spirituality has come to the New Age through indirect and direct sources. Indirectly, Asiatic religions have been incorporated into the occult-metaphysical tradition and have found their way into the New Age by way of Transcendentalism, New Thought, and Theosophy. Directly, the New Age has borrowed from Eastern religions, especially Hinduism and Buddhism, and their various offshoots found in America. The presence of many Eastern teachers and practitioners of Asiatic religions in America has created the spiritual subculture which gave birth to the New Age.

But as Diem and Lewis point out, the New Age maintains an idealized image of the East. This tendency is not new. For centuries European and American romantics have idealized the East and then criticized the West "in terms of that ideal." This utopian vision of the East found its way into the early occult-mystical bodies (Transcendentalism, Theosophy) and the first Hindu groups (Vedanta Society, Self Realization Fellowships) in America. Gradually this picture of the East "filtered out into American culture, and was thus readily available to the fifties Beats, the sixties counterculture, and the New Age movement of the seventies and eighties."[5]

For example, in his best seller *The Tao of Physics*, prominent New Ager Fritjof Capra has misinterpreted Asian religion. He has created an idealized Eastern spirituality that does not coincide with reality in the Orient and has used this vision to critique the West.[6] Other New Agers have even idealized the civilizations of Greece and Rome as a background from which to criticize American society.[7]

Second, religious pluralism has contributed to the eclectic nature of the New Age movement. Religious pluralism has a long history in America. Yet, for over one hundred years since the legal disestablishment of religion in 1789, such pluralism had little impact on American culture. As sociologists Wade Roof and William McKinney point out, "In self perception, if not in fact, the United States was a white country in which Protestant Christianity set the norms of religious observance and conduct." The White Anglo-Saxon Protestant (WASP) culture "shaped much of public life."[8]

So long as a common core of Protestant values could be taken for granted, cultural pluralism was manageable.[9] But in the 1960s the realities of an extended pluralism became apparent. Cultural pluralism mushroomed, and the common Protestant core could no longer provide the cohesion for national values. Immigrants from Asia and Latin America poured into America, Americans now traveled abroad much more, and many foreign students bringing non-Christian religions came to America.

This extended pluralism went beyond culture. It influenced morals, ideology, and religion. Secular, rational, occult-mystical, Eastern, and traditional Christian beliefs now competed with each other. William McLoughlin argues that from about 1890 to 1960 a national consensus existed around liberal Protestantism. This consensus had been shattered by the 1960s.[10] America no longer had a religious core. When it did in the past, pluralism in morals, beliefs, and religion did not seem so threatening.[11]

This pluralism in culture, values, and beliefs provided a seedbed for an explosion of fringe religions--including the birth of the New Age. In many ways during the sixties and seventies, America's traditional spiritual institutions were tested and found wanting. The new religions stepped in and filled the social, spiritual, and emotional voids left by many of society's overburdened institutions. Many people, especially youth, sought radical solutions to problems in economics, education, politics, and social relationships. Therefore, it was natural for young people to turn also to radical religious solutions--withdrawn communalism, mysticism, otherworldliness, the occult, Eastern religions, and the cults.[12]

When the counterculture of the sixties and seventies declined, the religious situation did not return to normal. The Judeo-Christian consensus had been shattered. Many people now turned to less radical, but still unconventional, outlets--the quasi-religions, self-help groups, spiritual therapies, and the New Age movement. Roy Wallis calls these nontraditional groups "world affirming religions."[13] Rather than withdraw from the world, individuals in these groups worked for both self-improvement and social change.

By the 1980s the religious order was deeply fragmented. In several ways, such a situation contributed to the growth of the New Age movement. As an eclectic movement, the New Age drew from many competing religious forces in modern America, attempting to synthesize many of their elements. Moreover, the New Age does not reject any of these diverse religions. All religions contain truth, but no one religion has a corner on the truth. An objective of the New Age is to establish a unity in religion--a faith drawing from Christianity, occult-mysticism, Eastern spirituality, and even science.

Individualism

Another longstanding component in American culture--individualism--goes hand-in-hand with the New Age movement. The New Age is but one aspect of the privatized, therapeutic, quasi-religions that have emerged during the 1980s.[14] As Melton writes, "the central vision of the New Age" is that of a "radical mystical transformation" on a personal level. The focus is on the individual, who awakens to new realities such as the development of new potentials within him or herself. Individuals may experience psychological or physical healing, a new view of the universe, the discovery of psychic capabilities, or an intimate experience within a community.[15]

Privatization and individualism in respect to religion is an important value in modern society. The voluntary form of religion--that religion is a matter of personal choice--has deep roots in American history. In America this religious individualism, of course, has been reinforced by capitalism, political democracy, and cultural pluralism.[16]

But a new type of individualism arose in the 1970s and 1980s. The earlier individualism usually resided within the context of a religious and cultural consensus and thus had more direction. Yet, as the old Judeo-Christian synthesis unraveled, the value system of the nation shifted dramatically. Life in the modern world had become fragmented. As idealism vanished from the American way of life, the deep-seated search for personal fulfillment increased. Many Americans could not find meaning in the values and institutions of the prevailing society. Therefore, they turned inward.[17] And as Thomas Luckmann points out, religion became "invisible,"a private matter. Each person would work out, from the available resources, a system of sacred meanings and values in accord with personal needs and preferences.[18]

The quest for personal fulfillment as a matter of individual experience is widespread in American religion. It is not limited to the new religions and spiritual therapies. As the authors of *Habits of the Heart* demonstrate, much of organized religion (including evangelicals, mainline Protestants and Catholics) has pursued a highly personalized agenda.[19] As historian Erling Jorstad notes, during the seventies and eighties "evangelicals talked less about watching and praying to avoid temptations and to be ready for Christ's imminent return to earth." Rather, they accentuated "the themes of self-discovery, personal growth, and fulfillment by the realization of one's potential."[20] Even within the liberal mainstream, many individuals sought personal fulfillment, often through spiritual therapies. Increased numbers of both clergy and laity attended workshops on personal growth and meditation techniques.[21]

The search for personal fulfillment and privatized religion was well suited to many of the new religions. The occult-metaphysical versions of the new religions are often more individual than corporate. In astrology and in groups such as Spiritualism, Scientology, and est, the emphasis is on self-fulfillment, rather than on any group life or social change. Likewise, in Eastern religions it must be recognized that much focuses on the experience of enlightenment, which is private and invisible. Eastern groups with a strong appeal to individuals and privatization are Yoga, Zen Buddhism, and Transcendental Meditation.[22]

But the quasi-religions, including the New Age movement, and spiritual therapies made the greatest appeal to those interested in self-fulfillment. In fact, some groups taught that salvation equals fulfillment, something that could be found only within the self. Individuals in these bodies utilize techniques to facilitate spiritual growth or, in more secular terms, to awaken inner experiences. Whether such a group is psycho-therapeutic, humanistic or religious in its focus, personal fulfillment is the primary objective of most of its activities. The primary concerns are how a particular technique can improve self-realization and how spiritual enlightenment can be acquired.[23]

The New Age is a movement with a dual focus. In fact, it might be considered as two movements--one with a global reform emphasis and another focusing on self-awareness and self-improvement. In the New Age, global activism and personal transformation go hand-in-hand. As *The 1989 Guide to New Age Living* indicates, "social change is most effective when accompanied by efforts to transform our own consciousness and redefine our own needs."[24] Personal change was to precede political action. Despite its global emphasis, the New Age must be seen as a victory for the privatization of religion.[25]

The Occult Revival

The key component in the New Age movement is the occult-metaphysical tradition. A dynamic occult tradition and a high level of occult activity is a prerequisite for the launching of the New Age movement. Did such a condition exist in modern America?

In the 1970s America experienced an occult revival. Yet this upturn in the occult should not be exaggerated. It did not come out of nowhere. The occult has had a substantial presence in America since at least the 1840s. What occurred in the 1970s in respect to the occult was an unprecedented peak in news media attention, publishing, and organizational activity. Of even greater significance, the worldview of occult-mysticism became widely accepted during the 1970s and 1980s, perhaps far more than at any time since the seventeenth century.[26]

In this so-called occult revival, two inclinations were noticeable, one focusing on specific phenomena and the other on a worldview. These two tendencies were not mutually exclusive, but involved considerable overlap. The first area of renewed interest concerned the occult practices (the occult "arts"). Most popular were astrology and several forms of divination (crystal gazing, palmistry, cartomancy, ouija boards, psychometry, numerology, prophetic dreams and visions, I Ching, and others). The list of other familiar occult practices includes magic, paranormal experiences, reincarnation, witchcraft, Satanism, and unidentifiable flying objects.[27]

Both individuals and groups practice these occult activities. Yet the occult lends itself to private activity, and in this realm most of the action takes place. Many new religions resemble Luckmann's invisible religions, but the occult carries this trend even further. There exist opportunities to worship with swamis, metaphysical churches, and even occult organizations (e.g., witch covens, Satanist groups, Rosicrucian orders, theosophical societies, Swedenborgianism, spiritualist bodies). Yet, community activities are not central. The occult is largely an invisible religion because it is personal, private, and not regularly institutionalized.[28] However, occult and quasi-occult practices are often utilized by some Eastern cults, metaphysical bodies, and the human potential and New Age movements.[29]

Of greater significance for the years since 1970 is the second tendency in the occult revival: the widespread acceptance of the occult-metaphysical worldview in the West. The occult-metaphysical worldview has many expressions, especially in Eastern spirituality, many psychotherapies, and the human potential and New Age movements.[30]

Towards the end of the seventies, a shift in the direction of the occult could be noticed. The early occult revival, ranging from the late sixties to the mid-seventies was largely a youth phenomena, closely related to the counterculture and the use of psychedelic drugs. The most pronounced aspect of this early occult explosion was the popularity of many occult practices, especially astrology and divination. In fact, many regarded the occult as a fad of the youth culture, somewhat of a "pop" religion, a means to proclaim the new Aquarian Age. As the more radical elements of the counterculture declined, a focus on the occult practices receded from public view and many occult groups continued on as isolated cults or modified their behavior, thus acquiring a more respectable presence in society.[31]

The second occult tendency, the prevalence of the occult worldview, was closely connected with the rising status of the occult. The occult-metaphysical worldview and some occult arts penetrated the respectable ranks of society and laid the basis for the human potential and New Age movements. The preoccupation with self-awareness and self-actualization presupposes the acceptance of many occult principles. A number of therapy centers and corporations have had their clients and employees engage in self-awareness exercises. In its higher forms, the modern occult must be regarded as a quasi-religious movement, an endeavor to discover valid proofs for the abilities that traditional occultism has always insisted were hidden within the human mind.[32]

In the occult world, the path to knowledge and enlightenment comes through experience. This longstanding occult method for acquiring knowledge now has parallels in modern society. A major epistomological shift, particularly in respect to obtaining religious knowledge, has taken place. The cognitive processes largely had been abandoned and experience now dominated. Indeed, as sociologist Ronald Enroth notes, "the thrust of the new religious groups--

whether Eastern mystical, occult, or aberrational Christian--is experience over doctrine, feeling rather than rationality." For many people, religious truth is not attained by the traditional modes of learning, but by mystical insight. Indeed, many people join new religious groups in pursuit of "peak experiences" and "moments of bliss."[33] Theodore Roszak, a cultural historian with a positive view of the New Age movement, regards this emphasis on experience as the greatest discovery of the religious awakening of the 1960s and 1970s.[34]

Indeed, a basic prerequisite for the rise of the New Age--a vibrant occult tradition--was in place by 1970. The occult was alive and well, and by the mid seventies it had adorned itself in respectable clothes and had penetrated many levels of both secular and religious society. A healthy occult tradition provided the seedbed that gave birth to the New Age.

The Counterculture

The New Age movement is a post-counterculture development. It reflects trends in American society that became noticeable after the mid-1970s--an emphasis on self-improvement, a degree of narcissism, and a less radical approach to change. Yet, the counterculture years (ca. 1960-1975) gave birth to the New Age movement. New Age values and beliefs come out of the counterculture and have been modified to suit American society of the late seventies and eighties.

The years from 1960 to the early 1970s, loosely referred to as "the sixties," were troubled, tumultuous, and traumatic. The spirit of protest began with young Afro-Americans, who were unwilling to accept the slow pace of racial progress, and spread to young whites sick of bland middle-class life and angry at government policies.[35] As historian Sidney Ahlstrom writes, "never before in the nation's history have so many Americans expressed revolutionary intentions and actively participated in efforts to alter the shape of American civilization in almost every imaginable aspect"--from religion to the political process, from art to the economic order, from health to diplomacy. These years represent a watershed in American history. American society was severely shaken and in many respects permanently changed.[36]

During the sixties many elements in American society literally exploded. But the changes of the sixties grew out of the problems of the past. This turbulent decade acted as a catalyst to forces already in motion. By now long-term moral, theological, economic, and cultural processes were brought to a boiling point by the rapid social change and tremendous economic expansion that Americans had experienced during the affluent years following World War II.[37]

Science, technology, and urbanization brought much of this change. American fiscal and political practices could no longer cope with urban and industrial problems that had been developing since the late nineteenth century. Scientific and technological advancements seemed to have no limits. In the face of tremendous scientific advancements, transcendent reality faded from view. As a result, for many, the notion of the supernatural lost its force.[38]

Theodore Roszak tells us that technology played a major role in the creation of a counterculture. The advance of technology, science, and urban growth depersonalized human relationships, creating a thirst for intimacy and community that some fringe religions would fill. Moreover, all of this emphasis on rationality, technology, and science caused a backlash. A shift in the way people learned became noticeable. The cognitive approach and research were being replaced by intuition and experience. Of course, such means for obtaining knowledge are basic with many fringe religions, including the New Age.[39]

Gordon Melton notes the changes in science that influenced the growth of nontraditional religions during the counterculture years. By the 1960s the lines between parapsychology and the occult became less distinct with some parapsychologists engaging in occult activities. Throughout Western history, science and the occult have overlapped and they would do so again in the New Age movement. Second, the discovery of LSD had quasi-religious implications. While this mind-altering drug had been invented in 1938, it became popular in the 1960s. Soon psychedelic experiences became identified with the search for religious ecstasy.[40]

Third, "a revolution in psychiatry and psychology" opened the avenues to certain types of alternative religions. In particular "humanistic psychology took a positive turn toward religion and religious experience." Psychological techniques and principles became surrogates for traditional religious practices and beliefs. When combined with Eastern thought and practice, humanistic psychology "gave birth to the human potentials movement," which in turn advanced the cause of many new quasi-religions, including the New Age.[41]

During the sixties, social and political relations changed dramatically. The White Anglo-Saxon Protestant (WASP) power structure now came under serious challenge. The Protestant establishment had been in a decline since the turn of the century. But now immigration patterns created many new voters of a non-European background who repudiated this Protestant ascendancy. When a Roman Catholic became president in 1961 and Vatican II ended many of the Protestant-Catholic tensions, relationships between these two groups were drastically altered.[42]

American society saw other changes. During the fifties and sixties, the Supreme Court removed several legal pillars from the white Protestant power structure. Segregation became illegal and Afro-Americans achieved more civil rights. The court also outlawed the use of many Christian symbols in schools and public places. Moreover, feminists demanded equal rights between men and women, and environmentalists called for an end to the rape of nature.[43]

Yet President Johnson's decision to escalate the Vietnam War provided the catalyst for uniting the different protest movements of the sixties. Political cynicism now turned to violence, culminating in the tumultuous events of 1968 (the assassinations of Martin Luther King and Robert Kennedy, the chaotic Democratic convention). Youth and others continued to agitate for nearly five years. America now experienced a series of traumas--the riots of Kent State, Watergate, the resignation of President Nixon, and the collapse of the American regime in Vietnam.[44]

All of these developments helped to create an apocalyptic mind-set in American society during the sixties and seventies, says Ronald Enroth. "The invention of the atomic bomb began the current apocalyptic mood." The doomsday predictions by some environmentalists contributed to the apocalyptic mentality. Radical political views also promoted such a mood. Many believed "that the American government [was] beyond reforming and must be destroyed totally in order for something new and better to take its place." While an apocalyptic mentality could be found in both the secular and religious sectors, "it was perhaps the strongest in the counter-culture."[45]

Influence on Religion

This transformation of American social and political life had its impact on American religion, leading historian Martin Marty to speak of a "seismic shift" in the nation's religious landscape.[46]   Sidney Ahlstrom regarded the 1960s as a time when the "old foundations of national confidence, patriotic idealism, moral traditionalism, and even historic Judeo-Christian theism were awash. Presuppositions that had held firm for centuries--even millennia--were being widely questioned."[47]

Such upheavals and turbulence fostered the emergence of new sects, cults, and quasi-religions. The roots of the New Age movement go back through Western history and have important Eastern connections. Yet, the more immediate context is the counterculture. New Age ideology is built upon the foundation of the counterculture. The counterculture years opened the door to the new and the untested--hallucinogenic drugs, free sex, Eastern religions, and the occult.[48]   A number of sects and cults blossomed forth in the atmosphere of the counterculture.   Yogis and gurus promised enlightenment; meditation became popular; witches danced in the woods; Hare Krishnas chanted; and the baby boom generation became acquainted with non-Christian spirituality.[49]

Closely related to the rise of these alternative religions was the drug culture.   The counterculture years saw many young people attempt to elevate their spiritual consciousness through both organic and synthetic drugs.   Marilyn Ferguson sees drugs and the psychedelic movement of the sixties as promoting an interest in new realities and as a critical step in the later development of the New Age movement.[50]

Indeed, the counterculture paved the way for the New Age. The occult revival and the influx of Eastern religions gave the New Age its worldview. The revolt against science and technology promoted the subjective, experience-oriented approach to learning so prevalent in the New Age. The breakdown of the Judeo-Christian culture in America ushered in post-Christian America, lending some credence to the New Age claim that a new era in human history had begun. The issues of the counterculture years--peace, political reform, feminism, and environmental concerns--largely set the political and social agenda for the New Age.

Despite much continuity between the counterculture and the New Age, there are significant differences between these two movements, as Elliot Miller points out. First, unlike the counter-culture, the New Age is not basically "a youth movement but spans all ages." Second, New Agers do not stand out from the rest of society "by outward appearance"--dress or hairstyle. Third, hard rock music is not dominant with New Agers. Instead, they have their own New Age music. Next, the New Age is not as overtly anti-establishment as were the movements of the sixties. Fifth, while the sixties counterculture tended to be radically left politically, the New Age has synthesized a number of right and left elements. Sixth, New Agers do not emphasize free sex as did the hippies of the sixties. Finally, in contrast to the counterculture, the New Age movement is largely drug free.[51]

The Seventies and Eighties

The counterculture of the 1960s is usually seen as the immediate catalyst for the rise of fringe religions. But a number of events in the early seventies brought the counterculture to an end. As the counterculture receded in the seventies, many of the new religions connected with the counterculture also declined.[52] Most of the sects and cults of the counterculture were "world rejecting" movements that thrived in the climate of the sixties. But when the secular protest movements receded, their religious counterparts also declined.

The cults and occult slipped from public view. This did not indicate an end to new religions, but the passing of a phase. By the late seventies a change could be noticed. Attention had shifted from the cults and occult to the psycho-religions and quasi-religions, especially the groups loosely associated with the human potential and New Age movements.[53]

This change came about for several reasons. First, the political activism of the sixties gave way to a more conservative era, which some have called a "counter-revolution." Interest in political and social reform abated. People now focused more on career advancement and personal fulfillment than on changing American society. Historian Arthur Schlesinger, Jr., divides American history into private and public interest cycles. He saw the former taking off in the mid-1970s. Second, the affluence of the sixties declined. Social protest and nontraditional lifestyles were a luxury that ended with the economic turndown of the 1970s. Young people now conformed to society in order to further careers that might lead to prosperity in difficult times.[54]

The new religions that are popular in the 1980s, especially the human potential and New Age movements, have a closer relationship to these political and economic developments than would the counterculture groups. Personal transformation and self-fulfillment are important goals for individuals in these quasi-religions. These religions fit into the environment described by Christopher Lasch, namely that the seventies were a decade when people focused on their self interests.[55]

In fact, the New Age was especially at home during the 1980s. Professor Randall Balmer says that "No other religion more aptly fit the temper of the 1980s than the New Age . . . ." Though the New Age has an agenda for social change, many of its activities reflect the individualism and materialism of the eighties--self actualization, inner harmony, career advancement, and a comfortable lifestyle. The New Age is a religion of the babyboomers, people from about twenty-five to forty who dominate the New Age subculture. On one hand, they generally did not like Ronald Reagan. Yet they have embodied the values of the Reagan era.[56]

It would, however, be incorrect to push the differences between the sixties and the seventies and eighties too far.[57] Many of the changes occurring in the sixties became institutionalized. Thus, the counterculture of the 1960s was not a passing trend, writes Douglas Groothuis. While a number of its outward forms of protest are past history, "many of its deepest claims have simply changed costume" and are now part of modern culture. The "love-ins," drugs, permissive sex, Eastern religions, and occultism, which were open but not the norm in the sixties, became "well integrated into the general culture by the mid 1970s."[58]

The practices, objectives, and ideology of the counterculture did not disappear, but the methods of implementation changed drastically. "The radicalism and enthusiastic protest of the sixties gave way to a more . . . integrated view that developed in the 1970s." The hippies, now ten years older, did not abandon their Eastern spirituality and pantheistic outlook. "They simply accommodated it to certain social conventions." They may have cut their hair and improved their dress, but they did not change their worldview.[59]

The grown-up hippies now changed their approach to society. Rather than attempting to tear society down by violent protest, or even separating from it, they often infiltrated society from within, hoping to transform it this way. Still, some refugees from the counterculture despaired of changing society. Without changing their views, "they turned inward in hope of personal transformation," an objective that is basic for the New Age movement.[60]

Chapter 5

THE MODERN NEW AGE

The New Age took off in the 1970s. By this time all of its ingredients were in place. Two new components--Eastern spirituality and new developments in psychology--had been synthesized into the Western occult tradition. The post-World War II social climate--namely affluence, cultural pluralism and individualism--produced an atmosphere conducive to the New Age. Moreover, the counterculture produced the catalyst that set the New Age in motion. This chapter will provide a brief historical account of the modern New Age, including the formative years of the 1950s and 1960s and the years in which it took off, the 1970s and 1980s. Many of the activities, individuals, beliefs, and practices noted in this chapter will receive more elaboration elsewhere in this book. The intent of this chapter is to establish the historical context for such developments.

The Formative Years (1950s and 1960s)

While the New Age became visible in the 1970s, a number of early New Age or proto-New Age groups were active during the 1950s and 1960s. These early bodies and developments cover a broad spectrum--Eastern groups, many occult activities, changes in psychology, holistic health organizations, and communal bodies. Many of these bodies and developments fall within the broad umbrella of the New Age movement. Their objectives, beliefs, and values harmonized with the New Age vision.

Eastern Groups

Eastern spirituality gained a strong foothold in America during the fifties and sixties. Several of these Eastern bodies and teachers can be seen as either paving the way for the New Age or as early New Age groups--depending on how broadly one interprets the perimeters of the New Age.

While Zen Buddhism arrived in America during the early decades of the twentieth century, its greatest growth came during the fifties and sixties. Prior to the explosion of the 1960s, Zen became the big symbol of the spiritual counterculture in the 1950s. Zen was attractive to Americans for two reasons, writes Robert Ellwood. First, Zen is paradoxical. It is an exotic Eastern import, but one that has been readily assimilated in America. Second, Zen has exploited the desire of many Americans for a non-rational and experiential religion. Rather than challenging Western thought, Zen "throws sand in the mind's gear and brings it up against a blank wall."[1] The objective of Zen is to experience a reality beyond the intellect or to be in a condition beyond the intellect.[2]

George Braswell gives other reasons for Zen's appeal. Some people gravitate to Zen because they see it "as a religionless religion with no transcendent authority, no binding scripture, and no legislation of morality." Others have been drawn to Zen because of "its various therapies for the mind, emotions, and body." Still others have chosen Zen because of its emphasis upon silence, discipline, and order.[3] Zen helped to shape the New Age. Both emphasize the experiential and therapeutic elements. Each is a religion that in many ways is not a religion.

A number of early Hindu groups have been identified with the New Age or participated in its activities. Some of these bodies were closely identified with the counterculture. With the end of the counterculture, their membership has either declined or plateaued.

Two Hindu groups with a connection to the New Age arrived in America before World War II--the Vedanta Society and the Self-Realization Society. Swami Vivekananda brought the Vedanta Society to America around 1900. Its monistic philosophy, mysticism, and goal of a universal religion--all presented in a way likely to be understood by Americans--had New Age overtones.[4] In 1920 Paramahansa Yogananda came to America and taught here for over thirty years. He began the Self-Realization Fellowship, which emphasizes yoga as the path to self-realization or God-realization. The word *yoga* means union and the practice of yoga includes a number of physical and mental disciplines intended to bring union with God.[5]

The largest and most successful of the Hindu groups in America is popularly called Transcendental Meditation (TM) and officially named the World Plan Executive Council. Maharishi Mahesh Yogi arrived in the United States in 1959 and established the first TM organization. TM was very popular in the sixties but leveled off by the mid-seventies. However, it remains a stable organization and can be regarded as a New Age group. It focuses on self-improvement and has utopian social and political objectives, including ushering in a new age in human history.[6]

Two earlier Sikh groups have New Age connections. The Sikh religion was founded as an attempt to reduce conflicts between Hindus and Muslims, and draws elements from both religions. The Divine Light Mission came to America with the Guru Maharaj Ji in 1970. The Divine Light Mission has a syncretic belief system emphasizing the acquisition of Knowledge--that is, understanding the primordial energy or source of life. The Divine Light Mission declined with the counterculture and barely maintains an existence in America.[7] Sikh Dharma and one of its offshoots, the Healthy, Happy, Holy Organization (3HO) arrived in America in 1968. This group has maintained a stronger presence in America, focusing on health concerns and social issues.[8]

The mystical wing of Islam, known as Sufism, has produced several religious bodies in America with New Age overtones. The most influential has been the Sufi Order, brought to America by Hazart Inayat Khan in 1910. Sufism Reoriented, better known as Meher Baba, began before World War II but peaked during the counterculture years and has had a low profile since then.[9] Another Sufi group teaching mysticism and divine unity is Arica, founded in 1971 by the Bolivian Oscar Ichaza.[10] The Baha'i faith has more tenuous connections with the New Age. While it came out of Sufism, it has lost much of its mystical qualities. Yet it does teach some ideas prevalent in the New Age--oneness in world religions and the political order, and a coming new age.[11]

The most important event for new religions and the New Age during these formative years was President Johnson's decision to rescind the Oriental Exclusion Act. Gordon Melton tells us that the growth of neo-Oriental religions in the United States "can be traced to the movement of Eastern teachers to take up residency in America beginning in 1965." Arriving in the late sixties and seventies, these teachers brought Eastern ideas to America and provided the catalyst for the spread of Eastern spirituality. During these years, Eastern religions began a major missionary effort to bring their faith and practice to the West.[12]

Occult Activities

As noted in the previous chapter, the occult surged during the counterculture years. The occult-metaphysical worldview penetrated American culture. The occult arts also exploded during the sixties and have provided the basis for many of the New Age practices so prevalent in the 1980s.

Undoubtedly, astrology was the most popular aspect of the occult revival. During the sixties it burst on the American cultural scene. As a fad it peaked in the seventies, but on a higher level than it had existed previously.[13] Divination is the attempt to predict the future or uncover knowledge by means of some instrument or operator. Some forms of divination--Tarot cards, ouija boards, dreams, and predictions--again became popular during the sixties.[14]

Intuitive prophecy is divination through the prophetic powers of a charismatic individual. In this respect two twentieth century prophets--Edgar Cayce and Jeane Dixon--helped pave the way for related New Age activities. Edgar Cayce (1877-1945), the "sleeping prophet," founded the Association for Research and Enlightenment (ARE) in 1931, an organization that has current connections with the New Age. Cayce engaged in many occult activities. Most famous were his self-induced trances in which he would make pronouncements on many subjects--a method resembling New Age channeling.[15] During the 1960s, Jeane Dixon became an American legend, largely because of her accurate prophecies--especially her prediction of John Kennedy's assassination. She believes that the antichrist is now alive and that his powers will peak in 1999.[16]

The New Age and neopagan witchcraft are separate movements, but they overlap and have much in common. The revival of witchcraft in the 1960s and 1970s gained much public attention. Modern witchcraft is neither Satanism nor the heretical witchcraft that existed in Europe from the fourteenth to the seventeenth centuries. Modern witchcraft is a religion based on the revival of the ancient, pre-Christian religion of Europe. Central to modern witchcraft is the practice of several varieties of magic, including divination, incantations, astrology, and herbology. The next most prevalent characteristic among modern witches is their love of nature. For most witches, the Deity exists in nature.[17]

Psychic and spiritualistic phenomena are longstanding occult arts. A partial list would include spiritualism; several types of psychic experiences generally labeled as extrasensory perception (ESP); ghosts and poltergeists; astral projections; levitations; apparitions; and possibly even reincarnation.

Spiritualism again surged during the 1960s, providing an important precondition for the New Age, especially one of its most popular practices--channeling. In part, this new interest developed because Spiritualism was an aspect of the larger occult revival occurring at this time. In fact, prominent individuals gained public attention for Spiritualism. In particular, James A. Pike, an Episcopal bishop, gained media attention for Spiritualism. He attempted to contact his deceased son by means of a televised seance, thus bringing Spiritualism into the homes of millions of Americans. Moreover, his book on Spiritualism, *The Other Side*, became a best seller and served to arouse interest in Spiritualism.[18]

Reincarnation is a belief in the preexistence of souls and the reincarnation of souls into different bodies throughout history. In post-World War II America, an interest in reincarnation grew, with about twenty-three to twenty-five percent of the population expressing some belief in it. Several developments promoted this interest. In the mid-1950s a book was published that popularized the subject and ignited a controversy over it. Morey Bernstein used a technique called age regression to hypnotize Virginia Burns Tighe. He took her back to what appeared to be a previous life as Bridey Murphy in nineteenth century Ireland.[19] Another factor is the exploding interest in Eastern religions in America, nearly all of which uphold a belief in reincarnation.

Members of UFO cults often have some New Age background or share many beliefs with the New Age, especially an impending new age for humanity. The modern history of unidentified flying objects

(UFOs) began in 1947 when Kenneth Arnold saw nine bright disks in front of his plane. Since that time, tens of thousands of UFO sightings have been made. Most of these reports have been satisfied by scientific or rational explanations. However, for about ten percent of these sightings traditional answers have been unsatisfactory. It is this percent that has prompted occult explanations. Around such answers, UFO cults have developed, usually based on the expectation of contacts with spiritually advanced beings from outer space. These space beings communicate "their messages through a 'channel,' that is, through the claimed human contactee. Thus was born the contemporary language of the 'channel'"writes Catherine Albanese.[20]

Part of the occult-metaphysical tradition is Native American spirituality. In the 1960s Native American teachers communicated their spiritual traditions to many non-Indian Americans, thus fanning the early flames of the New Age. In particular, New Age shamanism, ceremonies, and paraphernalia have close connections with Native American religions. A leading example is Sun Bear, who in 1966 founded the Bear Tribe Medicine Society, which teaches the Native American tradition to non-Indians.[21] In 1968 Carlos Castaneda published *The Teachings of Don Juan: A Yaqui Way of Knowledge*. This book sold millions and attracted many to Native American shamanism and spirit guides.[22]

Developments in Psychology

In the fifties and sixties psychology underwent several transitions. Some of these changes significantly impacted religion, including the New Age movement. More specifically, the New Age movement was one of the results of transpersonal psychology, which in turn came out of humanistic psychology and the human potential movement.

For much of the first half of the twentieth century, psychology was dominated by its two major schools--psychoanalysis and behavioralism. Freudian psychoanalysis saw human beings as products of social conditioning. Skinnerian behavioralism made human beings a collection of stimulus and response mechanisms. Key figures in rejecting these psychological orthodoxies were Abraham Maslow, Carl Rogers, Fritz Perls and Rollo May. Together they were pioneers of humanistic psychology.[23]

At the center of this new movement was Abraham Maslow. In the 1950s he established humanistic psychology, known as the "Third

Force," to distinguish it from the First and Second psychologies of behaviorism and psychoanalysis. Reacting against these two orthodoxies, humanistic psychology wanted to restore human dignity. As John Allan notes, Maslow assumed "that the human being is basically not a collection of neuroses nor a bundle of conditioned reflexes, but good and instinctively inclined towards improving himself."[24]

Humanistic psychology attempts to scientifically study healthy people. Its focus is not on treating the mentally ill, but on helping the well improve themselves. Several methods can be used to help people achieve their greatest potential, but John Mann singles out two concepts. First is the "peak experience," which Maslow defined as "a generalization for the best moments of life, for experiences of ecstasy, rapture, bliss or greatest joy." These experiences help the individual to transcend the psychological barriers to self-improvement. Second is the "life force," which emphasizes the release and flow of vital energy.[25] This flow of energy has many names, but it occupies an important place in the New Age.

Humanistic psychology was transported to society through several vehicles. Early links were forged between humanistic psychology and personal growth centers, the most important being Esalen. The Esalen Institute began in 1962 and has had a tremendous legacy in the New Age movement. In the early sixties, Esalen made important connections with Maslow and Carl Rogers, the intellectual architects of humanistic psychology. In 1964 Gestalt therapist Fritz Perls moved to Esalen and started the era of encounter groups. A while later, Will Schutz came to Esalen and began an eclectic approach to group therapy known as "open encounter."[26]

The influence of humanistic psychology has been enormous. Its assumptions have been widely accepted in Western society. More specifically, humanistic psychology gave birth to a "fourth force"--transpersonal psychology. Maslow's premise "that human consciousness linked humanity with the fundamental realities of the universe became the basic premise of transpersonal psychology," writes Robert Burrows.[27]

This "fourth force" has a mystical and spiritual dimension, which merged psychology and religion and forged direct links to the New Age. As a formal movement, transpersonal psychology was launched by Maslow in 1967.[28] Yet this new school of psychology looks

forward instead of backward and must be related to the launching of
the New Age in the 1970s and 1980s--a subject for another chapter.

Early Stages of Holistic Health

The changes in psychology focused on personal transformation.
Another development--the holistic health movement--had the same
objective and is an important component of the modern New Age.
Holistic health endeavors not only to treat physical problems, but also
to present a comprehensive approach to health--one that cares for
body, mind, and spirit.[29]

The holistic health movement took off in the mid-1970s. Yet, its
roots run deep in Western history and have connections with mystics,
faith healers, shamans, and so forth. In nineteenth-century America,
there were health fads and attempts at alternative health care. In the
formative years of the New Age, the fifties and sixties, several early
holistic health organizations emerged.   In 1958 the early holistic
health center--Meadowlark--was established by Dr. Evarts Loomis.
The Esalen Institute also promoted holistic health ideas and several
leaders of the movement resided here.   In the late 1960s, the
Menninger Foundation did pioneer work in holistic health, focusing
on the physiological effects of Transcendental Meditation and Yoga.[30]

Early Organizations

The New Age also came by means of some early organizations,
the most important being the Universal Link and the related
Universal Foundation. Gordon Melton describes the Universal Link
"as the networking of groups and individuals" for the purpose of
increasing the level of spiritual energy. Within the Universal Link
were a number of communities of people with similar philosophies.
These communities were called "light" groups--that is, theosophical
and channeling groups that met to prophesy the coming of a new
age.[31]

Most prominent among these "light" groups was the Findhorn
Community, established in northern Scotland in 1965. Findhorn
became "the first full embodiment of a wide variety of New Age
ideals, including its attunement to nature spirits, channeling, and the
articulation of a self-conscious New Age ideology." Finhorn attracted

a number of early New Age leaders, including David Spangler, who resided there for several years.[32]

The New Age Takes Off (1970s and 1980s)

By the early 1970s the New Age had become a self-conscious movement. The occult-metaphysical tradition had absorbed elements from Eastern spirituality and the new psychologies, forming a more or less common philosophy.[33] Individuals sharing this philosophy began to form networks and organizations. Centers promoting a new spirituality emerged, allowing for an interesting exchange between New Age teachers and aspiring students. Journals were established for the purpose of spreading New Age ideas. A series of books by the theoretical architects of the New Age began to shape the movement. Practices (channeling, crystals, and so forth) commonly linked to the New Age began to gain attention.

Such activities gave the New Age a wider visibility. Gradually it moved from a self-conscious movement to one with some national recognition. While they did not always know what it was about, by the mid-eighties, many Americans had at least heard of the New Age movement. By the early 1970s some West Coast scholars, primarily sociologists, began to recognize this new emerging spirituality. They saw that it was neither identical with Eastern religions nor just another cult. Rather they understood it to be a new movement, a blending of several religious and quasi-religious traditions.[34]

The evangelicals also took notice of this new movement. They watched with concern the development of networks, the publication of New Age books, the rise of New Age music, and the sales of New Age paraphernalia. By the early eighties, the evangelicals began to take a critical stance against the New Age.[35]

At first the news media gave the New Age little attention, regarding its participants as hangovers from the counterculture--simply aging hippies.[36] But the mid to late eighties saw the secular news media get on the bandwagon. Thanks to several developments, the New Age became something of a household word. Two 1987 events--*Time's* feature article on the New Age and the publicity given to the Harmonic Convergence--made the New Age well known. Celebrities embraced the New Age; business corporations enrolled employees in New Age seminars; New Age books sold well; and in general, the New Age became part of the pop culture.[37] By the early

1990s, polls indicate that about one in four Americans are aware of the New Age. About sixty percent of the Christians in America accept some New Age beliefs and practices, even if they do not always associate them with the New Age.[38]

Periodicals

A variety of publications gave the New Age visibility. A decentralized movement needs something to bring its diverse elements together. Early New Age publications provided such cohesion. At first New Age networks were linked by newsletters, carrying various announcements and advertisements. A step up from these newsletters were the networking directories, which focused on the distribution of New Age information in a particular area. In the early 1970s, the model for such directories was *Common Ground*, serving the San Francisco area. Other New Age directories include *Free Spirit* (New York City), *New Frontier* (Philadelphia), *New Texas* (Austin) and *New Age Chicago*.[39]

In the early seventies, national magazines and journals began to appear. They focused on New Age issues rather than on the distribution of local information. In these periodicals, occult-metaphysical theoreticians began to articulate the New Age vision. The first of these magazines was the *East-West Journal*. Of the other early New Age journals the most significant were the *New Age Journal*, *New Directions*, *New Realities*, and the *Yoga Journal*.[40] Since then the number of New Age-oriented periodicals has mushroomed. By the early nineties the number stood at about seventy-five.

Spokespersons and Their Books

In the early seventies, New Age leaders began to set forth their ideas in numerous books, thus further articulating the New Age vision. The landmark book, *Be Here and Now* (1972) by Baba Ram Dass, can be seen as one of the opening shots of the New Age. Formerly named Richard Alpert, he was a psychologist at Harvard. In the 1960s Harvard expelled him for using LSD. He went to India, absorbing Eastern spirituality, and reappeared as Baba Ram Dass.[41] His "excellent Western academic background transformed by his new-found faith made him the perfect symbol of the New Age," writes Melton. Throughout the seventies, New Age participants eagerly digested his publications: *The Only Dance There Is* (1973), *Grist for the Mill* (1976), *Journey of Awakening* (1978), and *Miracle of Love* (1979).[42]

The 1975 publication of *A Course in Miracles* brought to the forefront a prominent New Age practice--channeling. *A Course in Miracles* is a lengthy book (nearly 1200 pages), allegedly channeled by Jesus Christ to Helen Schucman, a psychologist associated with the Presbyterian Hospital in New York City and Columbia University. Between 1965 and 1973 Schucman transcribed the words she had received from an inner voice. The stated goal of this message was to "remove the blocks to the awareness of love's presence, which is your natural inheritance." Its central ideas were "that nothing real can be threatened, and nothing unreal exists." These themes were a restatement of New Thought ideas. Since its publication, *A Course in Miracles* has become very popular in New Age circles, selling over 500,000 copies.[43]

By the mid-seventies, David Spangler had emerged as an important architect for the New Age movement. He resided at Findhorn for three years and became a channel for a disembodied spirit named "John." His 1976 book, *Revelation: The Birth of the New Age* presented the New Age vision to many in the 1970s. He followed this volume with several other books: *Towards a Planetary Vision* (1977), *Reflections on the Christ* (1977), and *Emergence: The Rebirth of the Sacred* (1984).[44]

Marilyn Ferguson became one of the New Age's most prominent intellectual theorists. In 1975 she began publishing the *Brain/Mind Bulletin*, a periodical reporting the latest trends in psychology, learning, creativity, and other areas. With the 1980 publication of her book *The Aquarian Conspiracy*, she became the chief apostle of the New Age. Her book has been called the Bible of the New Age--the clearest and most comprehensive statement of the New Age's goals.[45]

While Baba Ram Dass, Ferguson, and Spangler are probably the New Age's three leading theorists, the movement has had other important spokespersons. Mark Satin is one of the New Age's leading political strategists. His 1978 book, *New Age Politics*, presented a vision for a new political and economic order united under a loosely structured global system.[46] Donald Keys, a consultant to the United Nations, founded Planetary Citizens--an organization that attempted to make Satin's ideas a reality. Keys' thought on this matter can be found in his 1982 book, *Earth at Omega*.[47]

The artist Benjamin Creme had many early occult connections. In the late fifties, he became involved with the Aetherius Society, a UFO group, and began to receive inner messages. These messages ceased until the 1970s when Creme began to channel messages from Maitreya (the Christ) regarding his imminent appearance. Creme published two books on this subject: *The Reappearance of Christ and the Masters of Wisdom* (1979) and *Messages from Maitreya the Christ* (1980). In 1982 he took out ads in seventeen papers announcing that "The Christ is Now Here" and that his identity would be made known within two months. Creme's statements regarding the coming of Christ gained the attention of the evangelical community and catalyzed their opposition to the developing New Age.[48]

Important New Age spokespersons arose in a number of other areas. Mystic physicist Fritjof Capra has been at the forefront of the "new physics," arguing that "the concepts of modern physics often show surprising parallels to the ideas expressed in the religious philosophies of the Far East." His first book, *The Tao of Physics* (1975), sold over 500,000 copies.[49] Psychologist and editor Ken Wilber has been a leading figure in transpersonal psychology. In the *Atman Project* (1980) and *Up From Eden* (1981), Wilber has given Maslow's "peak experience" a religious dimension.[50]

Popular level publications have given the New Age tremendous visibility. Celebrities often provided leadership for New Age ideas. The actress/dancer Shirley MacLaine became something of a New Age guru and catapulted the movement into the limelight. Several million copies of her 1983 book, *Out on a Limb*, were sold. Her television version of this book was just as popular, spurring the sales of occult and astrology books in general. Her later books, *Dancing in the Light* (1985) and *It's All in the Playing* (1987), made the *New York Times* best seller list.[51]

Organizations and Groups

Publications were not the only way of promoting New Age ideas. A number of organizations, groups, and communes helped move the New Age vision into the mainstream of American culture. Some groups begun prior to 1970 have continued, furthering New Age ideas and practices in various degrees. Earlier Theosophical bodies are active in the twentieth century and still play a role in the modern New Age. A list would include the Arcane School, "I AM,"

AMORC, the Liberal Catholic Church, Association for Research and Enlightenment, and the Anthroposophical Society. New Thought bodies (e.g.,Unity and Science of the Mind) have incorporated much New Age thinking. A number of earlier Eastern groups still maintain viable and active organizations and generally can be considered as New Age. Included would be the following: Zen, The Farm, Vedanta Foundation, Self-Realization Fellowship, Transcendental Meditation, Krishnamurti Foundation, Sikh Dharma (3 HO), Sufi Order, Meher Baba, and the Arica Institute.

Other earlier but less easy to categorize groups relate to the New Age. UFO bodies still exist and they have New Age connections. Psycho-spiritual groups such as the Urantia Foundation and possibly Scientology are within the general New Age framework. While beginning earlier, the distribution of Native American spirituality to non-Indians has even increased since the counterculture years.

But there arose a number of organizations that were either new since 1970 or, if established before then, did not take off until the seventies and eighties. These organizations with New Age connections fall into several categories--Eastern spirituality, Theosophical-occult, psycho-spiritual, communal, the human potential movement, and holistic health groups. Perhaps the best known of these bodies are est, the Rajneesh Foundation, the Church Universal Triumphant, and Scientology.

Business corporations inadvertently facilitated the New Age. Desiring to improve productivity, they required their employees to attend training sessions. Many of these programs focused on stress management, interpersonal relations, and employee morale.[52] However, others were not this innocuous. They had clear religious dimensions and in some cases may be regarded as a quasi-religion. Their approach to self or corporate improvement assumed an occult-mystical worldview. These programs aimed at inner enlightenment and the transformation of one's consciousness. For methods they used yoga, self-hypnosis, and guided imagery. According to Erling Jorstad, corporations spent "as high as $30 billion a year for psychological training of employees, much of this in inner-renewal programs."[53]

A number of self-help and management training groups carried out the task of transforming the inner self and improving corporate productivity. Est (now the Forum) might be the best known of these organizations. Est, when spelled with lower-case letters, refers to

"Erhard Seminars Training." Est is also Latin for "it is." Kenneth Woodward says that est is "the *Reader's Digest* of the consciousness movement--a distillation of every self-help technique from Dale Carnegie to Zen, packaged for quick consumption."[54]

Est "is a form of secular salvation," writes John Clark. It is secular in that it denies being a religion at all.[55] Yet, est propounds a worldview and attempts to transform people and deliver them from difficulty. But est is more than a powerful therapy or a religion. It is a multimillion-dollar educational corporation that has trained hundreds of thousands of people since its inception in 1971. Est can be regarded as one of the New Age and human potential groups. As such it is right at home with the narcissism of the 1970s and 1980s. At a time when self-improvement has taken on the proportions of a quasi-religion, est has grown significantly.[56] But like many New Age groups, est is attempting to influence American society. Est's strategy for accomplishing this objective is to influence the nation's key institutions (schools, churches, news media, law enforcement) and to attract important people into the movement.[57]

The very core of est is a sixty-hour seminar held in convention centers across the country. The goal of this seminar is for people to "get it"--that is, the total transformation of the individual. When enough people "get it," society will be changed.[58]

Erhard regards "belief as a disease." Thus, the first step in transformation is to strip the mind of its belief systems.[59] When this is accomplished, est introduces the person to its own belief system, which is summarized by John Newport. First, est teaches "that the world has no meaning or purpose." Second, est says "that the mind imposes artificial meanings and purposes in the world." Third, and most important, each person is completely responsible for his or her own life. As an individual, "you are the cause of your own world."[60]

While not as well known as est, Lifespring and its offshoot, the Movement for Spiritual Inner Awareness (MSIA), is also a management training group. MSIA was begun by John-Roger Hinkins, who broke from ECKANKAR. MSIA and ECKANKAR are interrelated and came out of the Sant Mat tradition of India. Both groups also focus on mystical or soul travel--the mystical traveler exists simultaneously on all levels of consciousness and reaches the pure spiritual worlds. With the success of est, MSIA began its own seminars for self-awareness and self-transformation. Like est, they put the trainees through rigorous sessions, breaking down their previous belief system. More than 250,000 people have taken this training course.[61]

A Theosophical type of New Age group prominent in the 1980s is the Church Universal Triumphant (CUT). Founded in 1958 by Mark Prophet as the Summit Lighthouse, its name was changed in 1976. Since Mark Prophet's death in 1973, the organization has been run by Elizabeth Clare Prophet, affectionately called "Guru Ma" by her followers. CUT has centers across the nation, with its current headquarters on a 33,000-acre ranch in Montana. The group has received media attention because of its predictions of a nuclear holocaust and the subsequent preparation for such an attack, namely the building of underground shelters.[62]

Typical of a New Age group, the Church Universal Triumphant is a syncretistic mixture of Western occult and Eastern spirituality. Though never affiliated with the "I AM" organization, CUT has drawn many of its beliefs from "I AM." At the heart of the church's teachings are those regarding the "ascended masters." The Church Universal Triumphant, through its messengers Mark and Elizabeth Prophet, sees itself carrying on the work of the Great White Brotherhood. Elizabeth Clare Prophet claims to be "God's chosen earthly messenger for direct dictations [channeled messages] from a host of ascended masters including Buddha, Jesus, Saint Germain, Pope John XXIII" and so forth, writes Russell Chandler.[63]

Scientology's connections with the New Age are more tenuous. It is often not associated with the New Age. Yet Scientology is a psycho-spiritual group that shares several goals with the human potential and New Age movements. Along with these two movements, Scientology emphasizes self-improvement or self-actualization. Hundreds of thousands of people have come to Scientology seeking improved mental and physical health, a more attractive personality, a better memory, and so forth.[64]

Less obvious, but also like New Age groups, Scientology does have a vision for a new world. Scientology's ultimate goal is a "clear" planet. But this can come only when sufficient individuals become "clear"; that is, they have no neuroses or problems. The New Age is to be ushered in when enough individuals have been transformed. An early sign of a clear planet would be the elimination of crime, war, insanity, drugs, and pollution.[65]

In yet another way, Scientology shows itself to be a New Age group--the convergence of East and West. Though the central ideas and values of Scientology evolved from a Western occult and Eastern worldview, they come to the public in a Western technological package. In fact, Frank Flinn calls Scientology a technological Buddhism. The Scientological term "clear" resembles "the Buddhist concept of *bodhi*, which describes 'the one awake' or 'enlightened one,'" who has gained release from the entanglement of illusion and existence.[66]

L. Ron Hubbard (1911-1986) founded Scientology in 1954. Scientology began as Dianetics, a psuedo-scientific and psychological movement. Its original concern was with engrams, which are psychic scars that inhibit a person's full potential. However, engrams can be removed through the process of auditing, a question-answer therapy process to help the patient in looking for forgotten shock incidents. As this process continues, the negative impressions are pushed out of the mind and the client becomes "clear."[67] Scientology is the supernatural or occult phase of the movement. To the more psychological approach of Dianetics, Scientology has added the ideas of extra-terrestrial life, reincarnation, and a spiritual dimension.[68]

Another example of the blending of East and West in a New Age group is the Rajneesh Foundation International. Founded by the Bhagwan Rajneesh, this movement's spectacular rise and fall in the United States from 1981 to 1985 was connected with the escapades of its founder. He was deported from the United States in 1985 and his 64,000-acre ranch, which served as his headquarters, was shut down.[69]

The Rajneesh Foundation can be seen as a New Age group because it converged much from the East and West, and it had a vision for humanity. As Gordon Melton points out, Rajneesh endeavored to create "a new religious synthesis which brings elements of all the major religious traditions together with the new Western techniques of inner transformation and therapy, [many borrowed directly from humanistic psychology]."[70]

Rajneesh's vision for humanity emanated from his perception of the world's condition. In 1979 he warned: "If we cannot create the 'new man' in the coming twenty years, then humanity has no future. The holocaust of global suicide can only be avoided if a new kind of man can be created."[71] This new humanity could come only when enough individuals experienced transformation, enlightenment, or Buddhahood. Therefore, his mission was to bring enlightenment to humanity, beginning first with his followers.[72]

The real work of the New Age has not been done by these better known organizations. Rather, the New Age movement has been promoted largely by a host of smaller networks, organizations, groups, and communes--what might be comparable to "mom and pop" stores in the business world. These organizations may be the most important element in the New Age movement. On a daily basis, they work at transforming society according to the New Age vision.[73]

Throughout the nation many businesses further the New Age cause. Most of these business organizations are local. Some exist for only a short while. Most focus on some transformational aspect of the New Age. The range that these businesses serve is wide: the martial arts, meditation, psychological therapies, body therapies, and various forms of alternative medicine, plus a wide selection of New Age consumer products--health foods, natural vitamins, New Age and occult books, incense, yoga mats, meditation cushions, crystals, and oriental art.[74]

Standing out in respect to New Age organizations was the holistic health field. Such businesses were often more national in scope. Building on the foundation of the early holistic health centers, the movement took off by the late sixties. According to Melton, the landmark years of the holistic health movement in the United States were from 1968 to 1976--the time when numerous centers went up all over the country, especially in California. However, the watershed event for "the holistic health movement . . . . was clearly the founding of the American Holistic Medical Association (AHMA) in 1978" by Dr. Clyde Norman Shealy. The Association for Holistic Health is another prominent organization.[75]

While many New Agers are quite individualistic, a number of its members have lived communally. New Agers believe in cooperation and sharing--values basic to communal life. Yet economic sharing is not widespread in New Age communities. Instead, New Agers share a common ideology, value system, and living space. Usually these communes are ecologically conscious, with the people living a natural life, emphasizing natural foods and an environmental concern. While nearly all New Age communes have gardens, they are not dependent on farming for a living. Most people in these communes are educated, middle-class people who run businesses while living in a commune. The early New Age was built upon two prominent communes--the Findhorn Community and Auroville. Since the sixties, the number of New Age Communes has grown, forming an important component of the New Age.[76]

Practices

Perhaps no aspect of the New Age has gained more media attention than New Age practices. In fact, New Age practices have been the primary vehicle upon which the New Age movement has entered American pop culture. While they might appear too exotic and eerie, these phenomena are also instruments for making the New Age vision a reality. For the most part, New Age practices are intended to be instruments of transformation.

During the seventies and eighties, several New Age practices (e.g., channeling, crystals, shamanism) become household words. But there are many more practices than these popular ones. A later chapter will concentrate on this subject, so at this point only a few will be noted. Channeling is the New Age rage of the eighties. It has come in many forms and through many mediums. While not that noticeable during the seventies, crystals became a symbol of the New Age during the eighties. For the most of human history, people have believed that crystal stones were endowed with magical and occult powers. Shamanism, a premodern practice centering on individuals who supposedly have magical powers, is becoming popular during the 1990s. Its modern base in America has been in Native American spirituality. But in recent years it has gone well beyond this circle.[77]

The New Age also features other practices--many with roots deep in human history. The New Age has simply given these traditional occult practices some new wrinkles and at times a new interpretation. Dreams are regarded as a means for recovering spiritual information. Hypnosis has many New Age uses--some in therapy, others connected with the health field. Meditation, the technique for looking inward for meaning, is popular in New Age circles. Along with many aspects of the occult, reincarnation made a comeback in the 1960s and now enjoys great popularity in the New Age movement. Astrology and several paranormal practices enjoy a prominent place in the New Age, so much so that the New Age movement has been accused of simply recycling much of traditional occultism. Divination, especially Tarot cards, is also in use in New Age circles. By the end of the sixties Jewish spiritualism, especially mystical Kabbalahism, was even making a comeback.[78]

Chapter 6

NEW AGE RELIGIOUS AND PHILOSOPHICAL ASSUMPTIONS

New Age religious beliefs are difficult to determine. The New Age is a highly diverse movement drawing its inspiration from a number of sources--Western occultism, Eastern spirituality, modern psychology, natural science, and even Christianity. Such eclecticism has produced a movement with a hybrid belief system.[1]

The New Age has no high priest, no single spokesperson, and no creed. Moreover, all of its adherents do not hold to the same beliefs. Some ideas are accepted by some followers; other New Agers maintain a different set of beliefs. In addition, the New Age promotes change and evolution. Thus, New Age concepts are in constant flux. What is in vogue today may be out tomorrow.[2]

The paradoxical nature of modern Western thought has contributed to the hybrid nature of the New Age. As Ted Peters points out, people in the West both accept religion and reject it; they both accept modernity and reject it. The New Age does not see itself as a religion. It especially rejects organized religion and orthodox Christianity. The New Age prefers to view itself as scientific and as part of a personal growth movement. Yet, the New Age rejects modern secularism and is part of a rising religious consciousness that stands outside the institutional church.[3] Thus, the New Age is something of a quasi-religion.

The subjective nature of the New Age further complicates matters. According to Elliot Miller, most New Agers reject the reality of ultimate truth. For them, final authority resides in experience and intuition. "Truth is intensely personal and entirely subjective. Underlying much New Age thinking is a relativistic assumption that anything can be true for the individual, but nothing can be true for everyone."[4] The basis of the New Age movement rests more on a vision and on an experience than on a particular belief system. Therefore, as Gordon Melton suggests, the movement should be approached more from the vantage of its goals and ideals than by the beliefs which it maintains.[5]

In spite of these problems, the New Age has core assumptions to which most of its adherents would subscribe, in one way or another. While it may not always be clearly articulated, the New Age has a worldview--one that is penetrating Western society and offering an alternative to that of natural humanism and Christian theism. Ted Peters boils these beliefs down to eight teachings: holism, monism, the higher self, human potentiality, reincarnation, evolution/transformation, gnosis, and a New Age Jesus.[6] Douglas Groothuis regards monism, pantheism, human divinity, enlightenment, the unity of religion, and cosmic evolution as the core New Age themes.[7] Elliot Miller identifies basic New Age assumptions: everything is of the same reality; ultimate reality is Being and awareness; pantheism; human divinity; and a spiritualized doctrine of evolution.[8] Most of these assumptions, of course, are found in less systematic language in the writings of the major theorists of the New Age movement.

I have identified similar assumptions about the New Age, but I have shaped them somewhat differently. Also, while these same New Age beliefs are the basis for New Age activities in politics, economics, education, science, and health, I have saved these subjects for future chapters. In this chapter I will focus on the foundational New Age assumptions that have a spiritual or quasi-religious nature.

The Coming of a New Age

As its name indicates, the New Age movement concerns a belief in the coming of a New Age. It regards humanity as standing between two ages in human history--the Age of Pisces and the Age of Aquarius.[9] The emphasis on the coming of a New Age has varied among New Age spokespersons. While some individuals focus on other issues, they advocate a transformation of society that points to a new age.[10] However, some spokespersons speak more directly to the issue of a coming new age. Such individuals include an early forerunner of the New Age, Alice Bailey, and current spokespersons David Spangler, Benjamin Creme, and George Trevelyan.[11]

Millennialism is not the central assumption of the New Age movement. Rather, millennialism is the umbrella concept for many other New Age ideas. Yet the New Age view of the future does have a "millennial ring" to it and it must be considered as part of the longstanding Western millennial tradition.[12]

New Age Optimism

Barbara Hargrove examines New Age apocalypticism in the context of similar post-World War II movements. She sees New Age millennialism as different from that of the Jesus People and fundamentalist premillennialism. The Jesus People took a dim view of the future and were absolutely convinced that Jesus would come in their lifetime. Fundamentalist premillennialism, as represented in Hal Lindsey's best-seller *The Late Great Planet Earth*, "holds that social and moral corruption will increase until Jesus returns to take up his faithful . . . ." Unlike this pessimistic apocalypticism, New Age millennialism is to be "characterized by love and light." More like post-millennialism (which sees Christ coming at the end of a golden age) than premillennialism, the New Age groups take a "more positive interpretation of the end of the Age . . . ."[13]

In many ways Eastern spirituality has left its imprint on the New Age. But in one way it has not. Eastern spirituality is pessimistic and lacks a utopian tradition. The Eastern views of reincarnation, karma, and time as a cycle produce pessimism and fatalism. The cycle of misery simply repeats itself. On the contrary, the Western psyche is marked by optimism and utopian visions. Because the Western mind thinks of time as linear, problems become manageable. They are not doomed to be repeated. The past will not inevitably be reproduced. Thus, Western thought is characterized by optimism, not pessimism.[14]

The writings of prominent New Age advocate David Spangler reflect this positive view of the New Age. He contends that the world is entering a new age, a cycle when humanity becomes the "world savior,"a time when light enters the planet and the world experiences an "occult redemption." The New Age is to be "the age of communication" when humanity, nature, Christ, and God effectively communicate and come to realize their unity and oneness.[15]

The positive nature of the new age becomes even more apparent when New Age authors compare it with the old Piscean Age. In *The Turning Point*, Fritjof Capra points out many of the shortcomings of Western society. He magnifies these problems by setting forth an idealized view of a future world, which draws heavily on the wisdom of antiquity and the East.[16]

A Paradigm Shift

This coming new age is based not on some doomsday scenario but on a paradigm shift. In his 1962 book, *The Structure of Scientific Revolutions*, science historian Thomas Kuhn introduced the notion of a paradigm shift. While Kuhn restricted his concept of a paradigm shift to scientific theories, New Age writers would apply it to nearly every aspect of culture.[17]

"A paradigm is a scheme for understanding and explaining certain aspects of reality," writes Marilyn Ferguson. "A paradigm shift is a distinctly new way of thinking about old problems." The new paradigm includes old truth but when enough people begin to think differently, a paradigm shift has taken place.[18]

Capra believes that the modern Western world is in a state of crisis--one that has been brought on by the old paradigm. The paradigm of the old age has been formed by the rationalism of René Descartes, Isaac Newton's physics, and the Judeo-Christian tradition. Cartesian rationalism has promoted linear reason and has pushed mysticism and intuition aside. Newtonian physics gave the West a mechanized worldview. The Judeo-Christian tradition desacralized creation by removing God from it and opened the door to the exploitation of nature. The old paradigm has also produced a patriarchical order, an authoritarian and centralized political system, and a hierarchical social organization.[19]

A New World Order and the Coming of Christ

The new age based on a new paradigm will be different. While elements of the old order will be retained, there will be a convergence of East and West. Rationalism will be balanced by intuition. God, humanity, and nature will no longer be regarded as distinct entities. The environment will be nurtured because humanity is one with nature. A holistic view of science will replace Newtonian physics. Men and women will have an equal status. Society will be less hierarchical, and the political systems will be decentralized. Internationalism and localism will replace nationalism in global relations. Crime and war will be greatly reduced. Also, there will be one world religion, based on common mystical assumptions drawn from the religions of the world. Finally, instead of competition which fragments the world, cooperation will reign supreme.[20]

While most New Agers are working for a new world order, some connect the New Age with the coming of Christ. Of course, the Christ of the New Age is not the Jesus Christ of orthodox Christianity. The New Age separated the human Jesus from the office of the Christ or the divine Christ spirit, which has indwelt many great religious leaders through history (e.g., Rama, Krishna, Buddha, and Jesus). In fact, because Christ is divine and divinity indwells all people, Christ is within each person.[21]

New Agers such as David Spangler and George Trevelyan speak of the coming of Christ in only a very general sense--he manifests himself in all humanity.[22] However, other New Age teachers have gotten into specific predictions and even date-setting. Many Theosophists believed that a world savior would come in the person of Jiddu Krishnamurti. When he renounced this role in 1929, Alice Bailey predicted the reappearance of the Christ, who some called Lord Maitreya. Several groups and individuals emerging out of her Arcane School continued this line of prediction.[23]

Most prominent of these individuals was Benjamin Creme. He said that in 1945 Christ announced that he would return if certain global conditions were met (peace, economic sharing, human goodwill, and the reduction of authoritarianism). In July 1977 Maitreya informed Creme that he had taken a body and would descend from the Himalayas. Creme intensified his traveling and speaking on the matter and in 1982 took out full-page ads in major newspapers announcing the coming of Maitreya.[24]

The Harmonic Convergence of 1987 concerns an end-of-the-world prediction. In his book *The Mayan Factor*, José Arguelles contended that according to ancient Mayan calendars August 17, 1987, would be the beginning of the end. On that day three planets would line up with the moon and a twenty-five year period of trouble would begin, culminating in a catastrophe in 2012. This period could be headed off only if 144,000 followers would gather in various sites around the world "to resonate in harmony" for a new age of peace and unity. Thousands of people did meet on that date.[25]

The New Age belief in the coming of a new age fits well into the climate of the early 1990s. The Revolution of 1989, which ended Communism in Eastern Europe, and the breakup of the Soviet Union were watershed events--perhaps as significant as the French Revolution. The end of the Cold War and the reduction of the arms race parallel New Age objectives. A more liberal administration in the United States with apparently a greater concern for the environment suits New Age proponents. The late twentieth century is witnessing the convergence of East and West and the development of a new worldview in a post-Christian America. Most important, the end of a millennium in the year 2000 portends the coming of the new epoch, a new age.[26]

Transformation/Evolution

How will this New Age, this global paradigm shift, come about? According to New Age advocates, the methods will be evolution and transformation. New Age definitions of evolution differ significantly from those found in biological science. Evolution has a progressive and comprehensive meaning, referring at its highest levels to the psychological and spiritual growth of humanity. Moreover, unlike science, the New Age regards such evolutionary change as occurring over a shortened period of time--perhaps a single lifetime or generation. If such an evolution takes place, humanity will progress and life will be better for both individuals and the world.[27]

As Elliot Miller notes, "evolution is central to New Age belief." New Agers have great faith in the evolutionary process. "I believe that the most fundamental thing we can do today is to believe in evolution," writes Robert Muller, New Age proponent and former United Nations Assistant Secretary General. This faith in evolution underlies the New Age's optimistic assumptions that humanity will correct the world's current problems and establish a new order.[28]

Transformation means "forming over, a restructuring," especially the "transformation of (human) consciousness," says Marilyn Ferguson. She argues that social change depends not so much on the goodness of human nature, but the "transformative process itself," which people must trust. There are four basic ways people change their minds: change by exception, incremental change, pendulum change, and paradigm change. Only paradigm change will bring about transformation. In this dimension of change, the old information and new perspective are integrated, forming a new insight--one that is holistic and will facilitate the transformation process.[29]

Individual Transformation

According to Gordon Melton, "the central vision of the New Age is one of radical mystical transformation on an individual level." A person awakens to new realities such as the development of "new potentials" within him or herself, a new view of the universe, or the discovery of psychic capabilities. Also, he or she might undergo some new experiences such as psychological or physical healing, or interaction within an intimate community.[30]

Ferguson speaks of this transformation as a "journey without a final destination." While the process has stages, it can be triggered by a spontaneous mystical or psychic experience, often sparked by the use of psychotechnologies. Psychotechnologies are systems intended to bring about a "deliberate change in consciousness." They are the methods found in sensory isolation; autogenic training; biofeedback; hypnosis; meditation; self-help networks; contemporary psychotherapies; and in such systems as Arica, Gurdjieff, and Theosophy, as well as seminars such as Silva Mind Control, Lifespring, Actualizations and est.[31]

These psychotechniques do not contradict reason; they transcend it. They "help break the 'cultural trance'--the naive assumption that trappings and truisms of our own culture represent universal truths. . . ." Psychotechnologies enable the individual to "trust intuition, whole-brain knowing." Along this reasoning, "intuition, that 'natural knowledge,' becomes a trusted partner in everyday life."[32]

Other New Age thinkers place more weight on knowledge and choice. Willis Harmon describes transformation as something in which people gain a higher (but subjective) knowledge of "Self" and the "Whole." Individuals must cooperate with the transformation of human consciousness, which is part of a longer evolutionary cosmic process. Barbara Marx Hubbard believes that for the first time in history, humanity has the freedom to choose a new way, a new synthesis--one that will form a new humankind.[33] While Gary Zukav regards intuition as important, he does stress that "our species is again being given the chance to choose how it will learn, how it will evolve." The current cycle of evolution is ending, and humanity can choose the path of "conscious growth and conscious life."[34]

What results does this mystical transformation produce? In the New Age subculture, as Ted Peters notes, transformation is "the functional equivalent of salvation." Whether through a psychotechnique or the acquisition of a mystical knowledge, individuals are awakened to the spark of divinity within themselves. In the New Age, the path from humanity to godhood is the transformation or awakening process.[35] According to New Age historian Theodore Roszak, the great project of our day is "to awaken the god who sleeps at the roots of our human being."[36] Some New Agers claim that the exercise of psychic and paranormal powers and the belief in reincarnation confirm humanity's divine nature.[37]

The awakening process should bring about behavior changes in the transformed person. Transformed individuals, according to Marilyn Ferguson, become the "artists and scientists of [their] own lives." They are creative and have "new tools, gifts, [and] sensibilities."[38] George Trevelyan tells us that in the transformed person "the basic virtues of tolerance, honesty, respect for truth, cooperation and compassion will become ever more manifest."[39]

The Transformation of Society

The theme of a mystical transformation on the individual level does not preclude the transformation of society--it is only the prerequisite for a broader social transformation. As New Age advocate Jonathan Adolph says, "Developing a spiritual awareness is fundamental to bringing about positive changes in ourselves and society."[40] Writing before the end of the Cold War, Donald Keys says that the potential influence of the experience of transformation "cannot be left out of any sober assessment of the chances of human survival."[41]

The very heart of the New Age is that the vision of the transformed individual be imposed on the world. Therefore, as Gordon Melton writes, "the New Age is ultimately a vision of a transformed world, a heaven on earth, a society in which the problems of today are overcome and a new existence emerges."[42]

Such a condition will become a reality when a sufficient number of people become "awakened" to their potential and become aware of their divinity. Such individuals, particularly those in positions of influence, will transform society by means of a decentralized system of networks. Related to this thinking is the concept of a critical mass. According to this theory, says Ted Peters, "if enough people believe strongly in something, suddenly the idea will become true for everyone." The critical mass concept "assumes that a reciprocity exists between one's individual consciousness and the collective higher consciousness." New Ager David Spangler believes that transformation will come suddenly because a critical mass of people are "believing in and practicing the values and strategies of the new paradigm." Several New Age groups (e.g., Transcendental Meditation, Scientology) argue that if a certain percent of the world's population practice their particular procedure, the world will change dramatically. However, the critical mass theory has been examined by scholars and has largely been disproved.[43]

Related to the New Age notion of evolution is the Gaia theory. A number of New Agers, such as Donald Keys, believe that humanity is on the verge of a new evolutionary step: "the emergence of the first global civilization."[44] The idea of humanity evolving into a single consciousness can be found in the writings of Pierre Teilhard de Chardin, a philosopher who had a profound influence on New Age thinking.[45] More recently, the notion of one living civilization is called the Gaia hypothesis. This theory attempts to give a scientific basis to the pre-Christian beliefs that the earth is a living creature. Begun by James Lovelock, a respected British scientist, the Gaia hypothesis has religious dimensions. Named after the Earth goddess of ancient Greek and Roman mythology, Gaia has inspired spiritual feminism and a number of goddess festivals.[46]

The New Age vision of transformed individuals remaking society bears resemblance to the approach of many evangelical groups. To be certain, these parallels pertain to the method of social change, not to theology. Both groups believe that individuals must be transformed before society can be substantially improved. While New Agers believe that transformation is a mystical experience triggered by a psychotechnique, evangelicals believe that conversion comes by the power of the Holy Spirit.[47] When a sufficient number of individuals are transformed or converted, their impact will be evident and society will undergo a change. The New Age vision bears resemblance to evangelical post-millennialism, not the premillennial version.

Knowledge

As I said previously, for the New Ager transformation, or the awakening process, equals salvation. Transformation in turn is acquired by knowledge. The human problem is not sin--it is ignorance. For individuals to be awakened and for society to be transformed, ignorance must be dispelled. It is ignorance that blinds humans to their divinity. Because of ignorance people pollute the environment, create unjust social and economic structures, and settle their conflicts by violence. Ignorance is darkness, the lack of enlightenment. The new age will come when enough people acquire knowledge.[48]

A Subjective Knowledge

The knowledge that transforms individuals and society is not based on scientific or rational inquiry. Rather, this knowledge is Gnosis--subjective, intuitive, personal knowledge. It resembles the knowledge of the ancient Gnostics, which consisted of secret or esoteric wisdom regarding the workings of the world. Gnosis was a saving knowledge that enabled the endowed individual to transcend this evil material world and pass into the realm of light and spirit.[49] According to author Elaine Pagels, the ancient Greek language differentiated between reflective or scientific knowledge and knowing by experience or observation. The later is Gnosis--a personal knowledge often labeled in the modern world as higher consciousness or awakening.[50]

Marilyn Ferguson speaks of "direct knowing," which she regards as a mystical experience. Direct knowing does not reject science or rational thought; it transcends it. Unitary knowing is holistic. To experience this, people must disregard their old, limited way of perceiving; they must transcend the system. Direct knowing awakens individuals and takes them "out of the system."[51]

Gnosticism has been adapted to modern culture. It has impacted both mainstream religion and marginal groups, including the New Age movement.[52] Ancient Gnosticism in its strict form does not exist in the modern world. What has continued through history is the gnostic type. Professor of religion Carl Raschke sees the "latter day Gnostics" as in "revolt against the course of modern history."[53] Ted Peters speaks of "new age religiosity [as] perennial Gnosticism" because its answer to solving the human predicament is "a form of knowledge."[54] Catholic priest Stephen Fuchs contends that the objective of New Age proponents is "quite similar to the Gnostics: to re-create . . . a secret doctrine," a secret knowledge. This "esoteric element is an important trend in the New Age."[55]

It is not enough for the New Age to emphasize personal knowledge--it often downplays belief and reason. As Robert Burrows puts it, "ultimate reality is beyond rationality, [thus] reason must be abandoned." Also, "humanity's only limitations . . . are those imposed by belief." Therefore, "dismantling belief . . . is high on the agenda of many New Age programs."[56] For example, one est trainer told his trainees, "We're gonna throw away your whole belief system . . . We're gonna tear you down and put you back together."[57]

The New Age emphasis on intuitive, personal knowledge relates to their perceptions of the functions of the right and left hemispheres of the brain. The left hemisphere is believed to be the seat of rational thought, quantification, and analysis. Thanks to the Cartesian worldview, say the New Agers, for centuries the left hemisphere was held in high esteem. The right hemisphere is regarded as more intuitive and creative. New Agers consider their experiential approach to knowledge to be more in tune with the right hemisphere, which in their opinion holds the key to godhood. However, scientific research has not supported this sharp division between the right and left brain. Jerre Levy, a biopsychologist, regards the theory that the right hemisphere controls intuition and the left controls logic as a half-truth. For the regions of the brain to function properly, "they must integrate their activities . . . ."[58]

Reality

Despite much diversity, the New Age movement comes close to sharing a unified worldview. Most New Agers are monists--they believe that the cosmos consists of one all-embracing reality. Yet a minority within the movement have dualistic tendencies. They separate spirit from matter. Spirit is the ultimate reality and is good.

Matter is evil and largely an illusion--something that the spiritual-mystical person must transcend.[59]

The New Age maintains a teaching that is basic for much of Western occultism and Eastern religion--namely, ultimate reality is one, universal, and undivided. Ultimate reality is god, a life force, an inexhaustible cosmic energy. A single reality unites all of creation. In spite of outward appearances, all reality is one and that one is god.[60]

This monistic view of reality undergirds the thinking of many New Age spokespersons. George Trevelyan speaks of the oneness underlying all diversity as God and that divinity is "inherent everywhere."[61] According to Fritjof Capra, when consciousness awareness is attained, "all boundaries and dualisms have been transcended and all individuality dissolves into universal, undifferentiated oneness."[62] Marilyn Ferguson says that when a person experiences direct knowing (mystical knowledge), "there is no dualism, no separation of mind and body, self and others."[63] David Spangler believes that oneness "is the key concept of the New Age and the realization of this fact of oneness is the secret of new age living."[64]

While most New Agers believe all reality is divine, there are several ways of looking at this worldview. Robert Burrows points out three aspects of this New Age cosmic unity. First, creation emanates from this ultimate reality, which is "without qualification or attributes." This reality transcends all polarities, including good and evil. Next, divine reality is also "conceived as an all-pervasive energy or life force," frequently called the higher self or universal consciousness. Third, divine reality is often "seen as a dynamic interaction of opposing forces: male and female, light and dark, aggression and passivity, etc." These apparent opposites are to be "viewed as complementary aspects of the same fundamental divine reality."[65]

The notion of cosmic unity, that there is one divine reality, leads to pantheism (God is all and all is God). If reality is divine and without divisions, then everything must be god--human beings, animals, plants, and inanimate objects.[66] As Benjamin Creme tells us, "God is the sum total of all that exists in the whole of the manifested and unmanifested universe." Furthermore, God cannot be defined; he is beyond our "level of knowing." God is not a definite person but a presence that can be found in all things.[67] David

Spangler describes the ultimate reality as "life from which all form springs," as earth being its body and as containing all beings.[68]

The environmental movement, especially its more radical elements, tends toward a pantheistic worldview. New Ager Bob Hunter says that "it is not enough to feel worshipful toward Nature, one must view Nature as a manifested Godhead."[69] Conventional ecology is largely a political movement attempting to protect the environment from human exploitation. Deep ecology advocates a more radical approach to environmental matters, even encouraging people to have "a direct spiritual relation to nature . . . ."[70]

If everything is god, so is Jesus. But Jesus is divine "in exactly the sense that we are divine," writes Benjamin Creme. As noted earlier, the New Age has separated the human Jesus from the divine Christ. But Jesus is divine, "having perfected Himself and manifested the Divinity potential in each of us."[71] Spangler speaks of the Christ pattern throughout the world as demonstrating "a quality of divine consciousness."[72] Or as Ted Peters describes the New Age perspective: "Christ is the prototype or expression of the universal cosmic consciousness inherent in us all, and indeed in all lives."[73]

A pivotal New Age doctrine is that each individual is god. This belief provides the basis for the New Age vision of enlightened individuals and a transformed world. Enlightenment comes when individuals discover that spark of divinity residing within them. When enough people are enlightened, the world will be transformed and the new age will be ushered in.

Benjamin Creme tells us that God is "immanent in all creation, in mankind and all creation, that there is nothing else but God; that we are all part of a great Being."[74] But people are unaware of their divinity. According to New Age celebrity Shirley MacLaine, "the great tragedy of the human race was that we had forgotten we were each Divine."[75] Thus, the great task of each person is to discover his or her own divinity.

Because people are divine they have great potential. Widespread in the New Age movement is the belief that individuals have within them a tremendous untapped potential. All power and knowledge are available to the individual who discovers this spark of divinity. The individual must look within for this divinity. When it is discovered, the only limitations that the transformed individual has are self-chosen.[76]

Holism

Holism, sometimes spelled wholism, is a popular New Age concept. "The cardinal principle of wholism," writes Peters, "is that the whole is greater than the sum of the parts." For New Age advocates, holism means "the reintegration of what modern thought has pulled apart"--body and spirit, the individual and community, the masculine and feminine, and so forth.[77] The emerging new paradigm has a holistic and organic character. Unity in nearly all aspects of life is the goal of the New Age. Holism is the key to New Age thinking in religion, science, education, health, and economics.

On one hand, holism is closely linked to monism and pantheism. It is an expression of the New Age view of reality. Holism has a religious dimension. By means of a mystical experience one becomes aware of his or her divinity and achieves unity with god. This transformed individual now can think holistically.

On the other hand, the concept of holism is not the private domain of the New Age movement. It is an important general concept in the emerging post-modern world--the time in which we are now living when the intellectual assumptions of the Enlightenment have broken down.[78] For example, New Age futurist Alvin Toffler says that the Third Wave culture (the post-industrial world) "emphasized contexts, relationships, and wholes."[79] The concept of holism has penetrated the areas of science, economics, education, health-care, and mental health in ways not necessarily connected with the New Age.

New Age holism is closely connected with the systems theory, sometimes called the General Systems Theory. New Agers believe that a change must be made from reductionist thinking to the systems view. Reductionism is "the belief that all aspects of complex phenomena can be understood by reducing them to their constituent parts," writes Fritjof Capra. He also says that an overemphasis on Descartes' method has led to the fragmentation characterizing the thinking of the modern world, including the academic disciplines.[80]

Capra argues that modern physics has rejected the Cartesian view and has adopted a holistic and organic approach. The world is "no longer seen as a machine, made up of a multitude of objects, but has to be pictured as one indivisible, dynamic whole . . . ." From physics such holistic systems thinking has spread not only to the other natural sciences, but also to the social sciences, especially economics and psychology.[81]

New Agers acknowledge diversity in the world, but they strive for unity in diversity. They believe that everything is interconnected and humanity must begin to think holistically--that is, they must see the connection between the various parts. For New Agers such holistic thinking touches upon a wide spectrum of life--involving body, mind, and spirit; a different perspective on economic matters; the desire for a more egalitarian society; the rise of an ecological awareness; a greater emphasis on preventive medicine, including nutrition; more balance between intuition and rational thinking; and a shift to Jungian philosophy.[82] At least on a superficial level such thinking has caught on, so much so that as Toffler notes, the term holism has "crept into the popular vocabulary" and is "used almost indiscriminately."[83]

Occult Phenomena

The New Age movement features many occult beliefs and practices--reincarnation, channeling, astrology, psychic phenomena, past-life regressions, walk-in experiences, shamanism, UFO encounters, and many more. Such phenomena are widely accepted as authentic in the New Age subculture. These practices will be discussed in a later chapter. At this point, I will connect these phenomena with the New Age worldview. I will also look at reincarnation, which is not only basic to the New Age but also must be regarded as more of a belief than a practice.

The New Age Worldview

The New Age belief in occult phenomena is a natural outgrowth of the movement's worldview. The New Age is a blending of Western occultism, Eastern mysticism, parapsychology, a "supernatural" humanism, and positive thinking. Basic to these various components is a monistic worldview. If god is one and all is god, there cannot be a sharp dichotomy between the natural and supernatural realms. New Agers do not make an absolute distinction between the physical, human, divine, and spiritual aspects of reality.[84]

The New Age worldview can be seen as a throwback to the premodern world, especially drawing on the wisdom of antiquity. The occult worldviews of the Hellenistic era, whether they be monistic or dualistic, included belief in a multidimensional reality inhabited by spirits. Christian theism, which dominated in the West until at least the eighteenth century, taught the existence of a supernatural realm inhabited by spiritual forces. Only the natural humanism of the modern world rejects the possibility of supernatural causes and spiritual beings.

The New Age is a return to the mindset of premodern occultism and paganism plus a strong dose of Eastern mysticism. Such a worldview allows for the enlightened entities that communicate to the world through human channels or the persistence of souls that are reborn repeatedly. However, such activities are not viewed as supernatural but as a multidimensional aspect of one reality. Other occult practices, such as psychic phenomena, are seen as natural but not presently explainable by science. Edgar Mitchell, a former astronaut turned New Ager, says that "there are no unnatural or supernatural phenomena, only very large gaps in our knowledge of what is natural .... We should strive to fill these gaps of ignorance." Human beings have great potential and can bring such phenomena to pass if they utilize their hitherto untapped abilities. The universe also has a great reservoir of unused power. A wide range of occult practices are simply devices for plugging into this power.[85]

Many New Agers utilize occult phenomena for very practical reasons. They are tools for triggering the transformation process or acquiring greater self-awareness. New Agers often consult tarot card readers, astrologers, and professional psychics. They also visit spirit teachers, sometimes called ascended masters, who provide metaphysical teachings. However, they tend to avoid mediums who consult the dead and the trivial aspects of the occult (e.g., fortune tellers).[86]

Reincarnation

Reincarnation and karma are bedrock New Age concepts. Professor Paul Edwards defines reincarnation "as the view that human beings do not . . . live only once, but . . . live many, perhaps an infinite number of times, acquiring a new body for each incarnation." The doctrine of karma equates justice with retribution. The world is just and "everything good that happens to a human being is a reward for some previous good deed, and everything bad that happens to him is punishment for an evil deed." One can believe in reincarnation without holding to the doctrine of karma, but the opposite makes little sense.[87]

From the sixth to the eighteenth century, reincarnation existed in the West only when it was reintroduced by an outside source. Being rejected first by the Christian tradition and then by natural science, belief in reincarnation is currently staging a major comeback in the West. According to several polls, in 1980 about twenty-three to twenty-five percent of the American population believed in reincarnation.[88]

Beyond what the polls say, some indication of reincarnation's popularity are book sales and the attention given to it by the media and celebrities. About a million and a half copies of Shirley MacLaine's book, *Out on a Limb*, were printed. A number of other celebrities claim to believe in reincarnation. Some examples include country singer Loretta Lynn and Hollywood stars such as Sylvester Stallone, Glenn Ford, Anne Francis, Glenn Scarpelli, Audrey Frances, and Audrey Landers. Reincarnation also has been a recent theme of many comic books (e.g., *Ronin, Doctor Strange, Master of the Mystic*, and *Camelot 3000*). However, more Americans than New Agers believe in reincarnation. Reincarnation and astrology are two occult practices that have a relatively wide acceptance in the general population.[89]

Reincarnation has entered the New Age primarily by two sources: Theosophy and Eastern spirituality. Reincarnation well suits the New Age worldview and tendency to practice the occult. Moreover, as Ted Peters notes, "belief in reincarnation represents . . . a modest rebellion against Western science"--a characteristic of the New Age movement.[90] Also, as Melton says, the New Age focus on continual transformation leads to reincarnation. The transformation process is often a spiritual journey which cannot be completed in one lifetime. Thus, the belief in reincarnation allows one to pursue a long-term spiritual development over the span of several lifetimes. Furthermore, for the occult tradition and Eastern religions, reincarnation is the alternative to the Christian belief in life after death.[91]

Chapter 7

SCIENCE AND EDUCATION
IN THE NEW AGE

As in most areas of life, the New Age sees itself at the vanguard of changes in science and education. The New Age approach to science and learning grows out of its religious or philosophical teachings and is interwoven with its worldview. The keys to understanding New Age science and education lie in its concepts of wholeness and oneness. The cosmos consists of one essence, which contains the spark of divinity. Thus, reality contains no divisions.

New Age spokespersons condemn the fragmentations currently found in science and education. They insist that all areas of science are interrelated and that science itself is connected with other disciplines. New Agers deplore the division of education into narrow specialties and argue for a holistic approach to learning--one that transcends academic disciplines and connects body, mind, and spirit. In particular, they tend to merge science with religion and give the educational process a religious dimension. Science and learning in the New Age look inward and to the East. New Agers stress subjectivity more than would the advocates of "orthodox" approaches to science and education.

The Fragmentation of Western Thinking

New Age philosophers soundly condemn Western science. They reject what they perceive as its dualistic and reductionist methodology. Modern science separates mind and matter, objectivity and subjectivity, science and religion, the mystical from the scientific, and science from other areas of study. New Agers say that modern science has caused people in the West to think incorrectly. Their thought is fragmented. They think atomistically and divisively and thus divide the world into isolated parts.[1]

Marilyn Ferguson says that if "we believe the universe and ourselves to be mechanical, we will live mechanically." Moreover, "We fragment and freeze that which should be moving and dynamic." She also condemns the influence of academic specialization on science. "Specialization has kept most scientists from trespassing into 'fields' other than their own. . . ."[2] Fritjof Capra argues that the dualism and fragmentation fostered by the Newtonian system has had a negative impact on many aspects of life, including science, psychology, medicine, and economics.[3] Such wrong thinking has led to economic depression, the rape of nature, the pollution of our planet, social inequities, violence, and the insanity of nuclear weapons.[4]

A Mechanistic Cosmos

New Age spokespersons trace this problem to the development of Western science, especially physics. The origins of Western science go back to the sixth century B.C. Greeks. According to Capra, the Milesian school did not separate religion, philosophy, and science. In fact, it evidenced a "mystical flavor," and a monistic and organic view resembling the philosophy of ancient India and China. The break began with the Eleatic school, which assumed the existence of "a Divine Principle standing above all gods and men." With this thinking began dualism, the separation of spirit and matter that so characterizes Western thought.[5]

Furthered by the thinking of the Greek atomists and the ideas of Aristotle, the notion of the division of spirit and matter took hold in the West. But during the Middle Ages, philosophers evidenced little interest in the material world. Instead, they concentrated on spiritual matters, especially issues concerning God, the human soul, and ethics.[6] Still, the sharp break between spirit and matter had to wait the birth of modern science in the sixteenth and seventeenth centuries. During the Middle Ages the worldview was organic, not fragmented. Unlike modern science, medieval science rested on both faith and reason. In looking for answers to ultimate questions, medieval scientists considered matters relating to God, the soul, and ethics. In fact, religious issues predominated, and Europeans primarily maintained a supernatural worldview. The sharp distinction between science and the occult had not yet been made. In the premodern world, the average person regarded the occult arts as practical devices for meeting their daily needs (the cure of illness, information regarding the planting cycle, and business transactions).[7]

Descartes and Newton

René Descartes and Isaac Newton are the acknowledged fathers of modern thought. Fritjof Capra and a number of New Age theoreticians have made them the major culprits in respect to the fragmentation of Western thought. The New Age movement has not limited its attack to Christian theism--it has also launched a frontal assault on modern science and modernity itself.

The philosophy of Descartes paved the way for the mechanization of modern scientific thought. He viewed nature as being divided into two separate and independent realms--that of mind and matter. His famous statement, "I think, therefore I exist,"has influenced Western people to "equate their identity with their mind instead of their whole organism." Descartes prepared the way for a mechanistic concept of the universe by separating sharply the objective external world from the subjectivity of the human mind. Descartes emphasized objective rational thinking and influenced subsequent Western thought to distinguish the external world from human consciousness.[8]

The culmination of the Scientific Revolution--the development of modern science during the sixteenth and seventeenth centuries--was the work of Isaac Newton. He synthesized the ideas of his predecessors, namely Copernicus, Kepler, Bacon, Galileo, and Descartes. In doing so, he formulated the theory of the Newtonian universe--"one huge mechanical system, operating according to exact mathematical laws." This mechanistic worldview became the basis of nearly all science until the late nineteenth century.[9] This mind-set spawned what futurist Alvin Toffler calls "The Second Wave--the rise of industrial civilization."[10]

The End of the Newtonian World

Until 1900 most classical physicists subscribed to Newton's mechanical view of the universe. But dramatic changes came in the first quarter of the twentieth century that would forever alter how scientists viewed the cosmos. Newton's notion of the universe as a well-ordered machine was destroyed. Upon these early revisions, a number of twentieth century physicists built their theories of a more organic, holistic universe. New Age theorists have seized upon these ideas, which they interpret as supporting their more mystical, subjective science.

The New Physics

Newtonian physics regarded time and space as absolute. Several centuries earlier the views of Copernicus and Galileo had sent tremors through both the scientific and religious establishments. A similar explosion took place in the early twentieth century. Albert Einstein unveiled his theory of relativity, thus shattering Newton's view of absolute time and space. Einstein argued that time and space should not be seen as absolute and distinct. They were relative and were related to each other, to the speed of light, to energy, and to gravity. With Newton's view of the universe now in ashes, scientists began to search for new models of the cosmos.[11]

Einstein's ideas also generated another revolutionary trend in science: the theory of atomic phenomena. While Einstein largely developed his theory of relativity by himself, the work on atoms-- which became known as the quantum theory--was constructed over thirty years by an international team of physicists. Best known were Einstein himself, Max Planck, Neils Bohr, Werner Heisenberg, Erwin Schrodinger, Wolfgang Pauli, Louis De Broglie, and Paul Dirac. The quantum theory, also known as quantum mechanics or quantum physics, contends that units of energy are "discontinuously absorbed and radiated by subatomic particles." The term "New Physics" has been used to describe these two developments: the theory of relativity and quantum mechanics.[12]

Max Planck, a German physicist, pioneered the work in quantum physics. He contended that particles of light, called by various names--energy packets, quanta, or photons--acted unpredictably, not in the systematic fashion assumed by the Newtonian worldview.[13] The Danish physicist, Niels Bohr, followed up with his Principle of Complementarity.   According to this theory, instead of questioning the erratic nature of the subatomic world, one should accept it. The reductionist methodology should not be applied to electrons. To best understand them, they need to be viewed holistically.[14]

Another German physicist, Werner Heisenberg, later wrote his Uncertainty Principle.   Based on his study of the electron, he contended that the quantum realm could not be measured and charted adequately. In the subatomic world, fundamental reality was unpredictable. In the macroscopic realm, outcomes can be predicted because the various forces at work can be discovered.   On the contrary, events in the subatomic world cannot be predicted with any accuracy because all of the forces are not discoverable.[15]

Perhaps even more than Einstein's theory of relativity, quantum physics has destroyed the worldview of Descartes and Newton. As New Age scientist Fritjof Capra puts it, the theories of relativity and quantum mechanics have "shattered all the principle concepts of the Newtonian world view: the notion of absolute space and time, the elementary solid particles, the strictly causal nature of physical phenomena, and the idea of an objective description of nature."[16]

These two theories have dramatically altered the way physicists view reality. They see fundamental reality as run by chance, behaving paradoxically, and better understood by holistic (rather than reductionist) thinking.   Quantum physics also has changed the relationship between subject and object. The scientist is no longer seen as an impersonal, totally objective observer of events. The scientist is now regarded as an active participant in scientific ongoings.   The act of observing influences the scientist, thus interjecting an element of subjectivity into the scientific process.[17]

David Bohm

In demolishing the mechanical world of Newton and interjecting an element of unpredictability into the scientific process, quantum physics helped pave the way for New Age science. David Bohm, a Princeton physicist, furthered such a development. He went beyond quantum mechanics and advocated a holistic approach to the physical world. So much have his ideas appealed to the New Age theorists that they have claimed his writings as support for their science.[18]

In going beyond quantum physics, Bohm sided with the thinking of the post-modern mind. Ted Peters summarizes his thought. Bohm believes that reality is fundamentally "undivided wholeness in flowing movement." He regards the universe to be "a whole and everything in it is engaged in perpetual motion . . . . " Bohm acknowledges particular regions of space and time, which he calls subtotalities. But the universe is not fragmented, for "the relationship between subtotalities and the whole is governed by holonomy--that is, the law of the whole." But there is a certain looseness about the law of the whole, for it permits "a certain autonomy on the part of the regions within it." Bohm even appears to be attributing divine qualities to this holomovement. He thinks of the "whole as holy" but he avoids anything resembling a concept of God.[19]

A Subjective and Holistic Science

When taken all together, the new developments in physics paved the way for New Age science. The universe was no longer seen as an orderly machine run by an omnipotent God. The quantum physicists believed that reality was a random process governed by chance. (However, Einstein disagreed, saying that "God does not play dice with the universe.")[20] In breaking down the barrier between the observer and subject, science had lost some of its objectivity and had become more subjective. A level of holism had been injected into scientific thinking, with many believing that the whole is greater than the sum of its parts.

Peters calls New Age science "scientific wholism." He says that it combines three elements: "twentieth-century discoveries in physics, an acknowledgment of the important role played by imagination in human knowing, and a recognition of the ethical exigency of preserving our planet from ecological destruction."[21]

Essentially, New Age science is a throwback to the science and mind-set of the premodern world, especially the world of antiquity. As Marilyn Ferguson puts it, "Science is only now verifying what humankind has known intuitively since the dawn of history."[22] New Ager Paul Davies says it in a different way: "For the greater part of human history, men and women have turned to religion not only for moral guidance, but also for answers to the fundamental questions of existence."[23] Basically, the New Age has returned to such an approach--that of giving science a religious dimension.

Prior to the seventeenth century, Western people maintained a religious worldview that did not rigidly separate science from religion or the natural from the supernatural. However, this religious worldview in the West was based on Christian theism. The New Age has rejected the modern secular worldview, but it has not embraced Christian theism. New Age science is holistic, combining religion and science, the rational and the intuitive. However, the religion is not Christian theism but occult/Eastern monism. Modern science, say many New Agers, has gone full cycle, returning to the monistic and organic view of the Milesian Greeks. Fritjof Capra says that if physics leads the world to a mystical worldview, it will be going back "to the beginning, 2,500 years ago."[24]

Several New Age spokespersons have attempted to link the concepts of modern physics with the ideas of Eastern religions, especially Hinduism, Buddhism, and Taoism. In his award-winning book, *The Dancing Wu Li Masters*, Gary Zukav points to "similarities between Eastern philosophies and physics" that to him seemed "so obvious and significant."[25]

Fritjof Capra carried this argument much further. The aim of his best-selling book, *The Tao of Physics*, is to demonstrate the "essential harmony between the spirit of Eastern wisdom and Western Science." He argues that "the concepts of modern physics often show surprising parallels to the ideas expressed in the religious philosophies of the Far East." Capra says that the "New Physics" (the theory of relativity and quantum mechanics) forces people to see the world in a way very much like Eastern mysticism does--that is, they become aware of "the unity and mutual interrelation of all phenomena and the intrinsically dynamic nature of the universe."[26]

A Subjective Science

What results when science is linked to the worldview of ancient and Eastern mysticism? We are left with a science that has a more mystical, subjective, and religious orientation than does conventional science, including the "New Physics." Accent must be put on the word *more*. New Age scientists such as Capra do not rule out traditional scientific methods: "rational activities certainly constitute

the major part of scientific research, but are not all there is to it."
The rational part of research must be "complemented by the intuition
that gives scientists new insights and makes them creative."[27] In a
later book, Capra's approach is more subjective. He argues that
"Deep ecology is supported by modern science . . . but it is rooted in
a perception of reality that goes beyond the scientific framework to
an intuitive awareness of all life . . . ."[28]

Other New Agers take an even more subjective and mystical view
of science--one that appears to redefine science. Michael Talbot
speaks of "the confluence of mysticism and the new physics."[29]
Marilyn Ferguson cites many scientists to bolster her arguments,
which in essence say that much of scientific knowledge must come
from intuition, an enlarged awareness, and a mystical experience.[30]
The late Bhagwan Shree Rajneesh said his "religion is absolutely
scientific" but "it is a different science" than that taught in the
universities, which is an objective science. His science is "subjective
science."[31]

Quantum physics opened the door to more subjectivity in science.
Yet, New Age science has carried this subjectivity much further than
anything intended by the quantum physicists. Many New Age
spokespersons insist that there is no objective reality. As Beverly
Rubik puts it, "there is no absolute objective reality . . . . Objectivity
is only a man-made concept . . ."[32] Michael Talbot tells us that "The
entire physical universe itself is nothing more than patterns of
neuronal energy firing off inside our heads . . . ."[33]

According to most New Agers, ultimate reality is mind or
consciousness, which contains the divinity that flows through the
cosmos. Because the nature of reality is consciousness, the human
mind can construct reality. In the words of Shirley MacLaine: "I have
come to realize that 'reality' is basically that which each of us
perceives it to be. . . we each live in a separate world of reality."[34]
New Agers writing from a scientific perspective make similar
statements. Fred Alan Wolf says, "Everything depends on you. You
create the whole universe; you are the 'you-niverse.'"[35] Talbot tells
us that "Consciousness creates all."[36] According to Capra, "The
electron   does not   have objective properties independent of my
mind. . . . We can never speak about nature without, at the same
time, speaking about ourselves."[37]

Because of such thinking, New agers have redefined science and
religion. They have merged the two, creating something of a hybrid.

In fact, if this view of reality were to become widespread, the very nature of Western civilization would change. Traditionally, the Western mind has seen science as dealing with objective reality and religion relating to issues concerning an objective, personal God. New Age thinking has made both science and religion more subjective--and thus more compatible.[38]

The New Age has married science and religion. In the Western psyche, religion and science have been at odds with each other for several centuries, eventually separating into two warring camps. In the New Age mind-set, peace has been restored. As religion and science have become more subjective, merging two views of reality into one, they have become partners. Because of its empirical methods of verification, traditionally science has not addressed the questions of ultimate reality. This has been the domain of religion. But in New Age thinking, ultimate reality is consciousness (the mind). Thus, because science is more subjective, it is now addressing the questions of ultimate reality.[39] Paul Davies even goes so far as to say that "science offers a surer path to God than religion." In his opinion, science has reached the point where it can tackle "what were formerly religious questions."[40]

The New Age merger of science with the religion of occult/Eastern mysticism could spell the end of "objective" science as it is known in the West. Some New Agers hope that this will be the case. Marilyn Ferguson states the opinions of Gary Zukav, a mystic physicist. He believes that "we may be approaching the end of science." The reductionist method of Western science has its limitations. Thus "only direct mystical experience" and "enlarged awareness" can "carry us past the limits of our logic to more complete knowledge."[41]

The architects of the "New Physics" acknowledged the chaotic nature of the subatomic world, thus making science more unpredictable. But they believed that a real universe would exist even if there were no human beings to examine it. Einstein said that "The belief in an external world independent of the perceiving subject is the basis of all natural science." However, he did speak of an imperfect perception of the world. Thus, our "notions of physical reality can never be final."[42] Or as Richard Rube, professor at Stanford, puts it: "Authentic science is unreservedly committed to the existence of an objective reality. . . . Our knowledge of this reality must indeed be personal knowledge, but this does not imply that it is therefore subjective knowledge."[43]

A Holistic Science

A subjective science is one result of linking science to the worldview of the occult tradition and Eastern religion. Another product of such a relationship is a holistic science. Holism is a basic concept of the New Age movement and has been discussed in chapter six. At this point, I will briefly relate holism to New Age science.

Central to New Age thinking is its monistic worldview. The cosmos consists of one divine essence or reality. Consequently, everything is connected and interrelated, resulting in a cosmic unity. Holism penetrates nearly every area of New Age life and thought. But New Age science led the way. The revolt against Cartesian dualism began with the "New Physics." New Age scientists claimed these developments as supporting their claims and since then the rejection of dualism has become widespread within the New Age movement.

In citing the work of other scientists, Marilyn Ferguson tells us that "modern science has verified the quality of whole-making." Wholeness is "a fundamental characteristic of the universe." She challenges the scientific method, condemning the practice of trying "to understand nature by breaking things into their parts. . . . Wholes cannot be understood by analysis." Rather, wholes are dynamic, creative, and constantly evolving. They just come together.[44] Paul Davies also condemns the reductionist thrust of Western science. Problems are like a jigsaw, they "can only be perceived at a higher level of structure than the individual pieces--the whole is greater than the sum of its parts."[45]

Of the New Age scientists, the most forceful articulation for scientific holism comes from Fritjof Capra. In the *Tao of Physics*, he says that the very essence of Eastern mysticism is "the awareness of the unity and mutual interrelation of all things and wants." Building on this foundation, he argues that modern physics has the same outlook as do Eastern religions--"everything in the universe is connected to everything else . . . ." In *The Turning Point*, he tells us that "subatomic particles have no meaning as isolated entities but can be understood only as interconnections . . . ." In his opinion, "modern physics reveals the basic oneness of the universe. It shows that we cannot decompose the world into independently existing smallest units. "[46]

This New Age emphasis on a holistic science leads to the paranormal. According to New Age thinking, consciousness creates reality. Thus, the capabilities of divinity are within each person and the paranormal becomes possible. The paranormal is also within reach because everyone has access to the holographic domain.[47] Holography is the construction of something resembling a three-dimensional picture. Every part of the hologram contains the entire image. In this holographic framework, according to Marilyn Ferguson, "psychic phenomena are only by-products of the simultaneous-everywhere matrix." She regards individual brains as "bits of the greater hologram." Under certain circumstances, they have access "to all the information in the total cybernetic system." Such an approach takes the paranormal out of the supernatural realm "by demonstrating that they are part of nature."[48]

Deep Ecology

New Age science has not been confined to physics. The same New Age ideas--monism and holism--have had a significant impact on ecology. In fact, as with physics, New Age environmentalism is but an extension of the New Age worldview. In chapter six, which dealt with the New Age worldview, I addressed the subject of ecology. Environmental concerns are an important item in the New Age political agenda--a subject for the next chapter. Thus, in this chapter I will briefly note the New Age ideas on ecology, particularly as they relate to science.

Jonathan Adolph, editor of the *New Age Journal,* considers several issues as central to the "serious" New Age movement. Concern for the environment is one of them.[49] As a result, New Age leaders have launched a three-pronged approach to the environmental problems. In the realm of ideas, they attack not only the current practices of the industrialized world but the mind-set that has fostered the destruction of the environment. In place of what they perceive to be wrong thinking, they advocate a different worldview--one they believe will solve many human problems, including the environmental crisis. Finally, the New Age has practical programs for implementing this worldview--topics better suited for the chapter on politics and economics.

The Crisis

In respect to the environment (and perhaps in their overall thinking) the "whipping boys" for the New Age have been the mechanical outlook of Western science, patriarchal values, and the Christian tradition.[50] New Age historian Theodore Roszak traces the root of environmental problems to the Judeo-Christian tradition. Judaism's "insistence on God's unity, invisibility,and transcendence" led to an uncompromising rejection of idolatry. This "hot intolerance for nature worship and the pagan use of imagery" carried over into Christianity. The medieval church rejected paganism, nature worship, and magic, but it accommodated aspects of the magical tradition (depending on how one interprets the sacramental system and the cult of the Virgin). Yet, the fiercest and most uncompromising rejection of idolatry came from the Protestant tradition. What Judaism and Christianity (Islam too) have condemned as paganism and nature worship has been called animism or naturalism by anthropologists.[51]

Roszak also tells us that the estrangement from nature ingrained in the Judeo-Christian tradition found its way into "the psychology of scientific knowledge." He admits that the industrialists, not the scientists, have ravaged the environment. But the Judeo-Christian tradition and Western science have provided "an image of nature that invited the rape" and even gave license to it. Roszak points out Francis Bacon's call to humanity "to unite forces against the nature of things, to storm and occupy her castles and strongholds and extend the bounds of human empire . . . . " In the pre-industrial world of the seventeenth century, humanity could do little damage to nature, but the seeds were sown by Bacon.[52]

A number of New Age spokespersons continue down this path, pointing out the evils of Cartesian philosophy and Newton's mechanistic universe. The story has been told elsewhere in this book. Descartes' separation of mind and matter have promoted a dualistic, fragmented worldview. Newton's science turned the universe into a lifeless machine.[53]   As a result of such thinking, "nature is pronounced dead and desacralized," writes Roszak. Nature is no longer seen as living and sacred and thus can be exploited.[54]

Vishal Mangalwadi, a New Age critic, addresses the related issue of psychic vibrations. Many New Agers believe that "the earth is a living being with feelings and emotions." Dark energy forms--fear, resentment, aggression, and anger--have emotionally hurt the earth. Thus, the environmental problem must be seen in terms of a disturbance in the earth's psyche."[55]

People living in urban industrialized societies have paid an "intolerably high" price for the Baconian mind-set, which encouraged humanity to dominate and abuse nature, says Roszak.[56] Fritjof Capra and other New Agers spell out the disastrous effects that this fragmented, mechanistic worldview has had on the environment. Life on earth has become "physically and mentally unhealthy." A list would include "polluted air, irritating noise, traffic congestion, chemical contaminants, radiation hazards," and many others. Of greatest concern is the "nuclear madness" that has driven society to produce nuclear energy and--worst of all--weapons of mass destruction.[57]

The Solution

The answer to these environmental problems, say the New Agers, is for human beings to change their thinking. They must abandon the old dualistic, fragmented paradigm associated with the Christian tradition, Descartes, and Newton. In its place, they must embrace the holistic thinking linked with the new emerging paradigm. In reference to the environment, New Age author George Trevelyan says that "our salvation lies in learning how to THINK WHOLENESS." Such holistic thinking comes from a monistic worldview that sees all things--God, humanity, and nature--as one. Only a monistic, pantheistic worldview can insure a balanced view of nature that preserves the environment.[58]

Most New Agers go well beyond concern for the environment. They embrace the notion of deep ecology, which has religious dimensions. There are deep philosophical differences between "deep ecology" and "shallow environmentalism." Capra tells us that shallow environmentalism concerns the "efficient control and management of the natural environment for the benefit of 'man'".... [59] Yet, it entails no substantial break from the Baconiam or Cartesian mentality. Shallow environmentalism is part of the old paradigm.

On the other hand, deep ecology rests in a new philosophical and religious system. It recognizes that ecological balance entails a significant alteration in the way human beings see their role in the ecosystem. Capra and others argue that deep ecology can be supported by modern science, especially the systems approach. Yet, deep ecology goes beyond science. It is rooted in the "intuitive awareness of the oneness of all life . . . ." Human beings should no longer see themselves as dominating nature. Rather they should "feel connected to the cosmos as a whole." Such a change in ecological awareness is spiritual and must come by means of a religious experience.[60]

The religious and philosophical framework for deep ecology and the experience that it entails can be found in both the Eastern and Western traditions, says Capra. It is common in Eastern spirituality, especially Taoism. The universe is regarded as of one essence and dynamic. The philosophy of deep ecology has been a minority opinion in the Western tradition. Some ancient Greeks, especially Heraclitus, taught this view. The wisdom of deep ecology has always existed in the Western occult tradition. The views of Christian mystics, such as St. Francis of Assisi, have bordered on deep ecology. Even some Western philosophers, including Baruch Spinoza and Martin Heidegger, have embraced the essence of deep ecology.[61]

The Gaia Hypothesis

Deep ecology is also linked to a previously mentioned New Age concept--the Gaia hypothesis. The belief that the earth is alive received strong support in the 1960s when James Lovelock set forth the Gaia hypothesis--the planet is one single living organism. The photographs taken by the astronauts of the "Whole Earth" moved millions of people to emotionally embrace such thinking.[62]

New Age author Peter Russell argues for the scientific basis of the Gaia hypothesis. "The entire range of living matter on Earth . . . all appear to be part of a giant system able to regulate the temperature and the composition of the air, sea, and soil so as to ensure the survival of life." In scientific terms, this is called a homeostasis: a stable state of equilibrium between different but interdependent elements of an organism or group. Maintaining the human body temperature at about 98.6 degrees Fahrenheit is an example of homeostasis. Russell contends that by monitoring many key elements on earth--the atmosphere, the soil, and the ocean--Gaia (the earth) appears to be maintaining a "planetary homeostasis."[63]

The Gaia hypothesis, named after the goddess of ancient mythology, connects with New Age feminism. The notions of

"Mother Earth" and "Mother Nature" have interjected a strong strand of feminism into New Age ecology. New Agers believe that Christianity has fostered many patriarchical values, including humankind's dominance of nature. Instead, if people were to view Mother Earth as a goddess, they would respect her--not dominate and exploit her. The idea of regarding nature as a living personality, specifically a feminine goddess, has taken a strong hold in neopagan witchcraft in recent years. Such a concept has spilled over into the New Age.[64]

A Holistic Education

The New Age worldview and values carry over into education, which the movement sees as a cornerstone for transforming society. The New Age philosophy of education centers on several key concepts: holism, transformation, diversity, and a nontraditional approach to learning.

There are three interrelated facets to New Age education--its critique of the existing system, its philosophy of learning, and practical steps taken to implement this philosophy. However, as in many areas of the New Age, the movement lacks distinct boundaries. What is New Age education and what are just current trends in learning is not easy to determine. They overlap considerably. For example, much of the New Age criticism of contemporary education and its suggestions to correct these problems are shared by groups who have no New Age connections.

New Age Criticism and Alternatives

Several New Age spokespersons lash out at the current educational system and offer opinions as to how it should change. Peter Russell argues that education must be a lifelong activity, not "simply a preparation for adulthood." Moreover, there should be less emphasis on facts and information and more focus on a subjective element--"the development of the knower." Intuition, creativity, and personal development should be as highly valued as technology, science, and economic progress.[65]

Alvin Toffler is especially critical of the "back-to-basics movement" in American education. He regards it as an endeavor to enforce "Second Wave [the old industrial age] uniformity in the schools."

Attempts to insure uniformity are "essentially the rearguard actions" of a declining civilization. Instead, the Third Wave (the New Age) will encourage diversity and flexibility in education, as it does in most areas of life. In fact, Toffler challenges the notion that education must take place primarily in the classrooms. Rather, learning should be combined with activities in work, community service, political action, and even leisure.[66]

Instead of a piecemeal approach to reforming education, Fritjof Capra believes that the changes underway will result in a significant transformation of the entire system. These changes, he contends, began in the 1960s and 1970s. They did not take place so much in the academic institutions as in the general population and especially in the efforts at adult education. Quite often these educational changes were spawned by the social movements of these decades.[67]

Perhaps the most comprehensive critique of the old system and an accompanying New Age philosophy of education comes from Marilyn Ferguson. She compares and contrasts the assumptions of the old educational paradigm with those of the new. Under the old system emphasis is on content; under the new, it is on "learning how to learn." Learning is a process, not a product as with the old paradigm. The old educational system is hierarchical and learning is rigid, a "lockstep progress" (compartmentalization for age groups) emphasizing performance and the external world. The new system is to be egalitarian, flexible in respect to age groupings, and placing priority on self-image and the inner experience. The exploration of feelings is encouraged, and there is to be a liberal use of imagery, storytelling, and dream journals.[68]

Under the old paradigm, divergent thinking is discouraged, and emphasis is placed on "analytical, linear, left brain thinking." The new paradigm encourages divergent thinking and endeavors for a whole-brain education, complementing rationality with nonlinear thinking and intuition. The old system is concerned with normative standards of achievement and theoretical book knowledge. The new system measures a student's performance in respect to his or her potential and augments book knowledge with experiential learning.[69]

In new paradigm classrooms, there is "concern for the environment of learning"--colors, air temperature, lighting, and physical comforts. Classrooms under the old system are designed for convenience and efficiency. Under the old paradigm, education is determined by the educational bureaucracy and is seen as a social necessity for a specific time period. Also, learning is a "one-way street" with the teacher imparting knowledge. The new system "encourages community input" into the decisions that determine the content of education and sees education as a "lifelong process." Moreover, learning is a two-way process with the teacher also learning from the students.[70]

Ferguson calls this New Age educational philosophy "transpersonal education." It borrows its name and much of its approach from Transpersonal Psychology. It "focuses on the transcendent capacities of human beings" and encourages the learner to be "awake and autonomous." At the heart of transpersonal education is the education of the whole person--body, mind, and spirit. Transpersonal education is education's "counterpart to holistic medicine." Such education is transforming. It transforms the learner, the teacher, and society.[71]

Ferguson sees a widespread movement toward holistic education: "tens of thousands" of administrators, classroom teachers, and college teachers are "among the millions engaged in personal transformation."[72] Her perception of the influence of New Age ideas on education are exaggerated. Yet, some impact is visible. Over the last twenty years, education has witnessed substantial changes. Many of the modifications are compatible with New Age philosophy. Yet, all of these changes did not originate with the New Age movement and thus cannot be labeled as New Age.

New Developments

The major changes in education endorsed by the New Age took place during the 1960s and 1970s. Beginning with the student rebellion of the sixties, students demanded rights in education. Included on their list were the right to participate in the process of deciding course content and that the universities should offer courses on subjects of current interest (e.g., Black studies, ethnic studies, women's programs). The next phase of change came in the seventies. The number of traditional students between eighteen and twenty-two declined, and academic institutions experienced financial crises. As a result of this financial crunch, they turned to innovative educational programs.[73]

These changes were most obvious in the areas of adult education and alternative educational programs. Adults learn better in situations in which they have some control. Thus, they have to be treated more democratically. Alternative education resonates with New Age philosophy. Students can earn college credit in many non-traditional settings--correspondence work, standardized examinations, travel, and documentation of learning and work experiences.[74] Other trends complement the New Age. The New Age frowns on narrow academic disciplines. Thus, an interdisciplinary approach fits well the New Age emphasis on wholeness. The New Age focus on diversity and interconnectedness relates to the current trend toward multiculturalism in education.[75]

A number of educational developments occurring during the seventies and eighties have more obvious religious and New Age connections. During the 1970s Transcendental Meditation received government funds to bring its ideas into the public schools as Science of Creative Intelligence. Transcendental Meditation has Hindu overtones, and in 1977 a federal court declared it to be a religion and thus in violation of church-state separation.[76]

Another New Age educational philosophy receiving federal funds was "confluent education." Confluent education can be described as a holistic approach to learning using the five senses, rational thinking, feeling, and intuition. The architect of confluent education was the late Beverly Galyean. Her program was used in the Los Angeles Public Schools. Confluent education teaches the basic subjects with introspective techniques. The child is not regarded as a blank slate on which to inscribe information. Rather, in problem-solving the child is encouraged to draw on his or her past experiences and imagination. Feelings and subjective evaluations are considered an important aspect of the process. Confluent education combines a number of factors in learning--the five senses, intuition, rational analysis, and effective communication.[77]

As progressive as this might sound, confluent education has religious overtones resulting from its monistic worldview. Confluent education contends for the equality of educational values because all people have divine attributes. New Age critic Frances Adeney points out three occult/Eastern assumptions behind Galyean's educational philosophy. First, people are not individuals but part of the universal god or spirit consciousness. Second, because each individual is "part of the universal consciousness which is love, each child contains all the wisdom and love of the universe." Thus, children have great potential and have access to the universal mind, which can be tapped through meditation and even spirit guides. Finally, each individual "creates his or her own reality" by selecting what to perceive and how to perceive it. Such an idea rests on the "assumption that the physical world is illusion . . . . "[78]

Chapter 8

THE NEW AGE REACHES OUT:
POLITICS AND ECONOMICS

The heart of the New Age vision is the spiritual and psychological transformation of individual people. But this is only the first step. The New Age, as the name indicates, envisions a new world, a new era in human history. Thus, society must also be transformed. For this change to begin, a sufficient number of individuals must experience transformation. These people, who are an influential minority in society, then actively work for social change. Important arenas for this activity and primary vehicles for implementing the New Age vision are the political and economic systems.

The criticisms leveled by New Age proponents at the contemporary political and economic systems resemble those directed at modern science and education. The focus of this attack is the fragmentation of the modern world. Descartes and Newton have done it again. The forces they set in motion--rational, linear, reductionist, and mechanistic thinking--have infested politics and economics. New Agers regard the modern political and economic systems as fragmented, unjust, hierarchical, patriarchal, and obsolete. They must go, say the New Agers. According to Marilyn Ferguson, "The political system needs to be transformed, not reformed. We need something else, not just something more." Economist Robert Theobald sees the changes taking place as having "no parallel in human history."[1]

In most areas of thought and practice, the New Age movement is highly diverse. The New Age ideas on politics and economics reflect this pluralism. Yet, there are core principles and values that link the divergent strands of New Age political and economic thought. Holism, interconnectedness, oneness, decentralization, monism, and environmentalism are the driving principles behind New Age political and economic thought.

New Age political and economic theory must be seen as advocating a "Third Force"--an alternative to the prevailing systems in America. While New Age politics leans to the "Left," it cannot, in any strict sense, be regarded as either liberal or conservative, authoritarian or democratic, or as supporting the Democratic or Republican parties. Conversely, in economics the New Age gravitates to the "Right," but it does not completely embrace capitalism or socialism.[2]

New Age Politics

By the late 1970s, the New Age movement began to develop a political and social consciousness. The publication in 1978 of Mark Satin's *New Age Politics* and the formation of California's New Age Caucus provided an ideological and practical framework for the developing New Age political consciousness. Satin also began some short-lived ventures--The New World Alliance political movement and a newsletter, *Renewal*. In 1983 he began *New Options*, a newsletter in which he challenged the New Age's utopian visions. By the mid-1980s, Green movements were active in Western Europe and other parts of the world.[3]

Third Force Politics

Like other aspects of the movement, New Age politics is eclectic, drawing from many elements. "Strains of anarchism, Marxism, libertarianism, corporate capitalism, pacifism, comunitarianism, individualism, occultism, and romanticism coexist (albeit nervously) within the movement," writes Gordon Melton.[4] Some of these components obviously stand in opposition to each other. Thus, New Age politics is difficult to describe and categorize. The standard political labels--left or right, liberal or conservative--miss the mark.

Marilyn Ferguson describes New Age politics "as a kind of Radical Center. It is not neutral, not middle-of-the-road, but a view of the whole road." By this she means that on any one issue New Agers are not locked into a set position but examine various schools of thought, learning from their contributions and errors.[5] The slogan of the German Green Party is "neither left, nor right, but out front."[6] In their book, *Green Politics*, New Age authors Fritjof Capra and Charlene Spretnak characterize the Green Party as transcending "the old political framework of left versus right." They describe it as a party with both left and right features calling for "social responsibility and a sound, sustainable economic system, one that is ecological, decentralized, equitable, and comprised of flexible institutions. . . . "[7]

Mark Satin calls New Age politics both "third force" politics and radical politics. Unlike the conventional approaches to politics, third force politics does not focus "exclusively on the institutional and economic symptoms" of society's problems. Instead, it is a third force in that it goes to the "psychocultural roots" of a nation's problems. Moreover, New Age politics is not "a wimpy 'mean' between the so-called 'extremes' of American power politics." Rather, it displays a "radicalism that is neither left nor right." New Age radicalism is "modest enough to borrow what it needs from each of the old political 'ism's' but bold enough to transcend them."[8]

New Age politics has synthesized both conservative and liberal elements. For the most part, the New Age has adopted a left-of-center political agenda with liberal political and religious values. But the means of implementing these values resembles those methods of the conservative right. In fact, New Age politics has been accused of being something of a contradiction. But New Age spokespersons believe that its political values are only contradictory when seen from the perspective of the obsolete right-left political spectrum.[9]

However, sources outside the movement describe New Age politics as "spiritualized humanism" and as "spiritualizing the left."[10] Like many aspects of the New Age, its political values are rooted in the counterculture. The sixties and early seventies witnessed a youth revolt against the establishment. There were riots, demonstrations, and sit-ins. Many members of the counterculture embraced a Neo-Marxist and radical left political stance that challenged the policies of the Johnson and Nixon administrations.[11]

But as the counterculture waned, both religion and politics mellowed. The counterculture religious groups declined. While still maintaining their occult-mystical worldview, many of their adherents gravitated to the New Age or psycho-spiritual groups. The same trend can be seen in politics. Many on the radical left retained their political views but adopted a less confrontational approach to change and brought their ideas into the New Age and other awareness groups. Jerry Rubin, a leader of the youth rebellion in the sixties, is one example. In his 1976 book, *Growing (Up) at Thirty-Seven*, Rubin describes his journey from political protest in the sixties to the spiritual awareness movements of the seventies--yoga, est, and human potential therapies. He also expresses disappointment that these spiritual movements are not politically active. Yet, Rubin believes that the consciousness movement has the potential to merge spirituality and politics and thus bring change to society.[12]

The New Age embraces many traditional left-of-center political and moral values. It espouses a radical feminism. The patriarchal system must go. The sexes must be equal. Within the neopagan groups women are to be superior. Concern for the environment is of paramount importance. Most New Agers go well beyond political environmentalism and espouse a deep ecology with spiritual dimensions. Human rights are basic and must be promoted and enforced throughout the globe. Social justice is an important ethic. The United States and the world has too many people. Thus, government action must curb population growth. Peace and disarmament are objectives that must be pursued.[13] Internationalism and globalism are high on the New Age agenda and will be given further treatment later in this chapter.

New Age spokespersons also espouse some social values normally identified with liberal politics and religion. In the New Society, there is to be abortion on demand. Mark Satin attacks the monolithic institutions of society including "church-centered religion," "monogamy, heterosexuality . . . marriage" and "the nuclear family." He condemns those institutions, among others, because of their monolithic character--"they establish a kind of monopoly" over certain areas of life. Satin argues that there should be socially accepted alternatives in respect to sexual preference, the traditional marriage, and the male-dominated family. He also insists on the repeal of all laws "creating crimes without victims"--that is, all laws "prohibiting the production, sale, possession, or use of drugs" and all laws "regarding prostitution" and the regulation or prohibition of gambling.[14]

The New Age has not moved wholesale toward the Democratic Party. For example, chapter two of Mark Satin's book, *New Options for America*, is entitled, "The Democrats Won't Save Us." Yet, on the whole, they would seem to prefer the values of the Democratic Party over those of the Republican. Most New Agers soundly rejected the domestic and foreign policies of the Reagan administration. However, some did applaud President Bush's use of the United Nations to thwart the aggression of Saddam Hussein.[15]

Some New Agers have expressed fond words for several Democrats, including President Carter and presidential candidates Gary Hart and Michael Dukakis. In the early months of the Clinton administration, some newspapers labeled his style and policies as New Age. Yet, the national political figure most compatible with New Age values is former Governor Jerry Brown of California. He has been quoted as saying, "We're going to go left and right at the same time."[16] Donald Keys sees Brown's politics as "neither right nor left but rather appears in a triangular relationship to the two." Its intent is to be transformational. Brown's administration is a model for New Age politics. While it was "animated by a non-material, humane world view, it was generously grounded in applied pragmatism."[17]

Mark Satin composed a scorecard for rating Senators and Representatives regarding their support for the New Age agenda. Only twenty-one Congresspersons out of 535 scored 70% on his system. Of the twenty-one, nineteen were Democrats. These twenty-one Congresspersons he has called "post liberal (or Green or New Age) in fact" even if they are not recognized as such.[18]

I am not implying that the Democratic Party is New Age. Also, it must be noted that many people embrace these left-of-center political positions who have no connection with the New Age movement. But it would seem that New Age values are closer to those of the more liberal elements in the Democratic Party and that this party has been influenced more by the New Age than has the Republican Party.

The New Age movement also shares some characteristics with the political right. New Age spokespersons reject the big government bureaucratic mind-set normally associated with liberal politics. Rather, they favor a decentralization and localization of the political system. As Satin puts it, the New Age "solution does not call for top-down bureaucratic government, but for much more local autonomy than we have at present and much more planetary cooperation." Political power should not be vertical, coming from the top down, but horizontal and shared by many segments of society. New Agers also emphasize individualism, self-reliance and personal freedom. The vision of the New Age is not to be implemented by a central government but by means of voluntarism. Individuals working through numerous networks will make the New Age vision a reality.[19]

Some aspects of New Age politics are difficult to connect with either the right or left agenda. Marilyn Ferguson sees the old political paradigm as breaking down. This old consensus is based on elements common to both liberal and conservative politics. In its place a new paradigm is arising--one that avoids political polarization and head-on confrontation. Instead "it reconciles, innovates, decentralizes, and does not claim to have all the answers." It is government by consensus. Leaders and followers have an interactive relationship, "affecting each other." Politics in the old paradigm is either pragmatic or visionary. In the new, it is both. Political policy must be based on the New Age worldview, but it is practical. It transcends the old liberal-conservative traditions and draws on both. The new paradigm sees humanity in partnership with nature, not dominating it. Reform is not only external, but must begin with the transformation of individuals.[20]

In *New Age Politics* (1978), Satin has devised a New Age political "platform," containing many planks not common to either left or right wing programs. "Absolute good," as he broadly defines it, entails health for individuals, society, and the environment. Governments are to encourage "voluntary simplicity" in lifestyle. Minimum and maximum levels of income are to be established. Except for a uniform flat tax with few loopholes, most taxes are to be abolished. Small businesses are to be encouraged through government aid and loans. Corporate taxes are to be abolished but the size of corporations are to be limited by antitrust laws.[21]

By means of immigration restrictions, abortion, and improved birth control, the population is to be reduced to about 175 million. Many restrictions on work are to be repealed--minimum wages, licensing requirements, and protective laws for women and children. Small farms are to be encouraged by restricting the acres one could own. The environment is to be protected in many ways: recycling of wastes, the manufacture of durable goods that can be repaired, the use of renewable sources of energy, and the phasing out of nuclear power. Many laws and restrictions are to be eliminated or modified. Some examples include the previously mentioned laws concerning drugs and prostitution; the restrictions on health practices, thus encouraging nontraditional medicine; and compulsory education laws.[22]

A national health program is to be established, but preventive health care and the use of natural foods is to be encouraged. Defense spending is to be cut by 40 percent, but a civilian draft is to be re-established. The citizenry should never relinquish their power to a professional army. Moreover, all people are to be trained in the art of "nonviolent and territorial defense." Satin has updated some of these ideas in a later book, *New Options For America* (1991).[23]

Politics and Religion

The New Age political agenda contains elements ranging from the radical left to the Libertarian Party. Yet, linking together this wide spectrum of political views are certain religious values and a worldview. In addition to drawing from the radical left, Marxism, environmentalism, and radical feminism, New Age politics has its roots in Eastern philosophy, the occult tradition and Western psychology.[24]

Certain religious and philosophical assumptions provide the ideological basis for the New Age political agenda. New Age political spokespersons vary as to the degree they mix religion and politics. Individuals like Robert Muller extensively spiritualize their political agenda. Some others appear to take a more secular approach to politics. Yet, the same core religious beliefs have shaped the political ideas of most New Agers. These central ideas concern monism, holism, and a particular view of human nature and sin.

Monism and its derivative, holism, are the keys to much of New Age thought, including its political values. The cosmos is made up of one divine reality, say the New Agers. This oneness leads to a unity among all aspects of existence--divinity, humanity, and the plant and animal kingdoms. Oneness also has significant political implications. New Agers believe that they are gods and as Douglas Groothuis notes, humanity's "collective divinity demands political responsibility." Given the oneness of the cosmos, it is only natural for the New Age political priorities to concern "ecology, sexual equality, and world order (or unification)."[25]

High on the New Age political agenda is ecology. The New Age idea of oneness, wholeness, and unity go hand-in-hand with such an emphasis. The universe is not viewed as fragmented. Instead, a holistic worldview regards the entire planetary system as interrelated. The concepts of oneness and unity have something of a sacred character. Thus, most New Agers reject "shallow environmentalism" for "deep ecology," which has religious dimensions. Armed with a view that sees nature as sacred, New Age political thinkers support radical policies for protecting the environment.[26]

Global unity is central to New Age political thought and will receive further attention later. New Agers see the world as already unified by modern transportation and communication systems. But they also seek global political unification. There is to be a new world order characterized by internationalism. Nations are to be united politically and economically. Such political interdependence has a religious, perhaps even a sacred, character. It is rooted in the New Age monistic worldview. If god, humanity, and nature are all one, it follows that there should be no boundaries between nations. The nations of the world should be united politically, geographically, and spiritually.[27]

The equality of the sexes is basic to the New Age political agenda. Given the oneness and interconnectedness of the cosmos, the patriarchical nature of Western civilization must give way to more equality between the sexes. New Age feminist Charlene Spretnak believes that feminine politics has a spiritual base in the interconnectedness of all matter. In turn, this "global feminist movement is bringing about the end of patriarchy . . . and the beginning of a new era modeled on the dynamic, holistic paradigm."[28] Marilyn Ferguson applauds the shifting balance of power between men and women and believes that society is benefiting from such a change. Women are enlarging "their influence in policy making and government." Their yin perspective complements that of the yang, and together man and woman "can create a new future."[29]

New Age political theorists optimistically believe that their agenda will become a reality.[30] New Age politics has been called "the politics of transformation." New Agers call not for moderate political reform but for a transformation of the entire system.[31] Such a radical change presupposes a positive view of human nature. Humanity is divine. Thus, human beings have unlimited potential. Such a belief provides the basis for the dramatic and idealistic changes embodied in the New Age vision. The human character is not flawed by sin. Rather, sin is ignorance. Once enlightened, humanity will enact the political programs necessary to build a new society.

While not highly pronounced, New Age politics does have some occult connections. David Spangler sees Lucifer as "an angel, a being, a great and mighty planetary consciousness"--not the popular image of Satan created by the Christian tradition. Lucifer is to work with the Christ as a force of change advancing humanity toward a higher consciousness.[32]

Theosophy has influenced the New Age movement, including its political views. In particular, Alice Bailey has left her mark on New Age politics. In New Age politics, as Groothuis notes, there is a strand of "occult elitism." During the 1980s Benjamin Creme, one of Bailey's disciples, spoke of the imminent return of Maitreya (the Christ). The "Christ" would solve the world's pressing problems--hunger, pollution, war, and strife--and "usher in a one-world socialist government."[33] Important in Theosophical thought is the notion of "advanced spiritual entities," including Lucifer. When the New Age becomes a reality, some New Age thinkers believe that the planetary leaders will be a spiritual elite who are tuned into their divinity.[34]

Global Unity

The notion of global unity is basic to the New Age vision. Such a concept goes by a number of names: planetary unity, planetization, world order, planetary consciousness, and the new global society. Essentially, it means the movement of all people toward greater unity and interdependence--especially in respect to worldview, spirituality, politics, economics, and care for the environment. While they disagree over how this global unity is to be implemented, nearly all New Age spokespersons emphasize this cardinal belief. However, not all people who have advocated the idea of a unified global order are New Agers. During the twentieth century, several visionaries have promoted the notion of a world government.[35]

Mark Satin offers several definitions. "Planetization is the process of our species evolving in the direction of its natural unity by means of . . . planetary consciousness." International consciousness and planetary consciousness are not the same. International consciousness also views the whole world. But it does so from "the perspective of a particular nation-state or ideology, whose interests are to be held to be separate from and prior to those of the whole." On the contrary, planetary consciousness recognizes the oneness of all humanity and the interdependence of all life and of all nation-states. It is a perspective that places loyalty to the human community above loyalties to tribe, nation, or another social group.[36]

For the New Age, global unity is far more ideological than it is organizational. While it occupies a central position in New Age thought, few steps have been taken to implement this global society. As noted earlier, the New Age belief in planetary unity is rooted in its monistic worldview. New Agers teach that the cosmos is unified. Thus, there is need for a unified political system in harmony with the cosmic order. New Agers believe that the Cartesian and Newtonian worldview has brought about the nation-state and the fragmentation of the globe. The solution to this problem is enlightenment--a mystical experience in which individuals become aware of their divinity. When a sufficient number of people realize that "all is one," a new global society will be possible.[37]

The New Age vision of a planetary society is also grounded in several practical considerations--the survival of humanity and modern technology. Advocates of change must believe that the current system is failing. New Agers are optimistic about the future. But they view the present system as inadequate at best and perhaps leading humanity towards a catastrophe. Marilyn Ferguson believes that a political crisis exists. "Our institutions--especially our governing structures--are mechanistic, rigid, [and] fragmented."[38] Capra and Spretnak say that "Green politics begins with the recognition that the global problems [are] currently threatening our survival . . . ."[39] In *The Turning Point*, Capra believes that our fragmented world is unhealthy and that several problems menace humanity--especially nuclear power and weapons and the destruction of the environment.[40]

Donald Keyes believes that the world is in a great crisis that can be solved only by the emergence of a world community. In *Earth at Omega*, he says that "Humanity is coming to the end of the road. The world will organize as a community or human life will perish."[41] In *Planethood*, Ken Keyes and Benjamin Ferencz insist that human survival is in jeopardy unless the current international anarchy is replaced with "an international legislature to make laws for global survival, accompanied by international courts and international enforcement."[42]

Humanity is faced with problems that transcend national boundaries--overpopulation, starvation, environmental pollution, and nuclear weapons. Therefore, New Agers believe that there can be no national solutions to these issues. Such problems demand global cooperation. But New Agers go further. Human survival requires not merely global cooperation but planetary unity. Global problems will force humanity to "sink or swim" together. The human race cannot survive if humanity remains divided into nation-states that go their own way. Thus, New Age theorists closely link global interdependence and human survival.[43]

A "shrinking"world has prompted New Agers to seek global unity. They see modern transportation as linking the world technically. Modern technology can liberate people from the bonds of ignorance and political repression. "Satellite TV, fax, and computer networks" have given people the power to "transform the world," say Ferencz and Keyes.[44] According to Mark Satin, modern means of transportation and communication are "conspiring to inspire us to recognize our oneness and interdependence."[45] New Agers see these developments as early stages of the emerging global civilization. What must follow technical interdependence is a unity in politics, economics, and religion.

New Agers have great confidence in human evolution. Humanity is progressing to higher levels in most areas of life, including political relationships. Moving from the nation-state to planetary unity is seen as an aspect of planetary evolution. Global forces are at work that will make a new unified world order not only necessary but inevitable.

In the mind of most New Agers, the great enemy to planetization is nationalism. New Agers favor globalization and localization, but not the nation-state. While it would seem to be an incongruity, most New Age theorists want to combine political decentralization with global unity. The nation-state developed about the same time that the modern worldview took shape. Thus, New Agers see nationalism as an outgrowth of the Cartesian-Newtonian worldview. As the Cartesian-Newtonian mind-set has fragmented the world intellectually, the nation-state has divided the globe politically. Such political fragmentation caused by nationalism has parented many of the world's problems--war, ethnic-strife, imperialism, economic exploitation.

New Agers also regard nationalism as obsolete and unnatural. They see it as part of the old paradigm that is giving way to a new world order. Or, as Alvin Toffler puts it, the nation-state is part of the Second Wave civilization that is in decline.[46] Mark Satin believes that localism and regionalism are natural, but nationalism is not. Nationalism is a relatively modern development that has been forced on humanity by the large nation-states. He sees it as serving "as a kind of vulgarized religion" in the modern secular society.[47]

Political Decentralization or Centralization?

Most New Age spokespersons uphold planetary unity and condemn the nation-state. But here is where the agreement ends. The majority advocate political decentralization and global unity. They believe that there can be a global political system that preserves regional and local autonomy. But they are vague on how these two developments can be reconciled. However, other New Agers believe that this planetary unity should be implemented by a centralized government.

Mark Satin sees the nation-state and its top-down bureaucracy as something of a prison that has enslaved humanity. Government must be more decentralized and more manageable. He believes that localization will help bring about planetization. If regional and local political units "want to be more self-reliant," then they must cooperate more effectively. Satin says political power should reside primarily on the regional level. The region defines its relationship to the nation-state. Rather than advocate complete independence he opts for regional autonomy, something on the Swiss model or a modified version of the Articles of Confederation in the United States. But he does not favor a monolithic world government. Instead, he promotes an effective global communications system. This "planetary guidance system," as he calls it, "could exercise some control over global processes without having to deny different ideological systems the right of existence."[48]

Marilyn Ferguson also criticizes political centralization. Whatever the system--capitalist, socialist, or Marxist--she believes that "the focusing of great central power is unnatural" and lacking the flexibility "to respond to the fluctuating needs of people. . . ." She places great faith in networks of several kinds--political, economic, social, self-help, and so forth. "Power is changing hands, from dying hierarchies to living networks." These loose networks are vehicles for transforming society. How such networks relate to global unity is not made clear.[49] Alvin Toffler also emphasizes political decentralization more than global unity. He believes that decentralization in economic activity, communications, and other critical activities will naturally force a similar development in "government decision-making."[50]

Several New Age scenarios promote planetary unity with some variation of a global central government. Robert Muller takes a spiritual approach to global unity and sees the United Nations as the centerpiece of the new world order. His approach to planetary unity flows from his mystical monistic worldview. People must elevate themselves as "cosmic beings in deep communion with the universe and . . . re-establish the unity of our planet and of our beings with the universe and divinity." He believes humanity is evolving toward a global spirituality that will promote political unity. While there are many religions in the world, they are linked by a "common denominator"--namely the oneness and divinity of all beings in the universe.[51]

Muller acknowledges that the United Nations is not a spiritual organization. Yet, it is more than a political organization. He contends that "prayer and spirituality play an important role in the United Nations." In particular, he applauds the spiritual role of U Thant, the former secretary general of the United Nations. The United Nations is part of the new political paradigm, an "expression of a deep, evolutionary change which in the long run will transform the world for the best."[52]

Donald Keys sees humanity as evolving toward something entirely new--"the first global civilization." In *Earth at Omega*, he says that this new world "requires a new kind of person with a planetary perspective." Global unity must begin with the transformation of individuals. But it does not end here. These aware individuals must work for a global society with meta-organizations to deal with pressing international problems. In particular, he sees both the United Nations and the United States playing major roles in planetary unification. The United States is highly diverse in respect to culture and ethnic composition. But it also has immense international influence and can be a major driving force for global unification. While he acknowledges the weaknesses of the United Nations, he sees it as the first universal organization with paramount significance.[53]

In *Planethood*, coauthored by Ken Keyes and Benjamin Ferencz, some practical steps for global unity are spelled out. Of utmost importance, the United Nations must be an organization with sufficient strength to ensure global peace. The powers of the individual states making up the world system need to be limited. In their place, there must be international laws and a world government with the power to enforce these laws.[54]

But how can a system of international governance be created? If such an organization is too strong, there shall be global tyranny. If it is too weak, it will be ineffective. Ferencz and Keyes reject the option of a world dictatorship. Power, they argue, must be limited. On the other hand, a confederation is too weak. They regard the current structure of the United Nations as a confederation too powerless to prevent wars and ensure the peace.[55]

Ferencz and Keyes advocate a "world democratic republic." There must be "a democratic republic of the world" that can end international lawlessness and provide the global community with a level of government higher than the nation-state. They argue that it is time to reform the United Nations into an effective global government. The model for the strengthened United Nations is the United States. The United Nations must be changed from a confederation to something resembling a federal republic. As they point out, the United States government has sufficient strength to enforce laws throughout the land. Yet, the central government's power is not unchecked. Ultimate political power, they contend, still resides with the people and the individual states. The central government's power to interfere with the activities within individual states is limited. The authors see the United States as providing the model of unity with diversity. A strengthened United Nations will establish global unity but still allow much autonomy and diversity on the national level.[56]

A minority of New Age theorists prefer a centralized world government with strong powers. New Agers with strong occult leanings look to some type of elitist structure. Benjamin Creme believes that the Christ (Maitreya) will return shortly to prevent a global catastrophe. While he speaks of people participating in government decisions, the new world order will not be based on the current political systems, whether they be democratic, communist or fascist. Rather, political power will rest with a spiritual hierarchy, headed by the Christ. The various international political agencies, including the United Nations, will be under the control of these spiritual masters. The Christ will be the world teacher who will "outline the possibilities" of the new world order.[57]

The United Nations will be the major institution of the new order. It will be through the United Nations that the divine energy will flow. The affluent developed world must adjust its lifestyle and live more simply. The surplus will then be turned over to the United Nations. Under the hierarchy of the Christ, the United Nations will redistribute the world's goods according to need. Thus, Creme is proposing that a spiritual hierarchy and the Christ will run a new socialist world order.[58]

Democracy or Elitism?

Most New Age theorists speak of democracy and of citizens participating in the political decision-making process. But they do not necessarily mean a system like the modern representative democracies. In general, most New Agers do not believe that the democratic principle is working in the modern world. They are particularly skeptical regarding majority rule. Thus, their political thought contains both democratic and elitist elements.

Mark Satin condemns political centralization and insists that citizens should be active in the political process on the local and regional levels. Political power, he says, ultimately depends on the consent of the people. But he has little faith in the electoral process, especially majority rule. Political change must begin with the individual. When enough people achieve self-awareness and experience personal growth, social change will come.[59]

But as Satin notes, change does not have to wait for a majority of a society to experience self-awareness. "A critical mass will do the job." A critical mass is those concerned people who are committed to New Age principles and who are willing to move society democratically in that direction. New Agers differ on how large this critical mass must be. The range varies from two percent of the population, as advocated by Transcendental Meditation, to the twenty percent that Eric Fromm deems necessary. Whatever the number, Satin insists that "a minority of concerned people can and should affect the democratic process more strongly than a large number of apathetic people."[60]

Donald Keys does not advocate authoritarian rule. But he believes that modern democracies are not functioning properly. He regards democratic rule "as highly experimental" and based on many inaccurate assumptions. For example, the collective will often does not make the "wisest choices" or select the best leaders. Hopefully, in the next millennium, humanity will have progressed to the point where they can make better decisions and select leaders who are well qualified to govern.[61]

Benjamin Creme throws the word democracy around. But he means something much different. Humanity is to be ruled by the spiritual elite, the perfect masters. "Hierarchy is a fact in nature." All people are on the ladder of spiritual evolution. They must recognize that some individuals have ascended to the top of the ladder and are qualified to be rulers. At one point an egalitarian/democratic principle comes into play. All people are on the same spiritual journey and have an opportunity to reach the top of the hierarchy. In *Rebirthing in the New Age*, New Age proponents Leonard Orr and Sondra Ray also speak of political power residing with a "spiritual aristocracy."[62]

Alvin Toffler refers to a new "twenty-first century democracy." In his opinion, democracy must be reconstituted in "Third Wave [New Age] terms," which consist of three principles. The first principle is that of minority power. By this he means minority political opinions or groups, not necessarily cultural minorities. Seldom can a country reach a 51 percent consensus over any issue. When it happens, it is a fragile consensus. The majority often flip-flops over issues. Therefore, a firm minority opinion counts more than that of the majority.[63]

Toffler calls the second principle "semi-direct democracy." People need to stop depending on their representatives and start representing themselves. The breakdown of consensus, in his opinion, negates "the very concept of representation." Also, high technology makes possible the "electronic town hall." Representation will not entirely be dismantled. Instead, a combination of direct and indirect democracy will exist in the future.[64]

Toffler's third principle is called "decision division." There exists on the contemporary political scene a "decisional logjam." Some problems cannot be solved on the local level; others cannot be reconciled on either the national or international levels. Thus, decisions need to be divided up--some allocated to their appropriate levels and others dealt with simultaneously on all levels. At the heart of this principle is a decentralization of government decision-making.[65]

Political Organization

New Age politics has more theoretical focus than it has organizational structure. Nevertheless, several political organizations do exist. Such bodies usually exist for the purpose of advancing the New Age objectives regarding peace, ecology, and global unity. In addition, New Agers have infiltrated a number of organizations that cannot be considered as New Age.

In 1972 Donald Keys, U Thant, and Norman Cousins (publisher of the *Saturday Review*) established the Planetary Citizens--an organization devoted to transforming the world according to New Age principles. This political action group deals with a number of concerns, including ecology, social planning, and future studies. The Planetary Citizens have attracted an impressive list of New Age leaders. A list would include the following individuals: Edgar Mitchell (former astronaut), David Spangler and Peter Caddy (both formerly from Findhorn), Willis Hartman (futurist), Michael Murphy (from Esalen), and William Irwin Thompson (historian).[66]

During the late 1970s, Marxists, anarchists, and other far left groups came together to form the Green Party in West Germany. This party approached a range of political and social problems from an anti-capitalist and radical-feminist perspective. In particular, the Greens advocated neutralism for West Germany, unilateral disarmament for the West, and environmental concerns.[67]

The Greens are a fringe political party. But by the early 1980s, they had won several seats in the West German parliament. Most people who voted for the Greens did so because of the party's stance on the environment, not on disarmament. During this time the Green Party split into two groups--the Fundamentalists, who favored action outside the system, and the Realists, who were willing to work with the Social Democrats, the major left-of-center party. The Green movement has spread to other countries, but with less success than in Germany. A United States Greens Party has been formed, but it has only a marginal existence.[68]

There are several other New Age oriented political organizations. World Goodwill is a political lobby that shares nearly all the goals of the Planetary Citizens. Alice Bailey's teachings direct the values and actions of World Goodwill, whose objective is to promote "the Plan"-- a new world religion and government lead by "the Christ."[69] Another New Age type organization is Beyond War. Founded in 1982, this group's objective is to promote peace.[70] The militant environmental organization, Greenpeace, must be regarded as thoroughly New Age. In addition to these New Age oriented groups, the New Age movement has infiltrated a number of organizations who are not self-consciously New Age. These groups usually work for peace, ecological concerns, or women's rights. Some examples include the Sierra Club and the Audubon Society.[71]

Recent Political Developments

The New Age movement is fueled by optimism. If a new age is dawning, one would expect to see some signs of such a development. Therefore, New Age spokespersons interpret a wide range of activities as harbingers of the coming new age.

New Agers regard a number of recent events as furthering their political objectives--peace, decentralization, and global unity. Alvin Toffler interprets many of the political problems of the 1970s as signs of the death of the Second Wave (the industrial civilization).[72] Writing during the Reagan years, Donald Keys sees several trends as supporting New Age principles: the slowing down of the arms race and the movement of power from the central government "back to local levels."[73]

Most New Agers would be critical of the domestic policies of the Reagan era. Yet, Mark Satin saw some positive trends during these years. In particular, he detects the rise of the caring individual. These people "care deeply about self and others; they are equally committed to self-development and social change." They have a social concern but they are still individualistic and reject the liberal solution of throwing money at social problems.[74]

Writing in the late 1980s, Ferencz and Keyes interpret many events as furthering planethood. The Cold War is over. The Intermediate-range Nuclear Treaty (INF) promotes the cause of peace and is a first step to ending the arms race. The collapse of Communism in Eastern Europe is seen as furthering the cause of freedom and human dignity. Presidents Bush and Gorbachev "have agreed to reverse the arms race."[75] Several developments have helped the cause of global unity. The coming together of twelve European nations into close economic and political ties is seen as a model of international unity. The end of the Cold War has brought to a close the superpower stalemate in the United Nations and has freed this international body to play a significant role in global affairs. The speed with which George Bush summoned the United Nations to throw back Saddam Hussein's invasion of Kuwait is a model for stopping aggression. These and other events encourage the authors to conclude that humanity is moving toward planethood.[76]

New Age Economics

Mainstream politics and economics interact considerably. The same is true in the New Age subculture. Many New Age economic themes are a carry-over of its political principles. New Age ideas common to both areas include holism, decentralization, evolution, inner transformation, and cooperation. Moreover, in both politics and economics, New Agers regard their approach as something of a "third force" and take an idealistic view of the ancient and medieval worlds.

What is a New Age economy? New Agers say that it cannot be equated strictly with any particular economic system or -ism. It can be compatible with several economic systems: capitalism or socialism, private or public ownership, or a mixture of the two. In fact, because a New Age government would be diverse, a combination of private and public ownership would be preferred.[77] At any rate, a New Age economy cannot be defined as a system. It contains a diversity of elements and is something of an economic "third force."

Mark Satin defines a New Age economy from the vantage point of values, not production and distribution. "It is any economy that organizes its production and distribution in a way that is compatible with New Age ethics and political values."[78] Within this framework, considerable diversity is allowed, even encouraged.

Economic Values and Principles

Though the specifics vary from spokesperson to spokesperson, some core New Age economic values and ideas keep arising. Holism is as important in economics as it is in other areas of New Age thought. Fitjof Capra believes that "economics is characterized by the fragmentary and reductionist approach that typifies most social sciences." Economics has not been tied to other aspects of life, especially the social and environmental systems. Moreover, economics has been divorced from other academic disciplines, especially other social sciences. Capra blames all of this on the Cartesian and Newtonian system, which brought about the Scientific and Industrial Revolutions.[79] In addition to many positive benefits, these developments had several damaging economic consequences-- unchecked economic growth, fierce economic competition, rampant materialism, and environmental destruction.

To solve these problems, the framework of modern economic thought must be abandoned, namely the Cartesian-Newtonian paradigm. A new holistic mind-set must develop. "The economy is alive and integrated, more an organism than a machine," says Marilyn Ferguson.[80] Economic thought and development must coincide with a holistic view of life, one that connects economics with society, religion, the environment, and self-enhancement.

Excessive materialism must be curbed. Both capitalism and socialism are based on material values, and thus are "inadequate philosophies" to transform society. A voluntary simplicity in lifestyle must be encouraged. Such a way of life need not be sacrificial. "Voluntary simplicity is an attitude, not a budget," writes Ferguson. It involves individual choice. For example, one may choose to buy an expensive sound system while driving an old car. But simple living does involve certain principles--a willingness to recycle goods and to buy healthful, non-polluting goods. New Agers call this "appropriate consumption."[81]

Materialism should be replaced by an enhanced self-identity. Satin says that people must move from a "thing-oriented" lifestyle to a "life-oriented behavior"--one that places value on the non-material aspects of life.[82] While there is to be "material sufficiency,"spiritual values are to "transcend material gain." An individual's vocation has meaning beyond acquiring material wealth. A vocation is part of the transformation process that puts people in touch with their inner selves and with others. For the transformed person, a vocation is not a job and there should be no break between work and pleasure.[83]

The current notions of economic growth and the distribution of goods must be revised. Capra is not opposed to economic growth, but contends that it "will have to be qualified" and fit a scale that is appropriate for "the restructuring" of society according to New Age values. Unregulated economic growth has been tied to an expansion of technology and corporate power. Such developments have destroyed the environment and created an unequal distribution of wealth. There exists a great economic disparity between social classes in the Western world and between the West and the developing world. New Agers differ on the means--personal transformation, education, or government action--but nearly all agree that the patterns of economic growth and redistribution of wealth must change.[84]

New Agers see a limitation to the planet's resources. Those living in communes believe that it is impossible for most of the world to live on the level of the middle and upper classes in the United States.[85] Theodore Roszak says that humanity and the planet are threatened by "the bigness of things." The "insensitive colossalism" of the economic and political organizations endangers both "the rights of the person and the rights of the planet."[86]

While they are not unanimous over the issue, most New Agers advocate economic decentralization. Economic centralization is challenged--whether it be that of corporate capitalism or socialism. Centralized economic institutions set prices, control governments, and eliminate domestic competition. Moreover, they represent the ultimate bureaucratic mind-set. Whenever possible, economic institutions should be downsized to a human scale. Massive economic organizations are regarded as dinosaurs--inflexible, out of tune with human needs, and incapable of keeping pace with the demands of our rapidly changing society.[87]

Capra and Spretnak regard decentralization as the key to change in many areas of life. In order to restore an ecological balance, there must be decentralization "in government, business, and in most of our social institutions. . . ." Such an environmental balance also requires a decentralization or "redistribution of wealth, especially between industrial countries and the Third World."[88]

New Agers can be found favoring either capitalism or socialism. Yet, more prefer capitalism--a downsized capitalism that respects the values of a "life-oriented society." Satin gives three reasons why New Agers gravitate toward capitalism. First, there are historic links between the market economy, individual rights, and political democracy. Economic competition has promoted pluralism more than socialism has. Second, despite the economic concentration of corporate capitalism, capitalism on the whole has tended to disperse economic and political power throughout society. Lastly, the restraints imposed by socialist governments imply a negative view of human nature--something contrary to the optimistic view held by New Agers.[89]

Recent Economic Developments

As in the case of political developments, New Age theorists see current economic trends as portents of a new age or a new era in economics. Marilyn Ferguson optimistically interprets many societal trends, including those in economics, as opening shots of the new paradigm. Writing in 1980 she views many people as moving toward "a post-extravagant society." Americans are increasingly regarding "national and personal consumption as wasteful." She sees a trend toward economic cooperation--"carpools, learning networks, food cooperatives, and shared childcare"--as embodying New Age values. An increase in communal living and shared housing are even stronger indications of these values. She believes that a trend toward simple living is catching on.[90]

Changes are occurring in the business world. In the early 1980s, corporate America began to search for alternatives to the "old management paradigm." Many companies have begun policies of "job enrichment" and "humanizing the workplace," writes Ferguson. Some companies also have "undertaken stress-reduction training programs for their employees." Others have taken further steps, introducing a number of psychotherapeutic programs to enhance personal awareness and creativity.[91]

Such themes are echoed by both New Age critics and more neutral sources. In many cases, these corporate programs go beyond motivation and stress management to project religious dimensions. Journalist Annetta Miller tells us that "the New Age movement has gone corporate." In order to improve efficiency and productivity, a number of corporations are hiring New Age consultants "to change the way their employees think." Corporate giants paying for such quasi-religious motivational programs include Dupont, Proctor and Gamble, GM of Canada, TRW, Ford Motor Company, Scott Paper, Polaroid, and Pacific Bell.[92]

A number of New Age bodies have created subsidiary organizations that focus on corporate motivational programs. Werner Erhard of est established Transformational Technologies. Lifespring has its consulting spinoffs. Insight Personal Seminars and Managing Accelerated Productivity (MAP) have come from John-Roger Hinkins' Movement of Inner Spiritual Awareness (MISA). Scientology has established several consulting groups--Sterling Management and the World Institute of Scientological Enterprises (WISE). Charles Krone developed Krone Training or Kronings. Its ideas are based on the teachings of George Gurdjieff, a Russian mystic.[93]

The techniques employed in these New Age motivational programs are drawn from a combination of occult-mystical, Eastern, and human potential philosophies. They include chanting, meditation, biofeedback, encounter groups, hypnosis, and several more obvious occult activities--channeling, tarot cards, psychic healing, and the intervention of spirit guides. Against these training sessions some employees have raised two objections: the programs constitute mind control or promote values and practices contrary to their religious beliefs. As a result, a number of lawsuits have been filed against companies who require employees to participate in such programs.[94]

From a more secular perspective, several New Age futurists see signs of the New Age economy. John Naisbitt views the end of the Cold War and the decline of Communism as ushering in a new age of globalization. Nations will prefer economic cooperation to military confrontation. As a result, Naisbitt predicts that much of the 1990s will be "devoted to the full realization of one, single global economy." Another New Age trend identified by Naisbitt is that of a small-time entrepreneur economy. During the 1980s individualism has been on the rise--a fact that has led to an increased importance for small entrepreneurs in the global economy.[95]

Writing in 1980 (*The Third Wave*) and 1990 (*Powershift*), Alvin Toffler identifies several New Age economic trends--especially decentralization, demassification, and globalization. He says that signs of the "third wave" (the New Age) economy could be seen in the United States as early as the 1950s, namely the growth of high technology and the decline of the smokestack industries.[96]

Decentralization of the economy means encouraging small work units. Toffler believes that high technology will change the very character of work, shifting "millions of jobs out of factories and offices" to the home. In some ways this modern "electronic cottage" is a throwback to what prevailed prior to the Industrial Revolution, namely an economy centered in the home.[97]

Related to this decentralization is a demassification of the economy. The "second wave" (the industrialized world) has been characterized by mass production and mass humanity. The "third wave" with its individualism and diversity will witness a shift toward customization. Within a practical framework, many products will be customized to the tastes of the consumer. Toffler cites the T-shirt as an example. "The shirts are mass-made. But new, cheap fast-heat presses make it economical to imprint designs or slogans" reflecting individual tastes.[98]

Decentralization does not mean that the world will return to small, isolated economic communities. The third wave will witness the first "transmarket" civilization. Networks and technology will connect those small economic communities. Such communities will be interconnected and dependent on one another. Thus, a true globalized production and marketing system will develop.[99]

In many ways, New Age economic thought looks longingly to the premodern world. In doing this, New Age economic ideas follow a pattern common to New Age religion, science, politics, and medicine. In respect to economics, it is decentralization, the household economy, and just pricing that attracts New Age theorists. New Agers desire the economic values of the premodern world while using modern technology in a responsible way.

Chapter 9

THE NEW AGE TURNS INWARD: SALVATION THROUGH PSYCHOLOGY

In the New age, personal transformation equals salvation. While such a transformation may be spiritual, it also has many psychological elements. In fact, the New Age equivalent to conversion--self-awareness, self-realization, awareness of one's divinity, or whatever the name--may be triggered by a quasi-psychospiritual experience. For the New Ager the turn inward, the quest for the higher self, the search for divinity has both spiritual and psychological dimensions. Psychological wholeness can be found by turning inward--the same place God can be found.

The modern New Age stands on three pillars--the Western occult tradition, Eastern spirituality, and modern psychology as represented in its humanistic and transpersonal forms. While modern psychology is not identical with the occult and Eastern philosophy, the three share many assumptions and are compatible at many points. All three maintain a monistic worldview, a mystical emphasis, a subjective approach to truth, and similar devices designed to trigger a psychospiritual experience that places people in touch with their divine selves.

The Therapeutic Society

In the modern secular world psychology has become a surrogate for religion, perhaps even replacing religion as the primary vehicle for improving the quality of the inner life. Religion has lost much of its ability to meet deep-seated human needs. Thus, religion is being dismissed as largely irrelevant. Psychology now leads religion. It is regarded as better suited than religion to address the concerns of the inner life.[1]

In *Cults and Cons*, Kenneth Cinnamon and Dave Farson tell us that the movement from a ritualistic church service to the therapeutic session is a normal progression. As religion loses its force, people take responsibility for their own lives. "Self is the new god." The psychiatrist is becoming "the priest" and "the clinical psychologist the witch doctor." People are moving from their "hands and knees" to the "couch or chair." The litany prayer is being replaced by "the language of therapy." There is still an appointed hour, but instead of its being the weekly church service, it is the session with the therapist.[2]

Perhaps more than any other influence, psychology has shaped the beliefs and lifestyle of the modern world. People have turned inward for many of the same reasons that they have turned to the East. Western religion has lost much of its instrumental forms--namely its functional ability to meet human needs. As a result, it has been challenged by both Eastern religions and psychology. Western religion has focused on abstract exhortations and commandments but has not told people how to follow them. Consequently, the church is seen as not able to improve the quality of human life.[3]

With Western religion stripped of a key reason why people turned to it in the first place, many individuals have looked to psychology as a practical form of religion in modern secular society. People regard psychology as much more efficient than religion in solving human problems. In this respect psychology and Eastern religions have something in common. They both have filled a gap left by Western religion. They both focus on the individual and his or her inner well-being. Their goal is primarily release from suffering--personal suffering as well as the sufferings of humanity.[4]

People have turned to psychology for other reasons, too. In a pluralistic society, individuals are faced with what Alvin Toffler calls "overchoice"--a vast array of ideas and moral codes from which to choose. These people suffer from a kind of "choice-fatigue." As a result, they turn inward for guidance and meaning. The pluralistic social structure has no meaning, and as sociologist Peter Berger notes, "The individual's experience of himself becomes more real to him than his experience of the objective world."[5]

But the turn inward has presented a different set of problems. "The world of the psyche has few road maps," writes Douglas Groothuis. There often develops a crisis of identity. The journey into the inner world does not always produce the anticipated results-- namely, authenticity, direction, and assurance. Consequently, individuals are often left hanging and experience anxiety and stress. At this point some modern therapies step in. They attempt to give direction and guidance to the search for meaning.[6]

These therapies encompass a wide variety of activities and have a broad appeal. Since the 1960s millions of Americans have embarked on a journey of self-discovery and self-improvement. Ron Enroth tells us that a multitude of new mind-body therapies have sprung up and "blended into this stream of American consumerism in recent years." Some, like swimming, aerobics, jogging, cycling, and weight loss, are largely aimed at improving overall health by means of physical fitness programs. Others, such as bioenergetics and rolfing, focus on mind-body interaction, emphasizing physical and psychological treatments that unlock physical tensions. Still, some like Scientology, est, and Silva Mind Control concentrate on psychospiritual concerns.[7]

This world of personal growth has become subject to much abuse and exploitation. This is less true of the programs emphasizing physical fitness, whose results are more subject to verification. More problems, however, arise in respect to the psychological, emotional, and spiritual therapies. In their longing for self-improvement, as Flo Conway and Jim Sieglman say, America's searchers have no way of "interpreting their experiences." They have not been able to separate "the truly spiritual from the sham, or of distinguishing genuine personal growth from artificially induced sensation." As pointed out by Cinnamon and Farson, the message of these therapies is often something like this: "You are not now OK, but after you take our course, participate in this group, etcetera, you will be O.K."[8]

Definitions and Relationships

Many of these therapies are at work in several related and nearly interchangeable movements--the New Age, the consciousness revolution, the "New Consciousness," and the human potential (or human growth) movement. The New Age has boundary problems. There is considerable overlap between the New Age and many Eastern religions and occult groups. The lines between the New Age and most of the psychospiritual movements are even murkier--almost indistinguishable. While the New Age, the "New Consciousness," the consciousness revolution, and the human potential movements are not entirely identical, they are often viewed as interchangeable.

Definitions

The New Consciousness is a new way of looking at reality. It denotes a wide range of groups that embrace an alternative worldview--usually a loose synthesis of elements drawn from occultism, mysticism, animism, spiritism, Eastern spirituality, and paranormal research. It also involves a heightened self-awareness, the realization of one's divinity and oneness with the cosmos. Christianity provided a new consciousness in the first century, one that came to dominate in the West for two millennia. But now in the West a wide range of groups--Hindu, Buddhist, Islamic, occult, and such--are offering a new approach to reality. Some Christian bodies are even offering new perspectives on reality.[9]

The terms *New Consciousness* and *consciousness revolution* are often used interchangeably. Both maintain an alternative view of reality. But the consciousness revolution focuses less on a worldview than on psychospiritual matters. While a monistic worldview is assumed, there seems to be more emphasis on the practical aspects of self-awareness. Kenneth Woodward says that in broad terms "the consciousness revolution represents a convergence of modern Western psychotherapy with the ancient disciplines of Eastern religions." The movement endeavors to put "seekers progressively in touch with themselves, with others, with nature and . . . with the fundamental forces of the cosmos."[10]

The human potential movement (or emotional growth movement) is a basic component of the New Age. Psychologist Harriet Mosatche defines it as "an umbrella concept used to encompass many different kinds of therapeutic techniques and offerings. There are group and individual therapies, mental and physical techniques, and various combinations of each whose purposes purport to be enhancement of psychological growth within the person and the breakdown of barriers between people."[11] While this movement maintains a monistic worldview and has a spiritual thrust, it focuses more on psychological matters.

Relationships

How do these movements relate to each other? The New Age, the New Consciousness, the consciousness revolution, and the human potential movement closely overlap and are indebted to each other. The New Consciousness focuses more on a worldview, not on personal growth. It is the broadest of the four groups; it contains the other three bodies and provides a worldview for them. For example, all New Agers embrace this New Consciousness, which they hope will usher in a new age. Many groups, not only the New Age movement, can be regarded as New Consciousness bodies.[12]

The consciousness movement or revolution, the New Age, and the human potential movement have self-fulfillment as a primary objective. Though the human potential movement is an essential part of the New Age, the two are not synonymous. The New Age is a broader movement. While building on the objective of self-fulfillment, it has other goals, including the vision of a new age which is free of crime, war, strife, pollution, hunger, and political divisions. The New Age also tends to be more mystical and occultic than the human potential movement, though this movement also contains these elements.[13]

The consciousness revolution has a closer relationship with the human potential movement. On one hand it grew out of the human potential movement and is nearly synonymous with this development, sharing most of its characteristics. On the other, the consciousness revolution is more eclectic, borrowing from an even wider range of sources. It is broader than the human potential movement, which has a more narrow focus. Aspects of the consciousness revolution appear to have more spiritual, mystical, and cosmic dimensions. The religious segments of the consciousness revolution most closely relate to transpersonal psychology, which is an outgrowth of the human potential movement.[14]

Psychoanalysis and Behaviorism

Before any of these psychospiritual movements could take off, the discipline of psychology had to change significantly. As indicated in earlier chapters, the field of psychology was dominated by psychoanalysis and behaviorism until about 1960. Psychoanalysis, or "First Force" psychology, can be seen as a form of psychic determinism. Freud believed that an individual's personality and lifetime behavior were determined by two factors: biologically inherited characteristics and the social influence of a child's first five years. Freud had a strong bias against religion. He neither believed in God nor practiced any form of religion. Freud's psychological system reflected his prejudice, largely portraying God as a father figure and a figment of the imagination.[15]

While Freud's psychoanalysis flourished in America during the twenties, thirties, and forties, dissenters arose. Freud's disciple, Carl Jung (1875-1961), questioned his mentor's total biological orientation and reduction of human behavior to a sexual impulse. He also challenged the anti-religious stance of the Freudian system, insisting that the spiritual side of a personality was not only real but important. His theory of the archetypes left room for the mystical and occult aspects of religion. In fact, facets of Jungian psychology dovetail quite well with many of the assumptions found in modern humanistic and transpersonal psychology and Eastern/occult spirituality.[16]

While not new, behaviorism (or second-force psychology) dominated during the fifties and sixties. Despite their disagreements, both behaviorism and psychoanalysis shared a basic presupposition--people are totally determined by their biological inheritance and social environment.   But behaviorism was more scientific than psychoanalysis, insisting on a return to more observable methods of investigation. Behaviorism believed that people were like animals--that is, a collection of stimulus-response mechanisms. As a result, human behavior could be modified by external factors. Humanity existed within a closed system that allowed no room for God, spiritual reality or human dignity. Best known of the modern behaviorists was B. F. Skinner (1904-1990). He systematized a comprehensive behaviorism that allowed little room for human free will and moral judgment.[17]

The rigidity, determinism, dehumanization, and anti-religious bias of psychoanalysis and behaviorism provoked a reaction.   The humanistic and transpersonal psychologies rejected these restrictions and took a different path. New Age theorists soundly rejected both psychoanalysis and behaviorism. Fritjof Capra links both of these systems to the old Cartesian-Newtonian paradigm. While Capra recognizes differences between psychoanalysis and behaviorism, he regards both as mechanistic and lacking a holistic, integrative approach to human problems.[18]

Humanistic Psychology

The movement against psychoanalysis and behaviorism was lead by Abraham Maslow (1908-1970). His 1954 book *Motivation and Personality* established the foundation for humanistic psychology. Maslow saw people as more than animals reacting to stimulus mechanisms. Rather, human beings were on a much higher plane.[19] He studied healthy people, not the mentally ill. As a result, he came to see humankind as basically healthy and capable of great personal achievement and self-transcendence.   In Maslow's opinion, human nature was good, not neutral or evil. Thus, instead of suppressing the inner nature, "it is best to bring it out and encourage it . . . . If it is permitted to guide our life, we grow healthy, fruitful, and happy."[20]

Maslow spelled out a hierarchy of needs. On the lowest level are physical needs such as food, liquid, sleep, and sex. Further up the ladder are safety needs (order and stability) and social needs (love and belonging). At the top of his hierarchy are the growth or self-actualization needs--beauty, truth, goodness, justice, goodness, truth, meaning, and self-sufficiency. These "being values" can be realized in "peak experiences" in which the individual transcends him or herself and becomes unified with reality.[21]

This transcendence or self-actualization is a religious experience. Not only did Maslow break the hold of the scientific, deterministic view of life, but he infused modern psychology with a religious dimension. He tells us that transcendence is a "mystical experience as classically described by the religious mystics . . . . " "Transcendence also means to become divine or godlike, to go beyond the merely human." But Maslow does not mean that transcendence is some supernatural experience because becoming "divine or godlike" is "a potentiality of human nature," not a gift of God.[22]

Maslow paved the way for a new psychological view of human nature--one that viewed humanity as basically good and containing great potential. He was followed by a number of psychologists, the most prominent being Rollo May, Erich Fromm, and Carl Rogers. May insisted that neither Freudianism nor behaviorism could deal with the real problems of life. His special contribution to humanistic psychology grew out his experience with European existentialism, which focused on an intense experience of being.[23]

Erich Fromm clearly linked humanistic psychology with a monistic worldview, describing his position as "nontheistic mysticism." He saw a relationship between Zen Buddhism and Western psychoanalysis, agreeing with the Buddhist writer D. T. Suzuki that the "Buddha is in all of us." Fromm united pantheism and humanism and saw the one within each individual.[24] Fromm described humanistic religion as "centered around man and his strength." In fact, "God is a symbol of man's own powers which he tries to realize in his life . . . ."[25]

In humanistic psychology, human beings are good and have unlimited potential. Thus, the job of the therapist is to place the client in touch with the higher self--the ultimate source of goodness and meaning. Crystalizing such thinking was Carl Rogers' "client-centered" approach to therapy. Because an individual has the answers within, the therapist is to guide clients, not instruct them. Rogers' methods have widespread acceptance within the psychological community, going well beyond the New Age. Yet, these ideas resonate with key New Age teachings.[26]

A number of core New Age assumptions correspond with those of humanistic psychology. Francis Adeney summarizes the major presuppositions of humanistic psychology. First, human beings are good and their natural bent is "toward goodness, toward growth." Second, "human potential is unlimited." Such potential is tapped largely through personal experience. Human autonomy is necessary because growth and values emerge from personal experiences that are not restricted by beliefs or social conventions. Third, "personal awareness is a valid life goal." The more self-awareness an individual has, the more alive he or she is.[27]

Transpersonal Psychology

In breaking out of the confines established by psychoanalysis and behaviorism, humanistic psychology prepared the way for a "fourth force"--transpersonal psychology. Humanistic psychology moved away from the rigid scientific cast established by behaviorism and gave psychology a more human dimension. In doing so, it blazed the trail for a new psychology with a spiritual focus. Humanistic psychology's focus on humanity was fine, but it did not go far enough. It was not "the be-all or end-all." Thus, with Maslow's blessing, humanistic psychology gave birth to transpersonal psychology.[28]

Transpersonal psychology is usually dated from the late 1960s. The leading figure in the early movement was Anthony Sutich. The year 1969 saw the founding of the Association of Transpersonal Psychology by Sutich and the publication of the first issue of the *Journal of Transpersonal Psychology*. In this issue, Sutich defined transpersonal psychology as "interested in those ultimate human capacities and potentialities that have no place in positivistic or behavioristic theory, classical psychoanalytic theory, or humanistic psychology." Transpersonal psychology is concerned with "becoming, individual and species-wide meta-needs, ultimate values, unitive consciousness, peak experiences . . . mystical experience (and) transcendence of self . . . ."[29]

Transpersonal psychology developed in the context of the mid-sixties. The counterculture was in full swing; interest in the occult mushroomed; Eastern religions fascinated many people and the drug culture gave others a chemically induced "altered state." These psychedelic states suggested possibilities that went beyond anything found in humanistic psychology. During the sixties the human potential movement and the hippie culture overlapped extensively, allowing for an infusion of the counterculture into psychology. Therefore, the cultural environment of the mid to late sixties was fertile soil for the development of a mystical psychology.[30]

While humanistic psychology had a spiritual dimension, it still focused on humanity and lacked a religious philosophy. Thus, religious ideas naturally filtered into the movement. To be truly self-actualized, a religious experience is necessary. For such religious ideas and experiences, humanistic psychology did not turn to Christianity but to the occult tradition and Eastern spirituality.[31]

As Francis Adeney points out, in any strict sense, "transpersonal psychology is not psychology at all." Rather, it blends "psychological concepts, evolutionary theory, and religious belief" in an endeavor "to give a cosmic explanation for all of life."[32] Transpersonal psychology embraces the monistic and pantheistic worldview of Western occultism and Eastern spirituality. Rejecting the anti-religious and even atheistic bias of Freudianism and behaviorism, transpersonal psychology declares that humanity is divine. Transpersonal psychology blends this monistic worldview with great confidence in human evolution and Western optimism. As a result, humanity has unlimited potential and is capable of a self-awareness that places individuals in touch with their divinity. To facilitate this consciousness expansion, transpersonal psychology also encourages Eastern practices such as meditation and yoga.[33]

Transpersonal psychology has not joined the ranks of mainstream academic psychology. But it does have a growing influence. A few universities offer masters degrees focusing on the study of human consciousness. Transpersonal psychology has also penetrated public education, especially confluent education. There are also a number of transpersonal theorists: Ken Wilber, Gerald Jampolsky, Charles Tart, and Arthur Deikman. Such individuals have attempted to integrate New Age thinking with transpersonal psychology. Of the types of psychology, the transpersonal variety is most compatible with the New Age vision of the transformed individual.[34]

The leading transpersonal psychologist identified with the New Age movement is Ken Wilber. In two scholarly works, *The Atman Project* (1980) and *Up From Eden* (1981), Wilber presents fourteen stages to psychological growth. One moves through these levels to the "highest stage," the "most realized" state. Here one experiences a higher consciousness, similar to Maslow's peak experience. At this highest level of transpersonal psychology the individual becomes enlightened and is in touch with the divine. In Wilber's scheme of things, Maslow's peak experience is a religious encounter. At this stage, psychology becomes the vehicle for implementing salvation, or--as the New Age advocates would say it--personal transformation.[35]

Human Potential Movement

The human potential movement has a two-fold relationship to the New Age movement. On one hand, it provides an important backdrop for the New Age. In part, the New Age grew out of the human potential movement. On the other, it is an essential component of the New Age. It is one of the vital networks of the decentralized New Age movement. The New Age and human potential movements share an important objective--self-fulfillment.[36]

Components

The core of the human potential movement is humanistic psychology. However, humanistic psychology lacks sharp boundaries. It moved from naturalistic to spiritual assumptions and incorporated transpersonal psychology and a wide range of therapies, activities, and techniques. Humanistic psychology spilled over into the broader human potential movement, which comprised an even wider spectrum of ideas and activities.[37]

Like the New Age itself, the human potential movement must be seen as a general rather than a specific movement. According to sociologist Roy Wallis, it consists of a collection of "independent groups, leaders, communication media, etc., which display no common structure of authority or membership," and which manifest a divergence of purpose and practice.   Yet these groups and individuals recognize that they share "a common commitment to the attainment of personal growth by self-directed means."[38]

Carl Raschke says that psychoreligiousity is the "use of psychological principles and techniques as surrogates for traditional religious beliefs and practices." According to him, "this is what the Human Potential movement is all about."[39]   It is, as Barbara Hargrove points out, a form of "personal salvation through the methods of humanistic psychology."[40]

The human potential movement is a synthesis of Western psychology, the occult and Eastern spirituality. The movement has moved from a focus on humanistic psychology to fully embracing an occult and Eastern mind-set.   In the human potential movement, Western psychology has undergone many Eastern influences. Conversely, many Eastern gurus are making use of Western psychology.[41] As Raschke says, "the human potential movement is a multilayered and eclectic blend of the new clinical psychologies with a dash of watered down Zen Buddhism, Yoga, or other forms of Oriental mysticism." But whether the focus is Western psychology, the occult, or Eastern religion, the gospel of the human potential movement remains the same: God is within the self; enrichment comes from discovering the self; and the transfiguration of society is through "the reintegration of individual psyches."[42]

There are a number of therapies, groups, and training programs whose committed participants would regard themselves as part of the broad human potential movement. Some therapies better relate to

Western psychology: encounter groups, Gestalt awareness training, Transactional Analysis, sensory awareness, primal therapy, bioenergetics, humanistic psychology, psychosynthesis, and biofeedback.   Other groups and practices are rooted in Eastern religions: transcendental meditation, Arica training, the Rajneesh Foundation, yoga, and the martial arts.   Still, some groups and therapies have more of an occult orientation or are difficult to categorize: est, Synanon, Silva Mind Control, Gurdjieff groups, psychic healing, and mind control training.   These groups and therapies do not function in isolation.   In fact, a hallmark of the human potential movement is the extent to which they interact with, overlap, and borrow from each other.[43]

Esalen

When one thinks of the human potential movement, two names come to the forefront--Abraham Maslow and the Esalen Institute. Maslow's ideas have already been noted.   In 1962 Michael Murphy and Richard Price founded the Esalen Institute in Big Sur, California. Since then Esalen has been at the forefront of the movement for the development of untried human potential.   As David Toolan notes, strictly speaking Esalen did not "give birth to the human potential movement, to the 'consciousness revolution,' and finally, to transpersonal psychology."   Rather, it provided the "search tools" for such developments.[44]

Esalen's goal has been to serve as an educational institution reaching "the cutting edge of knowledge to a greater degree than colleges and universities,"writes Gordon Melton.   It serves as a place where academics and professionals gather to share information on mental and physical health, government, education, business, and so forth.   Courses are taught on mysticism, meditation, comparative religion, psychotherapy, expansion of consciousness, and group awareness.[45]

In the last fifteen to twenty years, Esalen has undergone some shifts.   It has moved from a center for the exchange of ideas on psychotherapy to one on spiritual matters.   In part this transition has accompanied the shift from humanistic to transpersonal psychology. At Esalen there is now more Hinduism and Buddhism.   The atmosphere is more esoteric and contemplative.[46]

The individuals who have taught at Esalen read like a New Age Who's Who, plus a number of other prominent figures. Included on a short list are the following: Baba Ram Dass (Richard Alpert), Fritjof Capra, Willis Harman, Aldous Huxley, S. I. Hayakawa, R. D. Laing, Abraham Maslow, Timothy Leary, Rollo May, Ralph Metzner, Carl Rogers, Theodore Roszak, Bishop John Robinson, B. F. Skinner, Arnold Toynbee, Paul Tillich, Bishop James Pike, Alan Watts, and Fritz Perls.[47]

Precursors

Though the human potential movement began to take shape in a formal sense in the late 1940s, it has had several precursors in American history. As Rasche notes, the human potential movement may be seen as following in the steps of the earlier "mind cure" movement, whose proponents from Mary Baker Eddy to Norman Vincent Peale promised "health, wealth, and happiness for confused, lonely, and self-doubting people." The human potential movement differed with the "mind cure" school in regards to style and rhetoric but not in substance.[48]

As an organized body of knowledge, psychology originated in the nineteenth century toward the end of the Romantic revolt against the Enlightenment.   Psychology has developed primarily along the rigorous scientific lines of the behavioral school. But in forms like the human potential movement, psychology was related more to Romantic and organic themes. Because the Romantics emphasized freedom, spontaneity, feeling, and emotion, one constant theme in the Romantic movement was inwardness or the absorption in one's own mental and spiritual life. During the 1960s something akin to a new surge of Romanticism had extended across America. With it came an emphasis on exploring the frontiers of one's inner life. To turn inward was a way to "turn on." The inner world was seen as good and perhaps even divine.[49]

As Catherine Albanese points out, the new psychologies that encouraged this turning inward were "distinguished in several ways from the therapies of the past." Most important, they did not so much endeavor to heal the mentally ill as to bring ordinary people with usual problems "to the perfection of their capacity for happiness and creativity." Second, while the traditional psychologies had their basis in "the authoritarian model of the relationship between doctor and patient," the new therapies often have stressed different patterns: the community of peer relationships and the self-help techniques, like meditation, of some Eastern religions. Next, while the older psychologies employed a technical language that was scientific, the new forms used a somewhat religious vocabulary borrowed from the Eastern faiths. Finally, while the older therapies were seen as a temporary process, the new psychologies were devoted to the cultivation of techniques that should be used for a lifetime.[50]

Consciousness Revolution

Many of these psychological, emotional, and spiritual therapies are part of a large, culturally pervasive movement called the consciousness revolution. As the human potential movement turned East and became more mystical and spiritual, it gave birth to a closely related movement--the consciousness revolution. It embodies most of the characteristics of the human potential movement except that it is even more eclectic, spiritual, and mystical.

The consciousness revolution may turn out to be the twentieth-century psychoreligious counterpart to some of America's past religious awakenings. It endeavors to give individuals a psychoreligious mystical experience that puts them in contact with themselves and the universe. As Woodward says, its practitioners, methods, and rhetoric run the gamut from the serious to the sham. The movement's ranks include thousands of psychotherapists and psychologists and legions of gurus, swamis, and babas. Moreover, the movement inevitably has "attracted a sleazy new breed of self-anointed 'facilitators' who tamper dangerously with other people's psyches"--plus some charlatans who falsely feed unrealistic hopes for health, happiness, and holiness.[51]

Some authorities see the consciousness movement as being hastened by a decline of faith in family, church, and government. Encounter groups meet personal needs by offering instant intimacy in a society where mobility works against lasting relationships. Author Peter Marin sees the new consciousness therapies as but an aspect of the "new narcissism." They are a way "to avoid the demands of the world." The self replaces community, relationships, neighbors, and God. Psychiatrist Perry London says that body therapies "service people's sensory needs in a culture where leisure is so prolific that it must be made elegantly meaningful to be deeply savored." Theologian Albert Outler sees the "loss of the sacred" in our society as generating an excess of self-centered substitutes, ranging from "the inner directedness" of Carl Rogers and Abraham Maslow to the "hard-eyed egocentrism of Werner Erhard."[52]

Alvin Toffler says that "by the late 1970s a human potential movement . . . had spawned some 8,000 different therapies . . . ."[53] This estimate may be an exaggeration. Nevertheless, as Woodward claims, "the consciousness revolution, once confined to the youthful counterculture, has mushroomed into a mass movement, particularly popular with the more affluent individuals of society who can afford the time and money to develop their inner depths."[54] Ranging from inexpensive yoga classes at the YMCA to luxurious "awareness" cruises in the Caribbean, a vast network of therapeutic outlets is available to millions of Americans who are dissatisfied with their lives, looking for a direct experience with God, or just plain bored. The movement has "produced a lucrative market for packaged programs" designed to produce enlightenment. A partial list includes Silva Mind Control, est, Transcendental Meditation, Scientology, Synanon, and Arica training. These programs have promised a "new you to anyone who can pay for it."[55]

Can the consciousness revolution be regarded as a religious movement? At its furthermost frontier, as represented by transpersonal psychology, the consciousness revolution can be regarded as at least a quasi-religious movement. Woodward argues that "it brings Western psychotherapy 180 degrees from Freud's rejection of immortality as an illusion to an almost Buddhist rejection of the concrete world as illusion." A sense of the transcendent is present in transpersonal psychology, but the perspective is different from that of the Judeo-Christian tradition. One may have a direct experience with the divine without any necessary reference to God or revelation.[56]

As in the New Age, the emphasis is on me. I am the catalyst of change for myself. I am the focal point of my own universe. I have the potential to be divine, creating and experiencing my own reality. As a cultural movement, "the consciousness revolution feeds on the romantic notion that inner experience alone can transform reality" and that anyone can shape his or her life "into a perfect work of art." As a religious phenomenon, "it signals a return to Gnosticism, which always disparages common humanity in the name of higher truths."[57]

The New Age vision rests on the notion of the transformed individual. This transformation is an inward experience. As Marilyn Ferguson notes, for many "the trigger has been a spontaneous mystical or psychic experience. . .," which she calls "psychotechnologies--systems for a deliberate change in consciousness."[58] These psychotechnologies are a vital part of the New Age and several overlapping movements--the consciousness revolution and the human potential movement. And they come from a number of sources, especially modern psychology, Eastern religions, and the occult.

Chapter 10

HEALTH AND HEALING
IN THE NEW AGE

Health and healing are vital components of the New Age movement. Except for channeling, perhaps no aspect of the New Age has gained the public's attention so much as its belief in nonmedical forms of healing. New Age health remedies such as crystal healing, acupuncture, herbal remedies, and psychic healing are known to many people. For example, about forty to fifty percent of the members of the major denominations in America claim to believe in psychic healing.[1]

The quest for health and healing also have become open doors to the New Age. Marilyn Ferguson tells us that "The proliferating holistic health centers and networks have drawn many into the consciousness [New Age] movement." For many New Agers, "an involvement in health care was a major stimulus to [personal] transformation." Accompanying New Age health care is a new perspective on reality, a monistic worldview and perhaps even "altered states of consciousness."[2]

Hollywood stars have put New Age health and healing in the spotlight. Shirley MacLaine insists that "natural, holistic approaches [to health] worked better for me than medicines or drugs." She says that she no longer needs a family doctor. Experience has taught her "that orthodox Western medicine relied far too heavily on drugs." Instead, Ms. MacLaine now counts on the healing power found in crystal rocks, acupuncture, spirit messages, and sound therapy. She has learned "to work with the power of crystals" and claims that this discipline has "become part of my daily life."[3] Actress Jill Ireland believes that meditation combined with crystal power facilitated her successful recovery from cancer. She held a crystal in her hand, "drawing the healing energy into her" and then engaged in a "cancer meditation."[4]

New Age ideas on health have penetrated society. The New Age operates in the health field as an informal but widespread network. Transformation is at the heart of the New Age. At times transformation is a matter of healing--a physical, mental, and spiritual healing. Consequently, the New Age is getting its message out through chiropractors, massage therapists, psychologists, physical and mental healers, advertisements regarding alternative medicine, and bulletin boards in natural food stores.[5]

Definitions and Relationships

In recent years millions of Americans have practiced some form of alternative medicine. The terms *alternative medicine*, *New Age medicine*, and *holistic health* have been tossed around. What do these terms mean? How do these movements relate one to another? Because the New Age does not have distinct boundaries, it is difficult to draw a clear line between these movements.

Professor of religious studies Robert Fuller defines alternative or unorthodox medicine by contrasting it with orthodox or Western medicine. Since the Enlightenment, "medical orthodoxy has been defined by a commitment to the causal role of organic, or 'material,' factors in the etiology of disease." Western medicine opposes the pre-modern worldview which proposes "nonmaterial or spiritual causes of disease (e.g., sin or spirit possession) as well as corresponding schemas for therapeutic intervention (e.g., confession or exorcism)."[6]

On the contrary, alternative medicine can be defined as a system that believes illness and healing is caused by nonmaterial and nonmedical factors. Alternative medicine can be divided into two categories. There is the nonsupernaturalist variety. In explaining their various activities, these groups "make no claims concerning the presence or activity of extrasomatic energies." These nonsupernaturalist types are usually nutritional and exercise therapies that emphasize "preventive rather than curative practices."[7] They do not focus on supernatural or metaphysical aspects of health, whether they be of the Christian, occult, or Eastern variety.

The second type of alternative medicine is the supernaturalist version. While the term *supernatural* may be rejected by some of these groups, they all offer religious, spiritual or metaphysical explanations for disease and healing. Their worldview is based on the belief that extramundane forces exert curative influences upon the human realm. Such alternative approaches to medicine can be found in the Christian, occult, and Eastern traditions. Healing may occur because of forces beyond the material world, whether the source be the Christian God or a divine energy found in all living beings. This form of alternative medicine can be seen as a religious expression. More often than not, it leads to unorthodox religious beliefs and is linked to some nontraditional religion or quasi-religion.[8]

According to the CBS program "Anything for a Cure," one out of every three Americans has dabbled with some aspect of alternative medicine. The gamut of choices runs from well-accepted procedures such as chiropractic manipulations and health foods to exotic New Age or Eastern therapies. Alternative medicine is the broadest of the previously mentioned categories. It encompasses New Age medicine and the holistic health movement. These two movements are alternative medicines that assume nontraditional and spiritual causes of disease and healing. However, alternative medicine goes beyond New Age medicine and holistic health and includes practices with purely naturalistic assumptions.

New Age medicine can be defined as a holistic approach to health that believes wellness is regulated by some form of spiritual and mystical energy. According to holistic health physician Robert Gilder, "wholistic health is a state in which a human being is integrated at all levels of being: body, mind, and spirit." It is a "wholistic approach to creating and maintaining health," one that goes beyond any one particular treatment or therapy.[9]

In theory the New Age and the holistic health movement have separate existences.[10] A holistic approach to health is an alternative medicine that predates the New Age movement. Moreover, in theory the holistic health movement can contain individuals and groups who embrace either a spiritual or natural approach to health, but have no connections with the New Age movement. From another perspective, the holistic health movement can be seen as an important forerunner of the New Age.

But in practice, the New Age and the holistic health movements are one movement. "During the 1970s, the New Age Movement and the holistic health movement merged to the extent that it is difficult, if not impossible, for an observer to draw the line between them," writes Gordon Melton. They both embraced a number of the same alternative health practices and shared a similar philosophy. Thus, they naturally merged. One central concept philosophically unites the New Age and holistic health movements--"the individual person is responsible for his or her own life and for seeking out the means of transformation needed to achieve a better quality of life."[11]

Furthermore, New Age spokespersons view the holistic health movement as an important component of their movement. Likewise, holistic health practitioners regard New Agers as part of their movement and as important clientele for their businesses.[12] As a result, this study will use the terms *New Age medicine* and *holistic health movement* interchangeably. The holistic health movement is an expression of the New Age movement.

Social and Economic Factors

The 1960s, 1970s, and 1980s witnessed an amazing revival of alternative medicine, especially groups that postulated religious or metaphysical causes for disease and healing. The holistic health movement was one of these developments, arising in a social and spiritual climate conducive to alternative religions with unorthodox medical practices. On one hand, these groups maintain a continuity with the metaphysical healing traditions of the past. On the other, they do not completely reject modern medicine. Instead, as Fuller puts it, they regard their practices as "extra-, rather than pre-, scientific."[13]

The holistic health movement must be seen as a product of the sixties and seventies. Many of the occult and cultic groups that emerged at this time had healing dimensions. The holistic health movement shared much with these groups, including a monistic worldview and an emphasis on psychic powers. The worldviews of Christian theism and natural science were in retreat, paving the way for the occult/Eastern worldviews that permeate the holistic health movement. Therefore, the health practices of these alternative religions naturally spilled over into the holistic health movement.

The seventies and eighties have witnessed an explosion of self-help groups. As futurist John Naisbitt says, Americans have gradually become disillusioned with institutions "such as the government, the medical establishment, the corporation, and the school system . . . ." As Americans become "more self-sufficient" and "motivated by mutual self-interest" they have begun to help themselves and each other.[14]

Such a context gave rise to a growing interest in self-health care and disease prevention. People moved from a passive reliance on the medical professionals to more personal responsibility for their health. "Medically, self-help is taking responsibility for health habits, environment, and lifestyle . . . ." This emphasis on self-help resonated with a cardinal principle of the holistic health movement-- individuals are responsible for their own well-being. People began to exercise more, quit smoking, eat less, and adjust their diets. This trend toward self-help provided a catalyst for the emerging holistic health movement.[15]

In 1965 Lyndon Johnson rescinded the Oriental exclusion act, opening the door to a flow of immigrants from the Far East. This act brought many Eastern spiritual leaders to America, fostering the growth of Eastern spirituality and health practices. Richard Nixon went to China in 1972, beginning an era of better relations between the United States and China. This development made Chinese medical knowledge available to the West. Chinese medicine is a major component of holistic health, bringing to the movement practices like acupuncture, manipulative therapies such as acupressure, and many herbal remedies.[16]

A major factor in the growth of the holistic health movement was a widespread disenchantment with the current biomedical system. In recent years, the health-care system of the United States has come under attack from a range of critics from nearly every walk of life, including New Agers. It has been seen as too costly, unfair to the poor, sexist, racist, and generally inadequate. This attack on Western medicine is but one aspect of a more widespread condemnation of technology. But the holistic health movement has confronted Western medicine with a new challenge. This movement says that the modern health-care system has lost touch with issues that concern the human soul and spirit, and it seeks to bring these issues back into the practice of medicine.[17]

This dissatisfaction with the biomedical system brought two major changes. Western medicine, as Ferguson notes, is "undergoing an amazing revitalization." Medical professionals and patients alike are taking a more holistic approach to disease. In treating disease, they are complementing the traditional biomedical procedures with other considerations--diet, stress, and emotions.[18] Also, other individuals have turned to alternative health systems, especially those focusing on metaphysical causes for disease and healing.

The people turning to these alternative health systems during the seventies and eighties came from the middle and upper ranks of society. The rise of the holistic health movement was not an expression of desperation among the poor and uneducated. In fact, most of these alternative medical practices are not covered by health insurance and government programs. Some alternative health programs can be costly. Like the New Age as a whole, most people turning to holistic health measures are culturally and educationally sophisticated. In addition to a dissatisfaction with the biomedical system, alternative health systems also arose as an expression of spiritual hunger among the "yuppies"and prosperous babyboomers.[19]

Alternative Medicine in American History

The holistic health movement grew out of the social milieu of the sixties, seventies, and eighties. But it has much continuity with the past. A number of earlier alternative medical practices with religious dimensions paved the way for the holistic health movement. In fact, a number of these health treatments are currently practiced in holistic health circles. Even more important, a strong line of continuity exists between the philosophy of many of these early forms of alternative medicines and the worldview of the holistic health movement.

Throughout most of history and in many cultures, the diagnosis and cure of physical problems were entrusted to individuals with magical and supernatural connections. For thousands of years, mystics, faith healers, gurus, and shamans sought to treat illnesses by a variety of procedures, ranging from incision to exorcism. Only since the Enlightenment has the study of the human body and the approach to disease been largely removed from a supernatural context. In Western civilization, the scientific method gradually came to dominate the approach to health and disease.[20] By the 1840s the scientific approach to medicine had been established in America.

Against this medical orthodoxy, a number of alternative medical practices raised their voices in protest. Most of these unorthodox medicines were not self-consciously religious. Yet, nearly all of them had a religious-metaphysical dimension. Broadly speaking, there have been three periods that gave birth to a number of alternative health practices--the 1830s, the 1880s, and the 1960s. These periods generally coincide with what William McLoughlin describes as major shifts in American religion. During these decades the old religious consensus collapsed and a new one replaced it.[21]

Early Nineteenth Century

During the first half of the nineteenth century, Mesmerism and Swedenborgianism penetrated American society, registering a strong influence on a number of fringe religions. Close ties existed between these unorthodox religions and alternative health practices. Nontraditional religious theories tended to promote spiritual or metaphysical explanations for disease and healing. More specifically, both Mesmerism and Swedenborgianism proposed a harmonial model of the universe. An inner harmony existed between the spheres of the universe, with energy and wisdom flowing from the upper to the lower level. The deity was conceived as an indwelling cosmic force. This harmonial model provided the practitioners of alternative medicine with a rationale for their various therapies.[22]

The first half of the nineteenth century witnessed a flurry of religious activity. In addition to the events spurred on by the Second Great Awakening and revivalism, a number of fringe movements developed--Mormonism, the Shakers, Spiritualism, the Oneida Perfectionists, Transcendentalism, and a variety of millennial groups. The same environment also spawned a number of alternative health practices containing metaphysical assumptions. By mid-century, as Fuller notes, "America was awash in irregular, sectarian, healing systems." The best known were Thomsonianism, homeopathy, hydropathy, and a variety of dietary programs inspired by Sylvester Graham. While none of these systems logically entailed a metaphysical approach to disease and healing, an infusion of Mesmerism and Swedenborgianism helped to produce such an explanation.[23]

Many sectarian and cultic religious groups focus on a particular doctrine to the extent that such a preoccupation takes them outside the confines of mainstream religion. The same can be said for unorthodox medical practices. They often believe that one fundamental principle accounts for the cause of disease and healing. Thomasonianism insisted that disease had only one cause--cold--and only one cure--heat. The cornerstone of homeopathy is the doctrine that "like is cured by like." Small amounts of a substance considered harmful in a large quantity are prescribed for healing. Hydropathy believes that curative powers can be found in water. Grahamism focused on dietary practices, but at the heart of this system is the notion that people should eat only "well-made bread" made from unbolted wheat flour. This coarse bread would provide organic vitality without overstimulating the body. Grahamism's dietary practices influenced a number of religious communes and one large religious body, the Seventh Day Adventists.[24]

Late Nineteenth Century

A number of unorthodox medical practices developed in the second half of the nineteenth century. The best known are New Thought, Christian Science, chiropractic, and osteopathy. New Thought's foremost spokesperson, Phineas Parkhurst Quimby, contended that the source of health resides in a vital force, or magnetic fluid, running into the human nervous system through a "deeper level of the mind." Beliefs serve as floodgates or control valves, connecting or disconnecting the conscious mind from its unconscious dimensions. Quimby argued that "disease is the effect of a wrong direction given to the mind."[25] In a similar vein, Christian Science theology insisted that God created everything and thus all of creation is good. Following this line of thinking, the founder of Christian Science, Mary Baker Eddy (1821-1910), concluded that evil, sickness, and pain are not real. Rather, they are delusions created by an erring, mortal mind.[26]

A more serious threat to orthodox medicine came from chiropractic and osteopathic medicine. In the late twentieth century, both chiropractic and osteopathic medicine have largely abandoned their metaphysical approach to disease and healing. Chiropractic and especially osteopathy have gained widespread public acceptance. Yet, both systems are rooted in Mesmerism and for years maintained a metaphysical approach to health care.[27]

D. D. Palmer began chiropractic medicine in the late nineteenth century. Palmer was influenced by Spiritualism and other occult ideas and brought a monistic and emanationist cosmology to his ideas on health care. Such a monistic approach to healing was not unique. A number of alternative medical practices followed this path. Rather, Palmer's originality came in his claim to have discovered the physiological route through which the divine spirit directs the individual. The path of Innate, the Universal Intelligence, began in the brain and was transmitted by the nerve system. Thus, the key to health can be found in the correct alignment of the vertebrae along the spinal column. Like other advocates of alternative medicine, Palmer claimed to have discovered the single cause for all disease-- deranged nerves.[28]

Andrew Taylor Still (1828-1917) began osteopathy in the late nineteenth century. Like Palmer, whom he probably influenced, Still believed that all diseases were caused by the failure of the nerves to properly regulate the fluids of life. However, perhaps his Methodist background prevented him from completely abandoning the notion of a transcendent God in favor of a divine force flowing through human beings. While he maintained some metaphysical assumptions regarding physical health, he never defined them as Palmer did.[29]

There were many other alternative medical practices in American history. But most operate according to two principles, which Catherine Albanese says has been transmitted to New Age healing. First, healing entails a harmonization of the body's energy "so that they resonate with larger natural forces and laws." Second, healing means a journey into "the realm of nonmatter in which the subtle forces transmute into material substance."[30]

Holistic Health Takes Off

The modern holistic health movement has been built on a number of precedents--especially the many alternative medicines that developed in the nineteenth century. Modern holism also has been promoted by a host of publications and organizations, of which only a few can be mentioned.

A number of key books have brought the holistic health message to the public. Jan Christian Smuts' *Holism and Evolution* (1926) may be the first book to promote the early holistic health cause. In the late sixties and continuing into the seventies, books on holistic health proliferated. Rene Dubos's *Man, Medicine and Environment* (1968) critiqued the assumptions of Western medicine. Led by Paavo Airola's *How to Get Well* (1974), a number of books on natural healing appeared. Works on art and music therapy reached the book stores, including Ashley Montagu's *Touching* (1971) and *Touch for Health* (1973) by John Thie *et al.* More general books critiquing the medical establishment and setting the goals of holistic health were published. Some examples include *Healing for Everyone* (1975) by Evarts Loomis and J. Paulson, Rick Carlson's *The End of Medicine and the Frontiers of Science and Medicine* (1975), and *Holistic Medicine* (1979) by Kenneth R. Pelletier.[31]

The real work of the holistic health movement has been done in the numerous holistic health centers that sprang up nationwide, but especially in California. As mentioned in chapter five, the earliest holistic health center began at Meadowlark in 1958, followed closely by two mental health institutes with holistic health programs--Esalen and the Menninger Clinic. But the real surge came from 1968 to 1976, which Gordon Melton calls the "landmark years." During these years, numerous health centers and other important holistic health organizations were established. The year 1978 witnessed the watershed event for the holistic health movement--namely the founding of the American Holistic Medical Association (AHMA) by Dr. Clyde Norman Shealy.[32] In the late 1970s the book *Wholistic Dimensions in Healing* edited by Leslie Kaslof listed eighty holistic health organizations in the United States and Canada.[33]

Melton also describes the general characteristics of these holistic health centers. Their programs are comprehensive, taking a holistic approach toward health, and tailored for the needs of each client. Emphasis is on activating the individual's potential toward self-care. Health is conceived "as a positive state, not merely an absence of disease ...." Thus, emphasis is placed on the promotion of wellness, including diet and exercise. These clinics regard health care as a partnership between the clients and the health care professionals, who include medical doctors plus a wide range of other specialties. Health care decisions do not come from the top down; rather, they involve not only the professionals but also the lay people.[34]

Holistic Health Philosophy

The holistic health movement is diverse. As the authors of *New Age Medicine* indicate, no single group, organization, or type of practice represents this movement. Moreover, it is constantly being reshaped by its practitioners, who include scientists, physicians, osteopaths, chiropractors, sociologists, psychologists, healers, mystics, nurses, and lay people. Organizations that promote or practice holistic health range from large establishments with impressive budgets and facilities to some marginal storefront operations.[35]

Religious Overtones

In spite of such diversity and considerable quackery, at its serious levels, the holistic health movement has a more or less identifiable philosophy. Holistic health advocate Rick Carlson says that holistic health can be viewed three ways: as a concept, as a movement, and "as a mode of practicing the healing arts." Its impact as a movement and as a set of practices has been minimized by fraud in its ranks and because of resistance from the medical establishment. But as Carlson notes, holistic health has had its greatest influence as a concept. Aspects of its philosophy have penetrated traditional medicine since the 1970s and have facilitated change in the way Western medicine is practiced.[36]

Assuming a broad definition of religion--that an individual is placed in touch with higher beings or powers--then holistic health can be said to have a religious or spiritual philosophy.[37] The holistic health movement has many sincere practitioners whose immediate objective is to alleviate an individual's disorders. But prominent holistic health spokesperson Kenneth R. Pelletier indicates that holistic health has a more important objective--namely the "fundamental reorientation of life style and personal philosophy." By personal philosophy, he is referring to individuals' understanding of themselves, the universe, and the nature of reality.[38]

In *Holistic Medicine*, Pelletier tells us that basic philosophical changes are occurring in the current medical paradigm. "Central to this revision is the concept that all stages of disease are psychosomatic in etiology, duration, and the healing process." Pelletier is speaking of more than the psychological and attitudinal factors in physical healing. Rather, this psychosomatic interaction entails a fundamental revision in the concepts of causation. Drawing from the Chinese yin/yang philosophy, Pelletier says that the new medical paradigm will depict God as a spiritual energy exerting causal influences in the physical realm.[39]

The spiritual dimension of holistic health is evident elsewhere. Holistic health proponent Richard Miles tells us that "holistic health is a point of view about the Universe, about human life in the Universe and about how one finds . . . the fulfillment of self-actualization."[40] Even the basic premise of holistic health has religious overtones: "Every human being is a unique, wholistic, interdependent relationship of body, mind, emotions, and spirit." Such a seemingly straightforward statement entails an interpretation of reality and causality that is incompatible with the assumptions of natural science.[41]

The philosophy of the New Age and of the holistic health movement is essentially the same--namely a monistic, holistic worldview that rejects both Christian theism and the Cartesian mind-set of the modern world. The entire universe consists of one undifferentiated, impersonal reality--sometimes called "Universal Consciousness," "the one," or "Life Energy." Or, perhaps to placate those still hung up on Christian terminology, it may be called "God." If all of the cosmos is one, then all human beings are god or gods.[42]

This monistic, pantheistic worldview is evident in the holistic health movement's approach to healing. Western medicine has divided the human being into cells, organs, and systems. Disease is caused by bacteria or other agents that can be treated by drugs. New Agers argue that since people are one with the universe, a divine energy force flows through each individual. Healing occurs when people learn to manipulate this invisible flow of life energy. Since humanity is divine and one with the universe, physical and other healing can take place when individuals become aware of their oneness and divinity.[43]

Such ideas are not new. Many practitioners of the alternative medicines arising in the nineteenth century believed that the key to health was the proper flow of this divine energy throughout the body. For over a century, Christian Science, Science of the Mind, Religious Science, and other "mind science" groups have contended that sickness is an illusion. Therefore, the key to health is for human beings to realize that they are perfect spiritual beings. The revival of the occult and the influx of Eastern religions in the 1960s and 1970s reinforced this approach to healing that is so much a part of the holistic health movement.[44]

Major Precepts

The authors of *New Age Medicine*, Paul C. Reisser, Teri K. Reisser, and John Weldon, say that ten precepts can be found in holistic health. Running through most of these themes is the New Age monistic philosophy. Not everyone who adheres to these precepts or even advocates the practices that will be noted later is related to the New Age movement. Nevertheless, these themes are a way to view the conceptual framework of the holistic health movement.[45]

First, "the whole is greater than the sum of its parts." Holistic health has an "overriding concern for the whole person--body, mind, and spirit." Such an approach to health focuses on the premise that a human being is more than a collection of cells, tissues, and organs. Rather, a human being consists of body, mind, and spirit. A physical disorder does not occur in a vacuum. Attitudes, emotions, and lifestyles also have a significant bearing on health.[46]

The holistic health movement does not have a lock on such a concept. Concern for body, mind, and spirit is gaining a widespread acceptance in the traditional medical community. Yet, the "holism" in the holistic movement rests on the New Age movement's rejection of the Cartesian-Newtonian paradigm. Fritjof Capra tells us that because of the Cartesian paradigm "the human body is regarded as a machine that can be analyzed in terms of its parts . . . ." As a result of concentrating on small fragments of the body, "modern medicine often loses sight of the patient as a human being . . . ."[47]

Kenneth Pelletier also says that because of the "Newtonian reductionist view of world . . . a person is viewed much like an automobile." Consequently, "a patient is seen as a disabled mechanism . . . ." In place of Western medicine, he suggests a new medical model--one that takes a holistic approach to disease and healing. While this new model will not ignore biomedical factors, it will view the individual as a whole person, taking emotional and psychological factors into consideration.[48]

Second, "health is more than the absence of disease." Holistic health advocate George Leonard says that conventional medicine regards an individual as well if he or she "has no symptoms or falls within a normal range in a series of diagnostic tests." Yet, such a person might eat a harmful diet, get no exercise, smoke heavily, and be emotionally stressed. Holistic health practitioners would regard such a person as sick.[49] Capra says that "although medicine has contributed to the elimination of certain diseases, this has not necessarily restored health." Illness may be expressed in another mode than physical disease.[50] Marilyn Ferguson sees "disease or disability as a process" that may be at different stages. Emphasis should be on "achieving maximum wellness, [or] meta-health."[51]

Third, "individuals are ultimately responsible for their own health or disease." New Agers think of the patient as a client or a co-worker with the physician, actively participating in the healing process. Ferguson says that in the new health paradigm the patient "should be autonomous," a partner with the health-care professional. Each individual has a wise healer inside him or her. She says that in a sense, "there is always a doctor in the house."[52] Capra criticizes the paternal role that the physician assumes in our society, which has "conferred on physicians the exclusive right to determine what constitutes illness, who is ill and who is well, and what should be done to the sick."[53]

Fourth, "natural forms of healing are preferable to drugs and surgery." In American society natural forms of health--exercise, diet, health foods, vitamins--have become tremendously popular. The holistic health movement has capitalized on this trend. Some radicals would dispense with traditional medicine, relying entirely on natural forms of health. More moderate holistic health advocates, such as Kenneth Pelletier, see natural forms of health in a complementary relationship to traditional medicine.[54]

Fifth, "any method of promoting health or preventing disease has the potential for being holistic, but some methods are more innately holistic than others." Holistic health advocates acknowledge that any health measure, even the procedures of biomedicine, have the potential for being practiced in a holistic manner. But deep down, they have a profound disdain for conventional medicine and push a number of alternative practices with a close affinity to occultism and Eastern spirituality.[55] These specific practices shall be examined later.

Sixth, "health implies evolution." As noted in chapter five, evolution is a key New Age concept. But it is not used in the sense of Darwinian biological evolution. New Age evolution is both personal and societal. Individuals have the potential to steadily improve their lives. When enough individuals are transformed, society will evolve toward a new age. In respect to health, personal transformation will not only result in improved physical and psychological well being, but people will be in touch with the divine power within. When the New Age arrives, health care will undergo a radical change and holistic health will be the norm.[56]

Seventh, "to understand health and disease, we need an alternative model, one that is based primarily on energy rather than matter." The concept of energy is basic to the New Age and critical to the holistic health movement. New Agers argue that Einstein proved that matter and energy are one and the same. Transpersonal psychologist James Fadiman says that "we are not primarily physical forms. We are primarily energy . . . ." This energy is not merely a force that flows through us--it is us.[57] In presenting a space-time model for health, holistic health physician Larry Dossey contends that "the boundary of our physical self, our skin, is an illusion."[58]

This universal, omnipresent, spiritual energy comes in many forms, of which humanity is but one manifestation. This impersonal life force goes by many names. In Eastern religions it is the equivalent of God. The Chinese call this energy "Chi." To the Japanese it is known as "Ki." Hinduism refers to this energy as "Prana." To avoid an Eastern appearance, the New Age calls it "bioenergy." Individuals have given this life force a number of names. To Franz Mesmer it is animal magnetism. D. D. Palmer designated it as The Innate. William Reich calls it Orgone energy. In *Star Wars*, George Lucas named it The Force.[59]

The assumption that individuals are energy in the form of matter has significant implications for health care. For many alternative medicines in past American history, the flow or blockage of universal energy is the key to health. Disease is not regarded as a physical problem. Rather, it results from unenlightened consciousness or an imbalance of energy. In Eastern medicine, pain is regarded not as a symptom but results from an over-accumulation of energy in a particular area of the body. The cure is also in the realm of the mind. Health will be restored when this universal energy flows freely and is properly balanced. In the holistic movement, many therapies-- both physical and psychic--are designed to promote the flow of energy.[60]

Eighth, "death is the final step of growth." The extension of life
is a preoccupation with the holistic health movement.   Kenneth
Pelletier believes "that it is clearly possible to extend life significantly
beyond 100 years while maintaining a high quality of life."[61] But in
the face of such optimism, suffering and death do occur.   Thus,
necessity requires the holistic health advocates to take a positive view
of death, viewing it as an illusion or a means of passage to a higher
realm.[62] Others such as Dossey believe that if we abandon the linear
concept of time, the fear of death will fade.[63]

Ninth, "the thinking and practices of many ancient civilizations are
a rich storehouse of knowledge for healthy living." In general, the
New Age takes an idealized view not only of the Eastern civilizations
but also of the premodern world.[64] Much of the New Age is a
throwback to the ancient world.   Therefore, the holistic health
movement has naturally turned to the wisdom of the ancient
civilizations.   These pretechnological cultures which take a
metaphysical approach to disease and healing are viewed as adopting
a holistic, integrated approach to health--one that is in tune with the
forces of the universe.

From these ancient cultures, the holistic health movement has
drawn many of its healing practices.   Magic and shamanism have
impacted paranormal healing.   Native American healing practices
from North and South America have been embraced.   Acupuncture
and acupressure with their Taoist philosophy came from China.
India's Vedantic Hinduism gave the West yoga and meditation
techniques.   From ancient Egypt came many esoteric healing
traditions, including the belief in pyramid power. While the Christian
tradition is eschewed, Jesus is regarded as a shaman, an enlightened
healer.[65]

Tenth, "holistic health must be incorporated into the fabric of
society through public policy." The more moderate holistic health
practices--diet, exercise, natural foods--are experiencing wide
acceptance in American society. Still, the holistic health movement
promotes some esoteric practices that keep the movement on the
fringe of American society. They want to change this position, by
government action if necessary. New Age proponents desire to have
their therapies reimbursed by Medicare, Medicaid, Blue Cross, and
so forth.

Despite their preference for a less intrusive government, a number
of prominent New Agers want the United States government to

implement a holistic health policy. In Mark Satin's "political platform," the government would legislate a comprehensive health program consistent with holistic health principles, including encouraging "various 'natural' and Eastern medical practices . . . ."[66] Marilyn Ferguson believes that a number of professionals are at work to make holistic health public policy.[67] Capra wants government legislation to restrict pollution and unhealthy products and to promote positive health practices.[68]

Holistic Health Practices

There are a wide range of holistic health practices loosely connected with the New Age movement. Like most areas of the New Age, the boundaries of its medical treatments are not clear. Many holistic health practices predate the New Age, sometimes by centuries. They are part of the longstanding alternative medicine tradition. The rise of the New Age has simply given these practices a new lease on life and a new clientele. A number of these treatments--chiropractic, herbal medicine, natural foods--are not that far out. They have considerable public acceptance. Still, other practices are closely identified with the occult tradition and have adopted a metaphysical approach to health and healing. Therefore, I am not implying that everyone who participates in a number of so-called holistic health practices is connected with the New Age.

Holistic health practices are so numerous that I will note only a few. Moreover, these treatments are difficult to categorize. But some classification is helpful. Thus, in a modified form I will use the format found in *Wholistic Dimensions in Healing* edited by Leslie Kaslof.

Integrative Systems

Kaslof speaks of "integrative medical systems." Osteopathy, chiropractic, homeopathy have already been mentioned. Today, osteopathy is accepted by the American Medical Association and is fully integrated into mainstream medicine. Chiropractic is also widely accepted, being included in government-funded health programs and receiving many insurance payments. However, along with spinal manipulations, individual chiropractors have promoted New Age therapies such as acupressure, reflexology, and nutritional prescriptions.   Also, chiropractic has given birth to some holistic health treatments such as applied kinesiology.   Homeopathy was discredited but is currently making a comeback, especially in England.[69]

Several treatments in Kaslof's "integrative" category have not been previously noted.   Naturopathy, at times called Nature Cure, is "a major building block of the holistic health component of the New Age Movement" and has experienced a comeback during the 1970s and 1980s, writes Gordon Melton.[70]   The *New Gould Medical Dictionary* defines naturopathy as "a therapeutic system embracing a complete physical therapy employing nature's agencies, forces, processes, and products, except major surgery."[71]   Naturopathy predates the New Age by several centuries.   It focuses on the whole person rather than a specific anatomical area.   Naturopathy treats people, not conditions, and wants individuals to live in tune with nature.   It favors building a healthy body to combat disease instead of relying on drugs.[72]

Applied kinesiology is a unique American therapy developed by George Goodheart in the 1960s.   Formal kinesiology is the study of the principles of the anatomy and how they relate to human movement.   Applied, or behavioral, kinesiology is a unique blending of kinesiology, chiropractic, and the techniques of Chinese medicine to produce an entirely new discipline.   Goodheart took standard muscle-testing techniques and combined them with Chinese concepts of energy flow.   Applied kinesiology stimulates specific areas of the body as a means of strengthening the muscle and restoring the energy flow.   The Touch for Health is a popular form of applied kinesiology developed by John Thie.   The heart of Touch for Health is that innate intelligence or energy runs through the body.   Health or disorder develops, depending on whether the flow is unimpeded or blocked.[73]

Nutrition and Herbs

Another of Kaslof's categories is "nutrition and herbs."   The use of herbs and certain foods to prevent and cure disease is widespread and has a long history.   Since the 1970s many herbalists, vegetarians, and health food advocates have jumped on the holistic health bandwagon and have been accepted as an important part of this movement.   Advocates of herbs and nutritional therapies have aligned themselves with the New Age for several reasons. They embrace the holistic health movement's concern for the health of the total person. Like the New Age they stand against the overuse of synthetic drugs, chemical fertilizing, pesticides, and processed foods. But more important, the New Age worldview and many nutritional therapies share a common worldview. For example, vegetarianism has had historic connections with the occult tradition.[74]

Heuristic Approaches

Kaslof's next category is that of "heuristic directions in diagnosis and treatment." A number of common holistic health practices roughly fall into this area. Acupuncture is the best known of the Chinese medical practices in America. It developed from Taoist metaphysical theory. Acupuncture holds that ch'i or energy flows through pathways called meridians. If the circulation of ch'i is blocked, a surplus or deficit of ch'i may result. Such an imbalance manifests itself in the form of pain or disease. Depending on the problem, certain points are stimulated by acupunctures or needles and heating. Supposedly, circulation will increase, thus eliminating or reducing the problem. Acupressure is similar to acupuncture in theory and practice. Instead of inserting needles, the pressure points are massaged with finger tips.[75]

Iridology and reflexology can be placed in the same category. The basic premise of iridology is that each part of the body is represented by an area of the iris. Therefore, a problem in any organ of the body can be diagnosed by a systematic observation of the eye. Such a diagnosis entails taking a detailed color photograph of a patient's iris and examining it in view of established charts. Iridology is not a tool used by ophthalmologists. Reflexology rests on a similar assumption--one part of the body is a window into all internal body parts. In this case it is the foot. Relief will come to a particular area of the body when the proper point on the foot is massaged.[76]

Biofeedback

Biofeedback's use is not limited to holistic health circles and it may be in a category by itself. By use of instruments measuring ongoing biological information, biofeedback is a technique for bringing nonvoluntary bodily functions such as brain-wave patterns, heart rate, and skin temperature under voluntary control. Biofeedback has been successful in treating several physiological problems, including migraine headaches. Yet, in some circles it has been used as an instrument for inducing psychic experiences and altered states of consciousness.[77]

Psychic Healing

Next in Kaslof's classification is "psychic and spiritual healing." Unconventional healing can be defined as restoring a person to a condition of health through some supernatural or metaphysical powers. It goes by many names--spiritual healing, psychic healing, faith healing, magnetic healing, and so on. According to psychic healers, the power for unconventional healing is probably drawn from an energy field surrounding us. Moreover, it can be used in conjunction with conventional medical treatment.[78]

In holistic health circles, the most common form of unconventional healing is psychic healing. This term refers to a number of practices in which the healer utilizes some kind of parapsychological power to facilitate the healing process. Psychic healing is usually placed in the category of psi phenomena--events that defy scientific explanation. Actually, the main difference between psychic healing and other forms of metaphysical healing is one of degree and emphasis. Both draw on forces beyond the range of scientifically verifiable activity.[79]

Most of these practices go back to the ancient world. They include psychic diagnosis, that is, any technique for acquiring information about a patient without using ordinary methods of inquiry. Most common are clairvoyance, psychometry, aura readers, and diagnosis by spirit guides. Psychic healing involves transferring from healer to patient some form of healing drawn from a mass of cosmic energy. The transfer may come from the laying on of hands or a vague prayer. A current example is the popular practice of "Therapeutic Touch" taught by Dolores Kriger. This therapy is essentially the religious practice of the laying on of hands for healing. While it is dressed up in scientific language, it is based on the Hindu belief that universal energy flows through the body.[80] Psychic surgery involves surgical operations relying on some unknown power rather than conventional procedures. It is practiced in South America and the Philippines. While some psychic surgery is linked to fraud, other cases have been closely observed and should be seen as occult medicine.[81]

A number of psychic healers are well known. During the first half of the century, Edgar Cayce (1877-1945) gained national prominence. In addition to his famous prophecies, he diagnosed illnesses and prescribed therapy while in a deep self-induced trance. He successfully healed hundreds of people. His legacy has continued in the Association for Research and Enlightenment (ARE), an organization promoting a wide variety of occult and metaphysical activities.[82]

In recent years Olga and Ambrose Worrall have gained considerable attention. Olga may be the best-known living American psychic. The Worralls believe that illness comes when an individual falls out of harmony with their nonphysical environment. Therefore, the role of the healer is to be a conductor between the supply of universal energy and the patient. The Worralls claim that their parapsychological healing methods are compatible with Christianity. Universal energy, they insist, comes from God. Yet their methods and philosophy are compatible with the occult-metaphysical healing tradition.[83]

Psychophysical Therapies

"Psychophysical approaches" is Kaslof's next category. Best known in this area are a number of massage and body therapies. Massage therapies have a long history, being practiced by many premodern and non-Western societies. "Massage is the art of treating body ailments and conditions by the manipulation of muscles and soft body tissue, as opposed to manipulation of bony structure in chiropractic or osteopathy treatments," writes Melton. In the sixties holistic health groups practiced a variety of massage therapies. With the merger of the holistic health and New Age movements, massage passed into the New Age. While massage can be purely a physical function, in the New Age it has acquired a "transformative function as a means to achieving not only physical health but also mental-spiritual wholeness."[84]

Body work therapies, the most common being massage, are practices using the body as the starting point for a process to transform the whole person. Most of these therapies aim to release energy imbalances and are overtly mystical. Rolfing, also called structural integration, is a body work manipulating deep connective tissue between bone joints. In order to relieve energy blockages and rearrange the body into a correct posture, trained rolfers give deep massages that can be very painful. Supposedly, the patient experiences an emotional release.[85]

Several other therapies also focus on the release of energy. Orgonomy, developed by William Reich, believes that disease comes when the free flow of "orgone" energy in the body is restricted. The release of orgone energy and the restoration of health would come by uninhibited sexual activity.[86] Like acupressure, zone therapy believes that the manipulation of certain places on the surface of the body releases energy and cures maladies in various bodily organs. In theory Do'in is similar to acupuncture. It endeavors to promote the free flow of energy by gentle massage, not needles. Through massage, diet, and exercise, polarity therapy strives to balance the positive and negative aspects of energy flowing through the body. Bioenergetics analysis is a form of psychotherapy. It endeavors to alleviate physical and emotional stresses by means of active and passive exercises.[87]

Other Therapies

This selective description of holistic health practices has barely touched upon the subject. Kaslof has another category, "humanistic and transpersonal psychotherapies." The theory of these therapies has been discussed in the chapter on psychology and the New Age. Many other holistic practices could be mentioned. There are a number of alternative cures for cancer (e.g., laetrile and Hoxey treatment). Some art, music, dance, and flower therapies are identified with the holistic health movement. Meditation and visualization therapies (the use of mental imagery to achieve a desired objective) are used in healing. The Twelve Step Program, designed for spiritual improvement, and Alcoholics Anonymous fall within the holistic health framework. Their holistic approaches to curing maladies are compatible with New Age philosophy. Chromotherapy, or healing with color, is an old occult therapy practiced in New Age circles. The list could go on. But the concepts are usually the same--a person is healed by a metaphysical force or the proper flow of energy within the body.

Chapter 11

THE "POP" NEW AGE:
OCCULT PRACTICES

As previous chapters have indicated, the New Age offers many practices clearly intended for mental or physical healing. In addition, there are a wide range of practices or rituals whose objective is more spiritual and occultic. A partial list would include the following: channeling, crystals, shamanism, UFOs, astrology, tarot cards, hypnotic trances, pyramid power, yoga, firewalking, rebirthing, meditation, and reincarnation. While the holistic health treatments are based on metaphysical assumptions, these listed practices and others have close links to the occult tradition.

Much to the chagrin of many New Age leaders, the media coverage has focused on such occult and metaphysical activities. Thanks to celebrities such as Shirley MacLaine, the exotic aspect of the New Age has captured the attention of the media, thus creating the impression of a movement preoccupied with sensationalism. Ms. MacLaine believes in reincarnation, UFOs, trance channeling, and pyramid power, and she wears crystals. Her books and seminars have made her the "super saleswoman" for the New Age movement-- and have made her a lot of money in the process.[1]

As noted earlier, Jonathan Adolph says that the New Age movement has its serious and fringe elements. He believes channeling, crystals, and other occult activities to be "at most fringe issues--distractions from the largely practical and down to earth matters" that are at the heart of the New Age vision.[2] In fact, the major writings of many of the leading New Age spokespersons largely ignore such phenomena. While such individuals assume an occult-metaphysical worldview, their focus is on the serious New Age--personal and social transformation, ecology, social change, peace, holistic health, political unity, gender equality, and so forth.[3]

The occult practices are the "pop" New Age, the faddish element. They rise and fall in their popularity. Such occult phenomena are big business. Psychics collect up to $250 an hour for their advice. Conversations with channelers can run from as little as $25 for a short discussion to $1500 for the weekend. Shirley MacLaine charges $300 per person for her seminars. Jack Pursel grosses more than one million dollars a year as the channel for a spirit named Lazaris. Publishers estimate the sales of New Age titles to be over $100 million retail. People spend over $100 million per year on crystals. Natural food stores estimate their sales to be over 3.3 million.[4]

This frivolous aspect of the New Age is subject to much abuse. Many of its claims have been disproven by modern science. At best, the evidence for psychic phenomena is dubious. There are cases of outright fraud. Still, a gullible public spends billions on occult phenomena. These occult practices have no apparent social value and portray New Agers as self-indulgent. Many critics regard these phenomena not as wonders to draw people into the New Age but as warts that turn the public off.[5]

Still, the New Age has many gateways and the occult practices are one way into the movement. Moreover, it is not always easy to separate the serious New Age from its hype and kooky elements. Individuals committed to the New Age vision also practice some occult rituals. Conversely, people more inclined to the New Age occult phenomena bring a worldview to their actions.[6]

Perspectives on Occult Phenomena

New Age occult phenomena can be seen as sensationalism. But there are other ways to view these practices. American society is highly individualized and religion has become privatized. In the New Age teaching that we all have a private "higher self" within us, this trend is carried even further. As Vishal Mangalwadi notes, the "total privatization of spiritual experiences, beliefs and rituals, with no inherent checks . . . has meant that the New Age has been able to churn out a 'spirituality' that can be considered anything from responsible to bizarre . . . ."[7] The occult phenomena are the most individualistic and strangest aspect of the New Age movement.

The New Age is a revolt against modernity. As has been noted repeatedly, New Agers point to Descartes and Newton and the modern mind-set developing from their ideas as the source of most human problems. Suzanne Riordan tells us that for those agreeing with this assessment, "the pendulum is swinging from a worldview in which there was no place for gnomes, goblins, and angels to one teeming with nature spirits, extraterrestrials and ascended masters."[8] The outburst of occult practices in the New Age and in society as a whole is related to a shifting worldview--one that is more amendable to the occult-mystical tradition.

The New Age occult practices also can be seen as religious rituals. Catherine Albanese tells us that most religions have in one way or another four components: a belief system, a social ethic, a community, and rituals. Rituals are a means of expressing or acting out the meaning of these beliefs and codes of behavior. Channeling, crystals, shamanism, and more are religious rituals of the New Age movement. Albanese also says that the New Age has two tendencies-- the speculative and the phenomenal. The speculative involves the theoretical and spiritual aspects of religion while the phenomenal focuses on those dimensions known through the senses. The lines between these two inclinations are not hard and fast. Still, the speculative New Age has tended to focus on ethics or a social vision. Conversely, the phenomenal New Age has "expressed itself in a strongly ritualized religion, one that emphasized cultic behavior."[9]

These New Age rituals are not all hype. Serious New Agers regard them as instruments of transformation. In most religions, rituals are intended to evoke a religious experience and to place one in touch with the transcendent. For many New Agers, occult practices are the doorway to another level of consciousness. Personal transformation is at the heart of the New Age vision. While this can be a gradual process, it can be triggered by an experience. According to Marilyn Ferguson, these triggers are often "a spontaneous mystical experience . . . ." She calls them "psychotechnologies [that] help break the cultural trance . . . ." and open the individual to new choices. Her list of psychotechnologies is much broader than the more obvious occult practices, but these elements are also present.[10]

Channeling, shamanism, astrology, crystals, and similar phenomena presuppose an occult-metaphysical worldview. This view of reality and its occult practices predate the New Age by millennia. Whereas the occult worldview is a vital component of the modern New Age, it is only natural that many in the movement engage in occult phenomena. If reality is one undivided substance, there can be no sharp distinction between the natural and supernatural realms. The New Age has embraced a premodern worldview which accepts the reality of spiritual beings, communication with other worlds, individuals with supernormal powers, and other such phenomena.

Channeling

Channeling is one of the New Age's most popular occult practices. Along with reincarnation, which this study has treated as a belief, and crystals, channeling has gained the greatest media attention. Of all the New Age occult phenomena, channeling is the most sensational and has drawn the scorn of critics. Many serious New Agers regard it as frivolous. Skeptical outsiders see it as a fraud or at best as some form of self-hypnosis. Channeling is also big business--raking in millions of dollars for the channelers. For this, it also has received serious criticism.

New Age psychologist Jon Klimo defines channeling: "Channeling is the communication of information to or through a physically embodied human being from a source that is said to exist on some other level or dimension of reality than the physical as we know it, and that it is not from the normal mind [or self] of the channel."[11]

Channeling is a form of spiritism--the attempt to communicate with a nonphysical entity through a human medium. It includes necromancy: communication with the spirits of the dead in a seance. However, New Age channeling focuses not on contacts with deceased relatives but on the communication of occult information from a spirit to living disciples.[12]

The Who and Why of Channeling

Channeling is perhaps the New Age's clearest manifestation of the occult. The occult entails secret knowledge beyond the realm of normal human understanding. To acquire this hidden or esoteric knowledge, one needs a teacher, an enlightened master, a medium (referred to as a channel in the New Age). In channeling, an entity from another dimension brings its wisdom to humanity through a designated channel. Channeling not only brings a message with an occult doctrine, it is also an occult practice.[13]

The channeling craze of the 1980s can be attributed to several factors. It took off for many of the same reasons that caused the occult revival of two decades earlier--religious pluralism, individualism, narcissism, Eastern influences, a revolt against secularism, and a subjective approach to learning. During the seventies and eighties, many of the occult practices declined while the occult worldview penetrated society. Rather than decline, channeling received new life during the eighties. However, some sources indicate that channeling is declining in the 1990s.[14]

To a large extent, the channeling mania of the eighties can be attributed to the influence of celebrities, especially Shirley MacLaine. Her third autobiography, *Out on a Limb* (1983), ignited an interest in trance channeling. *Out on a Limb* contains a smorgasbord of occult activities, including disembodied spirits who tell Ms. MacLaine about her former lives. A number of spirit guides emerge in her other books written during the eighties.[15] While Ms. MacLaine has exerted a staggering influence on channeling, other celebrities have become involved with this occult activity. A partial list would include Clint Eastwood, Richard Chamberlain, Burt Reynolds, the late Joan Hackett, and Mike Farrell of the *M*A*S*H** television series.[16]

Like the New Age population in general, channel enthusiasts are not the poor and uneducated. The price of channeling sessions, ranging from $25 to $1,500, rules such people out. Channeling's biggest audience are the upscale type who have embraced an occult-metaphysical worldview that lends support to such activities.[17]

Channeling has a psychological hold on many. We live in a time when people feel powerless and have low self-esteem. Therapists deal with such problems, but they take a long time. Also, the therapist is a mere human being. Our generation is looking for a quick fix. Thus, channeling offers them the opportunity to be zapped instantly by a spiritual being. People believe that they are being placed in contact with a realm of reality beyond their own and that they will receive wisdom transcending human knowledge.[18]

All of this becomes more plausible because we live in a secular world that is thirsting for a supernatural experience. As Martin Gardner says, "Psychoanalysis is no longer chic. Encounter therapies and group grope have gone with the New Age winds . . . [But] the dead are alive and talking to us."[19]

Early Developments

Channeling is not new. It is but a modern nuance of the ancient practice of spiritism. Throughout history its various forms have gone by several names: mediumship, revelation, necromancy, and spiritism. Those individuals functioning as intermediaries also have received several labels--seer, shaman, oracle, medium, and witch. Moreover, mystics in most religious traditions have had experiences resembling those of the modern channels. Also, leaders in most religions have claimed to have had experiences in which sacred information has been revealed to them from a spiritual source.[20]

Spiritism thrives today in much of the developing world. But in the West it has been largely rejected, surviving as a fringe phenomenon. Two movements have exorcised Western culture of spiritism. Christianity is a supernatural faith. Still, it has suppressed other expressions of the supernatural, not because they are considered to be nonexistent, but because their source was Satan. The Enlightenment also dealt spiritism a blow. Western confidence in reason relegated spiritism to the realm of superstition. Together, Christianity and the Enlightenment have prompted the West to lose the respect for sorcery, magic, and spiritism that traditional cultures still maintain.[21]

From a New Age perspective, Christianity and the Enlightenment have also robbed Western culture of a subjective source of knowledge. Christianity is based on a divine revelation, but that disclosure is limited to the Bible. The Enlightenment rejects revelation, replacing it with science and reason. Consequently, the West has not looked favorably on private, subjective revelations. With the weakening of both Christianity and rational thought in the modern world, the door has been opened to a flow of subjective knowledge. Modern channeling is one source of this subjective, esoteric wisdom.[22]

In chapters three and five, I have briefly described the historical development of spiritism. At this time, I will note only the points of transition between traditional spiritism and modern channeling. With Theosophy a major turn toward channeling can be detected. In traditional spiritism, mediumship usually involved communication with departed loved ones. Madame Blavatsky began to receive and transmit messages from entities who are more highly evolved than humankind--the superhuman masters or mahatmas. In this development can be found the roots of modern channeling.[23]

Blavatsky's followers built on her beginning. The masters began to tell her disciples about a coming new age and how they must prepare for it. Best known was Alice Bailey, who between 1919 and 1949 transcribed twenty-five books allegedly received from the Tibetan master Djwhal Khul (D.K.). From the teaching received from D.K., there developed an entire school of occult thought based on the concept of a cosmic hierarchy of planes of existence.[24]

During the first half of the twentieth century several "bibles"were channeled, claiming to be a revelation for the modern era. In 1907 Levi Dowling published *The Aquarian Gospel of Jesus Christ*, which supposedly was channeled from Visel, the goddess of wisdom. This "bible"contends that Jesus studied with many Eastern wise men and eventually joined a sacred Egyptian brotherhood. During the 1930s the *Urantia Book* was allegedly channeled by automatic writing to an anonymous source. It is the longest book ever channeled--2,100 pages--and reveals previously unknown information about Jesus and the history of the earth.[25]

Edgar Cayce does not fit the pattern running from Theosophy to modern channeling. He did not employ an identifiable spirit guide but spoke in his own voice while in a trance. Supposedly, he drew his information from the akashic record--namely, cosmic information about all that has occurred. Cayce's pronouncements or "readings" numbered over 30,000 and pertained to many subjects, including health, metaphysics, and prophecies of future events. His teachings were on occult philosophy, combining Christian and Theosophical elements.[26]

Modern Channeling

Gordon Melton dates the advent of modern channeling with the appearance of several channeled books in the early 1970s. In the sixties an entity named "Seth"contacted Jane Roberts of Elmira, New York. Twice a week Roberts would go into a trance and Seth would expound on metaphysical subjects. Using shorthand, her husband recorded the information, which was organized into several books including *The Seth Material* (1970) and *Seth Speaks* (1973). Roberts received messages and wrote other books until her death in 1983. The material received from Seth is intellectually credible and perhaps the most believable of the channeled revelations. Jon Klimo says that Seth is "probably the best known, most widely published channeled entity in the twentieth century."[27]

The second book marking the beginning of modern channeling was *A Course in Miracles*. In 1965, psychologist Helen Cohn Schucman began to hear an inner voice. Supposedly, the voice came from the biblical Christ. By means of inspired or automatic writing, over the next seven-and-a-half years Schucman transcribed a 1,200-page, three-volume text. Published in 1965, the stated objective of *A Course* is to "remove the blocks to the awareness of love's presence." It is an attempt to explain the illusion-like nature of our daily existence.[28]

Channeling took off during the eighties. In Los Angeles alone there were estimated to be over 1,000 channels. Channeling is big business, grossing from about $100 to $400 million a year. While there are many channels, the big three are probably J. Z. Knight, Jack Pursel, and Kevin Ryerson. Other well known channels and their entities include Dr. Peebles, who speaks through two Los Angeles channels; Mafu, channeled by Los Angeles housewife Penny Torres; and Verna Yater, who channels two entities--Indira Latari and Chief White Eagle.[29]

The best known entity is Ramtha, channeled by J. Z. Knight, a former housewife with a Baptist background now living in Yelm, Washington. Ramtha is a spirit entity who claims to have lived about 35,000 years ago. He resided on the lost continent of Lemuria and fled to Atlantis when that continent was destroyed. J. Z. Knight and her second husband were first contacted by Ramtha in 1977. He declared, "I am Ramtha, the Enlightened One, and I have come to help you over the ditch," which he explained to be limited thought. Thus began a period of nearly two years in which Ramtha contacted Knight and taught her.[30]

In 1978 Knight held her first public channeling session, introducing Ramtha to a larger audience. Over the next few years she developed as a professional channel. Her career took a gigantic leap forward when several celebrities, including Shirley MacLaine, attended her sessions and endorsed her work. Ramtha's followers grew to an estimated 35,000. In the mid eighties, Knight began Sovereignty, Inc., a corporation that promotes her ministries--channeling sessions, books, videotapes, and cassettes. About four thousand people have moved to the area around Yelm to be near the channel.[31]

While Ramtha is popular, he and Knight have been criticized and are suspect even in New Age circles. Some of Ramtha's predictions have totally missed the mark. Knight's display of newly acquired wealth has upset many. Some business ventures involving Knight and based on Ramtha's advice have gone sour. Worse still, Knight has been accused of fraud and some of her followers have contemplated legal action against her.[32]

Jack Pursel and his entity Lazaris are popular in the New Age community and have not aroused the suspicions that Knight and Ramtha have. Pursel was an insurance supervisor in Florida. He began to meditate regularly and in 1974 he claims that Lazaris contacted him. Lazaris depicts himself as a nonphysical entity. While he has identity, personality, and self-awareness, he has never been incarnated in a human body. Lazaris speaks through Pursel while he is in a trance. After two years of conducting sessions on a part-time basis, Pursel quit his job and became a full-time channel. He spends as high as forty hours of nonsleeping hours a week in a trance channeling for Lazaris. In recent years, Pursel has gained stature as a channeler, appearing on national television, publishing several books, and conducting many seminars and workshops.[33]

Another popular and respected channeler is Kevin Ryerson. His integrity has not been attacked and his pronouncements have been rated as about seventy to eighty percent accurate. Based in California, Ryerson began to dabble with the paranormal in his childhood. In his early twenties, he joined a group of Edgar Cayce's followers and subscribed to his teachings. About the same time, he began to enter trances at will. A spirit guide, John, supposedly the apostle of Jesus, contacted him on a regular basis. In 1976 he became a full-time channel, carrying on Cayce's tradition. Unlike Knight and Pursel, Ryerson became the channel to several entities-- five in all. Also, differing from other channels, his entities were not exalted beings. Ryerson was catapulted into fame by Shirley MacLaine. His sessions with the actress were recorded in her book *Out on a Limb,* and he portrayed himself in the movie version of the book. She also speaks favorably of him in her subsequent books.[34]

Style and Message

These entities and others allegedly speak from different periods in history and are channeled in different ways. Still, their messages largely echo each other in tone and substance. Moreover, their messages are based on the same monistic assumptions about the nature of reality.[35] In both tone, content, and assumptions the channeled messages resonate with the style and themes of the New Age subculture.

As Suzanne Riordan notes, the entities' "tone is passionate and imploring, sometimes angry, ironic, or admonishing, but . . . respectful." Also, their method of communication is "personal and direct." Reflecting the grassroots nature of the New Age movement, these oracles "have a decidedly egalitarian bent." Some entities held status positions during their life. But many did not and they appear to be "upstarts speaking with authority" on our origins, problems, and destiny.[36]

A theme running through these channeled messages is a bitter critique of modern civilization. The authority of governments, religion, and science have enslaved people. They have been forced to rely on external sources of authority, thus encouraging people to deny "the inherent wisdom and goodness of the Self." The oracles urge individuals to free themselves from the limitations placed on them by the political, religious, scientific, economic, and family institutions. These channeled messages point to violence, ecological disaster, wars, gender inequalities, AIDS, and economic disparities as signs that the old age is breaking down. On a more optimistic note, the entities also proclaim the coming of a new age--one in which these problems will be no more.[37]

The key theme of these channeled messages is "the twin doctrines, 'you are God/You create your own reality,'" writes Elliot Miller. The rational/scientific approach to acquiring knowledge and religious belief systems have obstructed the proper view of reality and self. People need to abandon their anachronistic beliefs and adopt a more subjective approach to learning. They need to realize their divinity, that the "human self is by nature unlimited," and thus create their own reality. Such ideas are not limited to channeling messages but go right to the heart of the New Age.[38]

Building on these central themes, Miller and other sources extract several other key ideas from the channeled messages. One, "you are your own savior." The oracles say they are not trying to save humanity, but only intend to help people realize their unlimited potential and thus save themselves and the planet. Next, they insist that our individual and collective problems can also be traced to a lack of love. We fail to love others because we do not love ourselves. Thus, self-love is a key to solving human problems. Third, the entities insist that death is an illusion. A fourth theme is the "Higher Self." A major goal of the channeled teachings is to connect an individual with his or her "Higher Self"--the most spiritual part of oneself, at times called the Atman, Christ, Buddha, Krishna, or God within. Last, these spirit guides play a "supplementary role to the higher self," inspiring people to higher goals.[39]

Channeling and Spiritism

In several ways, channeling represents a new stage in spiritism. Perhaps due to frauds in previous American Spiritualism, the word *medium* has been dropped in favor of *channeling*--a term adopted from the UFO contactee movement, which can be seen as a form of spiritism.[40] As noted earlier, the contacts are not made primarily with dead relatives but with spirit entities who gave humanity the benefit of their wisdom.

For the first time, the disembodied spirits have become better known than the channels. The old notion connected with Theosophy--that only special leaders can be mediums--has been abandoned. Mediumship has been democratized. Because they are not the teachers, average people can be channels. The spiritual instruction comes not from a human being, but from a wise entity from another world. In a sense, the psychic and guru are being replaced by a more highly evolved being. In another sense, channeling can be seen as a form of special revelation. Having turned from the special revelation of the Christian tradition, New Agers are embracing another means of acquiring knowledge about the origins, nature, and destiny of the human race.[41]

Modern channeling has also attempted to clean up spiritism's act by being more visible. Traditional seances usually took place in a dark room and left spiritism open to charges of fraud. Teaching still remains the primary function of these modern channeled entities. Yet channeling often takes place before large public audiences-- seminars in hotel ballrooms, television performances, and call-in radio talk shows.[42]

The Source of Channeling

What is the cause or source of this channeling phenomenon? Who or what is sending out these messages? Riordan says that it is difficult, "if not impossible, to determine *a priori* whether a given source is divine or demonic, subconscious or supraconscious, transcendental or pre-rational."[43] New Age psychologist Jon Klimo examines a number of psychological options, settling on the notion that channeling is "the activity of different kinds of subpersonalities communicating with one another."[44]   Ted Peters says that psychological studies prove that "channeling can be explained as a purely psychological phenomenon," especially a form of hypnosis.[45]

Nearly everyone--even those within the New Age movement--allow for the possibility of fraud in some cases. Evangelical critics add another factor--supernatural explanations. Elliot Miller says that there are three explanations for channeling: "psychological disassociation, conscious fraud, and actual spirit possession."[46] Russell Chandler offers six possibilities. He includes Miller's three categories, but he breaks the psychological factors into subcategories.[47]

Crystals

In the New Age subculture, crystals are everywhere. Crystal-conscious New Agers wear them around their necks, on their fingers, and in body pouches. They place them on their coffee tables and window ledges and hang them from the ceilings and bedposts. They drop them in toilet bowls and bathtubs. They stash them in their purses, briefcases, and pockets. Some even go so far as to drink powdered rock crystals.[48]

During the 1970s crystals were only a marginal interest to New Agers. By the 1980s they had become the most identifiable symbol of the New Age movement. A 1987 issue of *Time* magazine best illustrates this point. The front cover featured Shirley MacLaine holding a quartz crystal. As the crucifix is a symbol of Christianity, so the crystal is of the New Age.[49]

On the surface, crystals appear to be a trivial fad. But to New Agers they are not a good luck charm or just a piece of jewelry. They are instruments of transformation and healing. New Agers do not believe that crystals have magical powers. Instead, they insist that crystal power can be validated by science. Also, they believe that crystals assist the mind in working change.[50]

While crystals took the front stage in the 1980s, they have a long history. Men and women have been fascinated with crystal substances since the beginning of history. They have been viewed not just as jewelry but as stones with occult and magical qualities. Some were alleged to have healing powers. Others were used as amulets and talismans--objects with powers to benefit and protect their owners. Crystals were also believed to have a certain astrological significance, denoting characteristics in individuals. Eventually gems became associated with months of the year and became birth-stones. People believed that crystals could reveal future events, and thus the crystal ball became the time-honored tool of fortune-tellers.[51]

In more recent history, as Melton points out, Edgar Cayce gave a boost to the use of crystals in the occult world. He related crystals to the legendary lost continent of Atlantis. He insisted that they provided the energy for Atlantis, and eventually their misuse destroyed the continent. Cayce also believed that crystals had inherent powers and could thus benefit individuals, healing them and developing their psychic powers. A number of Cayce's followers, especially Frank Alper, continued and further developed Cayce's ideas on crystals.[52]

The prominent position held by crystals in the occult tradition made it likely that they would be embraced by the New Age movement. In fact, as Robert Fuller notes, crystals have become "something of a rite of passage through which many modern Americans have entered into the spiritual path chartered by New Age principles." Crystals are rituals which resonate with the New Age's teachings and are a way of expressing these beliefs.[53]

New Agers believe that the ability to perform physical healings and psychic feats resides within each individual. Such power comes from the higher self. But people have erected mental fences, which not only limit their ideas but also block the flow of cosmic energy from entering their minds and bodies. However, crystals supposedly can alleviate this problem by helping the individual to realign his or her energy flow.[54]

New Agers place great emphasis on vibrations. They believe that the spiritual world operates according to scientific principles. Thus, they go to great lengths to explain scientifically the cause and effect of crystals. New Agers believe that spiritual or healing energy is transmitted at high vibration levels or frequencies. Because crystal is nearly devoid of color, New Agers believe that it is a refractor of divine white light. According to Daya Sarai Chocron, crystals act "as a catalyst, a conductor of energy." They both receive and transmit energy. Crystals give off energy in the form of vibrations. This energy forms a field around the crystal. The manipulation of this vibratory energy, often by meditation, facilitates the transformation process in individuals.[55]

Thus, crystals are used in a variety of New Age therapies. Most important is the role that crystals play in New Age healing. Crystal healing assumes a metaphysical worldview, which believes that physical illness is a disruption of energies in the etheric (spiritual) bodies. Crystals facilitate healing by restoring harmony between the physical and etheric bodies, which is the source of spiritual energy. Crystals are also used in acupuncture, psychic healing, meditation, magic, visualization, channeling, astral or soul travel, and various forms of divination. New Agers wear them on their bodies to attract the opposite sex, acquire prosperity, and bring general good luck.[56]

The use of crystals in electronics (computer chips, watches, radios, lasers, and others) has enhanced the status of crystals. This has added to the aura of power surrounding crystals. But there is no scientific evidence that crystals can store energy. Thus New Agers have turned to talking about the role of crystals in transforming paranormal spiritual energies--something which science does not measure.[57]

Astrology

The New Age has been called the Age of Aquarius. This name indicates the significance of astrology for the New Age. Yet astrology and the New Age are separate movements. Not all New Agers embrace astrology. Conversely, many astrology adherents are not New Agers. Still, the two movements overlap, and astrology plays an important role in the New Age. To be sure, the New Age has modified astrology and given it a new twist. The concern of this section is not on traditional astrology, but how astrology relates to the New Age movement.

"Astrology is the belief that the planets and stars and universe beyond--the heavens--have a direct and personal influence on individuals," writes Ruth Tucker. Underlying such a belief is the assumption that the universe has an overall order, and this order impacts our personal characteristics as well as the daily course of life. The manner in which the universe influences people "depends on the various 'signs' within the twelve 'houses' (divisions) of the zodiac, which represent twelve consecutive periods of the calendar year." The date of a person's birth determines his or her sign. For example, a Scorpio was born between October 24 and November 22.[58]

Astrologers say the sun moves slightly in relation to the stars of the zodiac (an imaginary belt in the heavens). About every 2,000 years the sun passes through one of the twelve degrees or symbols of the zodiac. It takes about 26,000 years to pass around the entire zodiac. Each symbol of the zodiac has characteristics that influence or determine the fate of humanity for that duration of time.[59]

For the last 2,000 years, the sun has been passing through the zodiac of Pisces, symbolized by the fish. New Agers believe that this accounts for the dominance of Christianity during this period. As Stephen Fuchs indicates, they say that "the symbol of the fish signifies something that is mute and dull, utterly ignorant, always passive." New Agers understand this to be "the chief characteristic of rule by the Christian clergy."[60]

Astrologers and New Agers believe that the sun is entering into another 2000-year period or zodiac, symbolized by Aquarius, or the water carrier. As to when the Age of Aquarius begins, astrologers do not agree. The suggested dates range from 1781 to as late as the year 3000. Some dates in the intervening period include 1844, 1900, 1962, 1983, 2000, and 2160.[61]

Despite differences over the dates, astrologers and New Agers generally agree as to the characteristics of the Age of Aquarius. Unlike the Piscean Age, the Age of Aquarius will be energetic and highly intelligent. Supposedly, humanity will enter a period of independence and strength, an era when humans are "likely to achieve self-realization and self-salvation." As a result of such individual transformations, the Age of Aquarius will be a time of peace, harmony, unity, freedom, joy, accomplishment, science, and inspiration.[62]

Astrology can be traced to at least 3,000 B.C. The original astrology of Chaldea began with a close link to religion and maintained this relationship up to the time of the Macedonian conquest of this area. As it spread throughout the Near East, it merged with the syncretistic religions of the Hellenistic world, gradually losing its religious core, and became Western astrology. As a magical science and no longer a religion, astrology could coexist with other religions, if they accepted magical beliefs outside their own systems. Most important, astrology had become primarily an instrument for predicting the fortunes of people and nations, especially for the rulers and powerful people.[63]

By the seventeenth century in Europe, educated people began to discard astrology. The religious and political institutions now denounced astrology as superstition and relegated it to the ghetto of occultism, along with many other occult practices. The Enlightenment dealt it a further blow. As a result, astrology went underground, becoming a folk belief or an occult teaching taught by clandestine groups. A brief revival occurred during the French Revolution of the 1790s, but in the 1890s Europe witnessed a resurgence of astrology--one that spread to America and has continued until the present day.[64]

As with so many of the occult practices in America, Theosophy contributed to the revival of astrology. But of importance for this study, Theosophy appeared to give a new twist to astrology that the modern New Age movement has built upon. One of Madame Blavatsky's associates, Alan Leo (1860-1917), published a series of books introducing a psychological interpretation of astrology and inviting the general populace to encounter the mysteries of esoteric knowledge.[65]

These nineteenth-century developments, plus a strong astrological presence in the United States during the first half of the twentieth century, all provided the backdrop for astrology's resurgence during the 1960s. Nevertheless, the revival of astrology in the sixties and seventies is best connected with the general resurgence of the occult. This awakening of astrology was independent of the New Age and would have come with or without this movement. Yet, these two movements feed into each other and astrology has become an important practice in the New Age.[66]

Along with a fascination with reincarnation, the growth of astrology is the best barometer to measure America's interest in things occultic. Drawing his information from professional astrological societies, Gordon Melton says that in 1990 there were "more than 10,000 professional astrologers in the United States, serving more than 20 million clients, in addition to those who read astrology magazines and the astrology column in the daily newspaper."[67]

The total number of casual and serious astrologers would be more than thirty million--including about twenty-five to thirty percent of the Protestants and Catholics and even ten percent of those who call themselves evangelical Christians.[68] By 1988 astrology had reached the highest level of American society, the Reagan White House.[69]

The New Age has taken traditional astrology in a different direction. As it has done to most occult practices, the New Age has turned astrology into a vehicle for self-realization, one more way to acquire wholeness and personal healing. Modern science has destroyed the basis of astrology, demonstrating that the physical position of a planet cannot affect a person at birth any differently than it would at other moments in his or her life. While New Agers can be critical of modern science, they respect it enough not to push a belief totally untenable to a scientific worldview. As a result, they psychologize many of the tenets of traditional astrology to make them more acceptable.[70]

In its traditional form, astrology has been an instrument for predicting the future. New Age astrology minimizes the predictive element and maximizes its therapeutic power. Moreover, New Age astrology discards several key assumptions of traditional astrology. Contrary to traditional astrology, the new astrology is not fatalistic. It operates on the assumption that human personality is not fixed. Basic to the New Age vision is the principle that individuals are responsible for their actions and that they have unlimited potential. The stars are not seen as determining one's fate. Rather, they give individuals certain strengths and weaknesses that influence how they respond to life's challenges.[71]

Shoshanah Feher sees the differences between New Age and traditional astrology as one of degree, not absolute contrasts. For New Agers, astrology is more of a worldview than a predictive tool. While New Agers have rejected mainline religion, they are more religious than traditional astrologers. For New Agers, astrology is "experienced as a therapy--it deals with the mind (psychological tool) and the body or spirit (healing art)."[72]

Other Occult Practices

In addition to the phenomena previously mentioned, the New Age movement embraces a number of other occult practices. While most of these phenomena have a long history, the New Age has given them a new wrinkle. In several instances, the New Age has psychologized or spiritualized the old occult practice, using it as a tool for personal transformation.

UFOs

During the 1980s UFOs became popular in the New Age subculture. As noted in chapter five, the UFO movement began in the 1940s. The movement can be divided into two categories. There are the ufologists who believe that flying saucers are real and that the political establishments have suppressed evidence proving their existence. When scientific proof is meager, what has begun as science often turns into religion. Out of this development came the UFO cults. Rather than discuss UFOs in a scientific framework, these cultists spiritualized the phenomena, relying on inward states of mind and occult information. A number of these UFO cults are flourishing in New Age circles.[73]

In 1952, when George Adamski claimed that a UFO occupant met and talked with him, the UFO sightings took on another dimension. He wrote several books on the subject, and many other reports of contacts with visitors from other planets followed. Some of the contactees (those contacted by UFO occupants) continued to seek answers about the nature of UFO visitors. But a second group viewed the UFOs from an occult perspective. Having made contact with what they claimed to be extraterrestrial beings, they committed themselves to telling others the message of the space people. The movement had acquired a religious dimension.[74]

Gordon Melton says that through these early contacts, the space people began to articulate a message. While it varied over the specifics, the general thrust was the same. The space people were more highly evolved beings who were coming to aid the occupants of Earth. "They brought a message of concern about the course of man, whose materialism is leading him to destruction." However, the space people offered a means of salvation. Humankind could avoid the coming destruction by following their message of love.[75]

An interest in UFOs began to slowly emerge in New Age circles during the seventies. New Age gurus began to make reference to UFOs. David Spangler incorporated a belief in UFOs in his planetary and interplanetary vision.[76] Benjamin Creme insisted that "all the Hierarchies, of all planets, are in communication." Moreover "the U.F.O.'s . . . have a very definite part to play in the building of a spiritual platform for the World Teacher" (the Christ).[77]

During the eighties, several books ignited a further interest in UFOs. Shirley MacLaine's best sellers *Out on a Limb* and *It's All in the Playing* revived a faith in UFOs. Two successful books (*Communion* and *Transformation*) by science fiction writer Whitley Streiber also contributed to the growing New Age fascination with UFOs.[78] A 1987 Gallup Poll showed that 50% of Americans believed in the reality of both UFOs and extraterrestrials.[79]

While they overlap, there are two types of New Age contactees. Some claim to have physical contacts with the Space Brothers. These contactees serve as intermediaries or mediums for the extraterrestrials, bringing their message to humanity. However, most New Age contactees claim to have had a psychic or spiritual contact with the space beings. They see themselves as channels transmitting the teachings of space entities to earthlings. For them, the psychological impact of the UFOs is more important than their physical reality.[80]

The teachings of these space entities resonates with the New Age vision. These beliefs are a version of the New Age monistic philosophy drawn from occult and Eastern spirituality. The message relayed to Ruth Montgomery from a space being said "that each of us is something of God, and that we are all one. Together we form God, and it is therefore essential that we help each other, so that all may advance together." Each person has a spark of the divine within him or her and an individual's spiritual quest is to fully realize his or her cosmic oneness with God. Such a message is a familiar New Age teaching.[81]

Shamanism

Shamanism appears to be gaining popularity in the New Age movement. Anthropologist and promoter of shamanism Michael Harner tells us that "shamans . . . are the keepers of a remarkable body of ancient techniques that they use to achieve and maintain well-being and healing for themselves and members of their communities." In more primitive cultures they are called witch doctor, medicine man, sorcerer, seer, wizard, and magician.[82]

As Harner also notes, "a shaman is a man or woman who enters an altered state of consciousness--at will--to contact and utilize an ordinary hidden reality in order to acquire knowledge, power, and to help other persons." Shamans also employ spirits to perform their tasks.[83] Thus, shamanistic religions are ecstatic, or trance-based. Their adherents "believed that while mystics or shamans are in the trance state they have direct experiential knowledge of the divine and can serve as channels of communication between the human community and the supernatural," write Irving Hexham and Karla Poewe.[84]

In the New Age subculture, interest seems to shift from one practice or philosophy to another. During the seventies the focus was on Eastern spirituality, especially Zen and yoga. In the eighties, channeling was the major fad. But in the 1990s, there appears to be a shift of interest toward shamanism and Native American spirituality.[85] In fact, individuals of the New Age sub-culture have shamanized Jesus Christ, interpreting his healings and miracles as proof that he was a shaman.[86]

Why has shamanism caught on in the New Age movement? Shamanism has always had a strong hold on less developed societies, including Native American communities in America. In part, the New Age emerged at the same time Native Americans were reviving their cultural and religious roots. Both the New Age and Native American spirituality share a common magical worldview. They both believe that secret power is available to those who seek it, especially to charismatic individuals. Moreover, New Agers tend to romanticize Native American spirituality, elevating it to a lofty position. Thus, as Native American spirituality gained a place in the New Age culture, shamanism became popular with many New Agers.[87]

The holistic health movement opened another door for shamanism to enter the New Age movement. While shamans perform a number of religious and social functions for their respective communities, their primary focus is on health and healing. Both New Agers and shamans take a holistic approach to healing--seeking physical, psychological, and spiritual healing. "Like shamanism, one of the characteristics of the New Age movement is a marked emphasis on healing, and like shamans, many New Age teachers unite the roles of spiritual guide and healer," writes James Lewis. Both shamans and holistic health healers take a metaphysical approach to healing, relying on nonmedical forces to perform their tasks.[88]

Shamanism has other avenues into the New Age. New Agers have a major environmental concern, viewing themselves as one with nature. Thus, they are attracted to the way shamans are mystically tuned into the forces of nature. Also, the New Age focus on channeling bears close resemblance to the shamanistic trance state.[89]

But as Robert Ellwood and Harry Partin note, New Age shamanism is not "identical with primitive shamanism." The greatest difference between the two is that "the primitive shaman is part of an integral culture whereas the modern religionist is expressing a sense of alienation." These authors do not speak of a new shamanism, but of "a rediscovery of certain motifs of shamanism as effective counters to the values of a technological, rationalistic culture in historical time."[90]

These modern shamans, says Brooks Alexander, "are psychospiritual soldiers of fortune, seeking wisdom and power. They are both autonomous and rootless." They appear to be interested in individualistic actions in a pluralistic society that provides them with no clearly defined social roles.[91]

Chapter 12

EVALUATING THE NEW AGE

In any evaluation of the New Age, several problems arise. Because the New Age is a multifaceted, multifocused, decentralized movement, its influence is difficult to estimate. It has no central organization to report its membership numbers and progress. When New Agers disclose the movement's size and effectiveness, they often exaggerate their estimates. Moreover, the New Age is a cultural movement in transition. Consequently, it is constantly shifting. What is in today may be out tomorrow.

The New Age lacks clear boundaries. Thus, what is New Age and who is in the movement is unclear. A number of fringe religions overlap with the New Age but are not part of the New Age *per se*. Not everyone who engages in New Age practices or utters New Age terminology is a New Ager. The New Age has no single spokesperson. It has no established creed or code. Consequently, its adherents do not always agree with one another.

What unifies the New Age is its worldview and assumptions regarding reality, God, human nature, and the basis of the human predicament. Thus, any evaluation of the New Age must focus on its worldview and various presuppositions. But people usually approach another worldview from the vantage point of their own worldview. Therefore, my evaluation of New Age monism will come primarily from the perspective of the Christian tradition. However, I will also assess the New Age from a more secular and neutral point of view.

But before doing this, we need to see where the New Age is going and how others have viewed it.

The Future of the New Age

Some authorities contend that the New Age is a fad that has peaked. They point to polls in the early nineties where only 28,000 Americans identify themselves as New Agers. The New Age has also received less media attention than it did during the late 1980s. There are currently fewer flamboyant gurus in America. Also, some New Age practices are passing fads. Certain observers interpret these developments as signs of a decline in the occult and Eastern religions in general and the New Age specifically. Moreover, some exaggerated New Age claims have been proven to be inaccurate both scientifically and historically.[1]

Professor of religion Randall Balmer believes that the New Age has "run its course." It is a religion suited for the social and economic climate of the 1980s. New Age religion embodied the "individualism and materialism" of that decade. Despite its lofty political goals, the New Age belongs "alongside yuppies, Michael Milken, Ivan Boesky and Ronald Reagan as yet another example of the self-aggrandizing tendencies of the entire decade."[2]

The New Age has some organizational framework and a worldview. But to have a lasting impact, it must develop more structure and bring more cohesiveness to its belief system. Christopher Lasch believes that the New Age is too eclectic to achieve this. "The mix of ingredients is too unstable to hold together, to provide a coherent explanation of things or even a coherent answer to the personal difficulties that attract adherents in the first place." The New Age stresses relativity and rejects any standard of objective truth. This "it's true if you believe it" approach to life is "appealing in the short run; but in the long run it works no wonders."[3]

Gordon Melton presents a mixed picture regarding the future of the New Age. To the extent that "the New Age Movement represents primarily an updating of the long-standing occult and metaphysical tradition in American life, it has a bright future." But as a distinct movement he believes that "the days of the New Age are numbered."[4]

Melton gives several reasons for this assessment. He contends that the New Age has built many of its occult-metaphysical teachings on contemporary science. However, science has moved beyond many of these New Age concepts, thus undercutting its worldview. Second, some elements and organizations within the movement have had more success in meeting the spiritual needs of religious seekers. These groups "will survive to become long-term religious institutions" while other New Age organizations "will fall by the wayside."

Third, the New Age has a large number of entrepreneurs (e.g., health-food stores, publishers, alternative health practitioners, bookstores). Many of these providers must compete with each other in a free market. Such competition undermines the New Age principle of global cooperation and has "weakened the movement." Last, evangelical Christians and the scientific community have attacked the New Age. While these confrontations have not seriously damaged the New Age, they are a factor in the movement's future.[5]

New Age Influence Will Endure

New Age cultural influence, in my opinion, is not a passing fad. Rather, it represents a deep cultural shift, one probably continuing well into the future. Aspects of the New Age are faddish and they will pass away. In fact, the name *New Age* most likely will be replaced by other designations. It has already become something of a generic term with little precise meaning. Thus, as a self-conscious movement the New Age may fade from the public view.[6]

As a cultural movement, the New Age can be compared to the counterculture. The counterculture spanned only about a decade and then passed into history. But its values and practices have continued, leaving their permanent mark on American society. I believe that the New Age will have a similar impact. It may decline as an identifiable movement, but its worldview and approach to human problems will continue. They have already been integrated into the American social fabric.

The small number of people who formally identify themselves as New Agers is a misleading figure. About twenty-five percent of the American population have engaged in some New Age activity. The booming sales of New Age books, health services, health foods, and paraphernalia are a better barometer of an interest in the New Age.[7]

The current approach to New Age book sales is an example of how the New Age is being integrated into American culture. Leading

New Age publisher Jeremy Tarcher does not want a separate category for New Age books. "The job of the 80s was to . . . establish an identity . . . . The New Age publisher's goal for the 90s is to find ways to integrate these ideas within the general culture rather than isolating them in a special category . . . ." New Age books speak to many issues, and bookstores are now placing them on the shelves for psychology, education, science, mythology, and religion.[8]

New Age influence, in one form or another, will have staying power for a variety of reasons. It has a foothold in American society and probably will not pass quickly. Most important, the cultural trends that set the New Age in motion show no signs of abating. In fact, some of these forces are accelerating and will probably continue to do so in the future.

The New Age draws heavily from the occult. America has a long-standing occult tradition. While Christianity has deeper roots and a much wider acceptance, the occult is not a negligible force. It is not declining in the 1990s. Rather, it has become more palatable to American society. According to a 1992 Gallup study, several occult paranormal beliefs and practices are accepted by forty to fifty percent of the members of the major American denominations.[9]

The occult is only one aspect of the growing mystical tradition. Cultural pluralism is continuing to explode in the nineties. An aspect of this pluralism is the further growth of Eastern spirituality--another component of the New Age. In the mystical culture of the 1990s, the lines between religion, the occult, and transpersonal psychology are becoming increasingly muddled. For many who have turned inward in the nineties, psychology has become a religion, an alternative altar.[10]

Such pluralism has created a syncretistic religious climate in America--similar to that of the Hellenistic era. As in that time, Christianity is competing against a vast array of cults and quasi-religions that overlap and have assimilated many elements. These religions draw their inspiration from occult, Eastern, psychological, and even Christian sources. In such an environment some variation of the New Age will continue to thrive.[11]

The 1990s has witnessed a "cafeteria," "grab bag," "do-it-yourself" approach to religion. On one hand, fewer Americans formally align themselves with religious organizations. Loyalty to brand-name denominations has declined. On the other hand, an increasing number of people see themselves as "spiritual" or "religious." They believe that you can have a deep relationship with God or the divine force, however defined, without attending religious services. There are lots of believers but few belongers. People have their own private, do-it-yourself religions. Some of these faiths are actually a spiritual "quick fix." In the spiritual cafeteria of the 1990s, which blends many practices and beliefs, versions of the New Age will remain a viable option.[12]

The religious vacuum of the nineties has contributed to the viability of the New Age. The intellectual currents of the modern world have weakened Christian theism. The challenge of natural humanism has created a spiritual void that occult-mysticism has rushed in to fill. But natural humanism itself has declined, creating an opening for new religions. As Martin Marty notes, in modern society, "God may have been eclipsed, but not by agnosticism or secular humanism so much as by belief-in-everything."[13]

Of utmost importance for the staying power of the New Age, its worldview has penetrated many levels of American society. The New Age worldview and cultural forms have touched nearly every aspect of American life. Business seminars, public school classes, health care, science, psychology, art, music, entertainment, and politics have all felt the influence of the New Age. In fact, New Age spirituality and therapies have made inroads into the churches. The lack of intellectual content in most churches and their preoccupation with interpersonal and emotional needs have opened the door to the New Age.[14]

Two other factors may contribute to the staying power of the New Age. As noted in chapter one, the New Age does not draw its clientele from the lower classes. Its followers are middle and upper class people, even celebrities and opinion makers. Such people are better suited to further the New Age vision. Second, the year 2000 is approaching. New Agers generally do not make doomsday predictions regarding the future. Rather, they are an optimistic lot, looking for a future golden age. Yet, the New Age is a millennial movement suited for the mood of the 1990s.

Religious Responses

Religious reactions to the New Age run the gamut from hysterical overreaction to nearly total acceptance. Is the New Age demonic, divine or something else?   At one end of the spectrum are the conspiracy explanations.   At the other are the religious writers who have incorporated large elements of mysticism and Gnosticism into their thinking.   Somewhere in between are some evangelicals who distance themselves from the more sensational attacks on the New Age while still rejecting the movement.

Evangelical Responses

The first and best known of the conspiracy interpretations is Constance Cumbey's *The Hidden Dangers of the Rainbow* (1983). Benjamin Creme's predictions that Maitreya (the Christ) would appear in 1982 alarmed Cumbey, a Detroit lawyer. In her book, she portrayed the New Age movement as a gigantic Satanic conspiracy designed to control the world, destroy Christians and Jews, and force the universal worship of the Antichrist. She insisted that "for the first time in history there is a viable movement--the New Age Movement-- that truly meets all the scriptural requirements for the Antichrist and the political movement that will bring him on the world scene . . . ." Reacting to Creme's predictions, Cumbey forecast that "the Antichrist's appearance could be a very real event in our immediate future."[15]

Cumbey argues that New Age conspirators have infiltrated many private organizations, government, and industry. She strongly objects to their open and bold plans for "a new mandatory world religion." Cumbey even sets forth the misleading accusation that New Agers are anti-Semitic and links them with Nazism. "Jews are no better off with the New Agers than they were under their predecessors the Nazis. . . . " The New Age movement, she contends, "parallels Nazism in every grotesque detail. . . ."[16]

The Hidden Dangers of the Rainbow caused a firestorm in the evangelical community. However, Cumbey's thesis lacks credibility. If the New Age is a cultural shift, a loose set of networks as this study has contended, it cannot be a tightly organized conspiracy bent on world domination as Cumbey insists. Moreover, there is no evidence that the New Age has Nazi connections.[17]

In general, Cumbey's arguments have been an embarrassment to the more moderate evangelical community. However, *The Hidden Dangers of the Rainbow* did turn the spotlight on the New Age. Since then a number of books on the New Age have come out of the evangelical community. Most have followed the sensationalistic pattern of Cumbey's book. Yet others have rejected the New Age, but in a less strident and more scholarly manner.

Following in the wake of Cumbey's best seller came a number of similar books. Capitalizing on the evangelical thirst for end-time conspiracies, these books have sold well in Christian circles. Cumbey wrote a sequel, *A Planned Deception* (1985), which basically defended the thesis of *The Hidden Dangers of the Rainbow*.[18] Texe Marrs penned *Dark Secrets of the New Age* (1987). Relying on his interpretation of Bible prophecy, Marrs insists that "The New Age appears to be the instrument that Satan will use to catapult his Antichrist to power. Once he is firmly entrenched, he will unite all cults and religions into one: the New Age World Religion." Marrs' book is basically a repeat of Cumbey's thesis.[19]

Also overreacting to the New Age, in my opinion, is researcher Dave Hunt. In several books, especially *The Seduction of Christianity* (1985), he portrays New Age mysticism as seducing the church. While he is correct in pointing out the extent to which mystical spirituality has crept into Christian circles, he makes some incorrect generalizations. Anyone faintly entertaining New Age ideas and practices is labeled as a New Ager. Some prominent Christians are accused of being New Age collaborators. Psychology, he says, cannot be Christian. Thus, even if Christians innocently use psychotechnologies they are in league with the New Age.[20]

Much more helpful are the writings of the more moderate evangelicals. On one hand, they criticize many aspects of the New Age and point out that its monistic worldview and mysticism are incompatible with historic Christianity. On the other, they generally view the New Age as a cultural trend rather than a Satanic conspiracy. Some writers in this category would be Douglas Groothuis, Elliot Miller, Russell Chandler, Karen Hoyt, Brooks Alexander, and Robert J. L. Burrows.[21]

These evangelical critiques of the New Age may have achieved the objective of alerting the churches to New Age teachings. But they seem to have had little direct impact on the New Age. The New Age movement has priorities other than responding to evangelical criticisms. Thus, as Gordon Melton notes, they have paid little attention to these evangelical attacks, regarding them "as a product of old age thinking which will pass away as the New Age emerges."[22]

Mystical Responses

At the other end of the spectrum from the conspiratorial theories, several religious writers have incorporated much New Age mysticism into their thinking and might even be regarded as New Agers. Catholicism has a long-standing mystical tradition. Its mystics have functioned both within and outside of the perimeters of Christian orthodoxy. Therefore, it is no surprise to see some Catholic thinkers moving in the direction of New Age mysticism.

One example is Fr. Bede Griffiths of the Order of St. Benedict. Since arriving in India in 1955, he has promoted the marriage of Eastern philosophy with Christian spirituality. He blames the world's problems on the modern industrial system and the Cartesian philosophy behind it. Griffiths believes that a true Gnosis exists within the church. Therefore, the church must recapture this mysticism--whether it comes from the contemporary East or premodern West--and synthesize it with the natural sciences. Still, Griffiths' view of God is closest to Christian theism. His ideas are drawn from Christian theism and Asian mysticism and represent an informal New Age syncretism.[23]

A former maverick Catholic with a New Age appeal is Dominican Matthew Fox. He cannot be regarded as a New Ager in any strict sense because he remained as a loyal member of the Catholic Church until his dismissal from the Dominican Order. He is now an Episcopalian. Fox promotes a new post-modern paradigm that establishes a common ground among all other religions, science, and ecological concerns. He rejects the two earlier paradigms, "the scientific mind-set of modernity plus what he dubs the 'fall/redemption' mind-set of traditional Christian theology," writes Ted Peters. Instead, he promotes his own "creation-centered-spirituality." In his theology he comes close to pantheism, asserting the divine origins and morally unfallen state of creation and that "god is in everything, and everything is in God."[24]

The New Age has apparently influenced Christians closer to evangelical circles. Prolific Christian writer Morton Kelsey employs New Age phrases and ideas. In *The Christian and the Supernatural*, he points to Jesus' psychic powers and concludes that he was a shaman.[25] Another example is Rodney Romney, pastor of a Baptist church in Seattle. In *Journey to Inner Space*, he contends that "To understand God is finally to realize one's own godhood." Romney also says that Jesus intended "to establish a world religion that would embrace every soul and synthesize every creed."[26] In *The Healing Gifts of the Spirit*, author and teacher Agnes Sanford notes some concepts that are close to the ideas of past-life regression.[27]

Positive and Negative Aspects

Opinions about the New Age differ. Evangelical Christians largely view the movement with alarm. Of any religious group, Catholics register the highest favorable opinion of the New Age--30% positive, 40% negative, and 30% undecided. On the whole, about 49% of the American population have a negative view of the New Age.[28] Yet, whatever the percentages, any fair appraisal of the New Age must note that the movement has its positive and negative aspects.

The New Age is too diverse to receive a blanket judgment, whether it be praise or condemnation. The New Age is a collection of individuals, networks, and groups. Some are legitimate; others are fraudulent. Some are sophisticated, while others are simplistic and naive. Moreover, the level of involvement that people have in the movement varies. Some individuals dabble at the edges of the movement and then go on their way. However, other people completely buy into the New Age philosophy and it becomes a way of life.[29] Thus, it is difficult to paint everyone related to the New Age with the same brush.

The Bright Side

In my judgment, the New Age's down side outweighs its good points. But the movement is not a diabolical plot. Thus, its healthy qualities must be affirmed to the point that such is possible.

There are some serious theological and philosophical problems with the New Age. Nevertheless, some New Age teachings can be commended. The New Age places a tremendous emphasis on holism. Western thought has been fragmented and divided. It has disconnected spirit and body, objectivity and subjectivity, humankind and the realm of nature, and male and female. The New Age aggressively and correctly attacks these dualisms. New Agers contend for a more integrated approach to health-care, education, politics, the environment, economics, and gender relationships. The New Age must be commended for its holistic approach to life.[30]

Closely related is the New Age's criticism of reductionist thinking in science and society. New Age physicist Fritjof Capra correctly denounces "the belief in the scientific method as the only valid approach to knowledge . . . ." He also condemns the view that life in society is "a competitive struggle for existence; and the belief in unlimited material progress to be achieved through economic and technological growth."[31] Evangelical professor of theology Ronald Sider says that New Agers "speak for millions in the West who rightly sense the failure of Western naturalism and materialism grounded in the 18th century Enlightenment."[32]

The New Age emphasis on holism and its condemnation of reductionism and materialism has provided the basis for its healthy position in other areas. In the personal sense, New Agers stand for cooperation, not competition. They also correctly desire unity and cooperation in politics. As a result, the New Age promotes internationalism rather than nationalism. Nations cannot function as isolated entities. Economic and political events in one part of the world often have a global impact. Unity and cooperation are also important factors in the New Age drive for peace in the world.[33]

Holism has probably had its greatest influence on the New Age approaches to health, the environment, and education. While the monistic worldview behind these activities may be unacceptable to several religious traditions, many of the specific practices are worthwhile. Preventive health and the New Age emphasis on proper exercise and health foods is commendable. A healthy body cannot be separated from one's mental and spiritual condition. The desire to protect the environment instead of exploit it has widespread acceptance in most religious and scientific circles. The New Age has made its mark on education, promoting creativity and spontaneity rather than the old rigid, stifling methods of learning.

From the human potential movement have sprung a number of psychotherapies that facilitate mental health. Biofeedback, assertiveness training, visualization, hypnosis, dream analysis, and meditation have their value. These and other therapies have helped people deal with stress, anger, fear and pain. In general, New Age seminars and training have helped people gain a sense of self-worth and confidence. However, these therapies are often in the gray area. They can involve occult mysticism and even fraud.[34]

In the modern world the East and West have come together. On one hand, the New Age has flowed from this convergence of Eastern and Western culture. On the other, the New Age is an attempt to address this development and to forge a synthesis between the East and West. While the New Age worldview is incompatible with the theism of the Christian, Judaic, and Islamic traditions, it has focused considerable attention on the issue of worldviews. People of all religious traditions and secularists have had to evaluate and come to grips with their own worldviews.[35]

Theological/Philosophical Problems

The New Age vision has been implemented only in "bits and pieces." Thus, any critique of the New Age should focus on its worldview and ideology. In fact, in my opinion, the New Age raises some serious theological and philosophical problems. Because the New Age movement is a hybrid, it conflicts with a number of religious traditions, especially those with a theistic worldview--Christianity, Judaism, and Islam. Yet, the New Age is strongest in the United States where Christianity is still the dominant religion. Thus, I shall evaluate the New Age primarily from two perspectives: the Christian tradition and logical inconsistencies within its own belief system.

To say that the New Age worldview conflicts with that of Christianity is to state the obvious. While there are points of agreement on practical matters, theologically the New Age and Christianity are in total conflict.

On one hand, it may not be fair to judge New Age beliefs from the vantage point of Christian theism. This is like criticizing a dog for not being a cat. Like dogs and cats, the New Age and Christianity are two different animals.[36] On the other hand, Christians have incorporated many New Age ideas into their version of Christianity. This is like mixing oil and water. Also, the New Age strives to establish a global faith, incorporating elements from many religious traditions, including Christianity. Thus, I will note the key areas of difference between Christianity and the New Age.

The New Age embraces a mixture of monism, pantheism, and animism. In the convergence between East and West in post-Christian America, which is embodied in the New Age, the lines between monism and pantheism and Christian theism have become blurred. Yet, this can present problems. From a Christian perspective, at best the New Age worldview is naive and unrealistic.

The New Age insists that ultimate reality, which is god, is One and impersonal. God is pure unmanifest energy and is one with the cosmos. Thus, there is no distinction between god and the cosmos. All is one. The emanations of God, which can be seen in the cosmos, are appearances. They present only a limited and deceptive view of reality. Thus, the cosmos is *maja*--the play of illusion.[37]

Christianity clearly distinguishes the God of Israel from the world. God is personal and manifests personal characteristics--love, anger, will, creativity, freedom, and responsiveness. Christianity holds that the world is a creation, which God has created. The world is not divine. All of its components--human beings, animals, and plants--are creatures. God transcends creation and is sovereign over it. God is not part of creation. There is, as Soren Kierkegaard notes, an "infinite qualitative difference" between the human and the divine. Theologically, we cannot equate ourselves with God. Also, we cannot equate God with the cosmos.[38]

An aspect of the New Age view of reality is its concept of human nature. As part of the cosmos, humanity also has an impersonal divine nature. Human beings therefore have no limitations. Not only do they have a divine nature, but they also possess the infinite power of the universe. Moreover, because of their divine nature, human beings are immortal. Ultimately, death does not exist. It is an illusion.[39]

According to the New Age perspective, the human dilemma is ignorance, a constriction of awareness. Considering humanity's divine nature, sin is not part of the New Age vocabulary. Social conditioning has established boundaries where there would only be Oneness. Reason and belief are the worst culprits. They have fragmented our understanding of reality and prevented us from a true perception of the One.[40]

The New Age perception of reality and human nature propels its vision of social change. Without the belief that human beings are divine, the New Age ideas on politics, economics, education, and deep ecology would have little basis. Such a view of reality is the cornerstone for the New Age vision of a holistic world.

Christianity has an entirely different view of human nature and the human dilemma. Human beings are part of creation, sharing in its potential and limitations. As persons they share many characteristics with God. But they are not God and are subject to him. In addition to the boundaries established by creation, human beings are further restricted by sin. Sin is a moral rebellion against God and has brought death and destruction into the world. Of great significance, Christianity regards the world as broken by sin and alienated from God. This brokenness is not an illusion; it is real.[41]

Taking contrary positions regarding the human predicament, the New Age and Christianity have different remedies for the problem. For the New Age, the solution is for people to attain a knowledge of their divinity. Such knowledge has many names--enlightenment, god-consciousness, Gnosis. It results in a fusion with the One. Christianity says that the power necessary to heal a broken world does not lie within. Instead, it comes from beyond, from God's grace. People need salvation, which is a gift of God--not enlightenment.[42]

Aside from any conflict with the Christian tradition, the New Age worldview has logical inconsistencies with its own objectives. The heart of the New Age vision is personal transformation. When enough individuals are transformed, society will be changed. But as New Age critic Art Lindsley points out, New Age monism and pantheism undercuts the New Age vision of transformation.[43]

Marilyn Ferguson contends that "The separate self is an illusion."[44] New Agers believe that individual personality is illusory. The distinction between individuals, between people and nature, and between humanity and God is unreal. This view of reality creates a major problem for the New Age. As Lindsley points out, the monistic and pantheistic perspective undermines "the possibility of real personal transformation and the individual potential." Moreover, these worldviews also tend "to work against social transformation." If, as the New Age proponents say, all is one, then "all individual social problems must be illusory." Social transformation, therefore, "would amount to reorganizing illusion."[45]

While the New Age can be critical of Western science, it is not anti-science. New Age proponents use scientific evidence, as they interpret it, to substantiate their views. But the New Age view of reality is not consistent with the scientific method. Scientific research assumes an objective reality. However, monism and pantheism insist that objective reality is an illusion. They lead to an escape from "concrete existence, into a life of meditation and isolation." Given the New Age assumptions, "scientific research would amount to systematizing illusion."[46]

The New Age assumption that objective reality is an illusion impacts other areas of the New Age vision. Everything is relative. Subjectivity runs rampant. Reality is whatever one envisions it to be. Such thinking goes beyond undercutting the impetus for personal and social transformation and the scientific method. It calls into question the New Age vision in politics, economics, education, and some aspects of health care.

The New Age perception of reality as an illusion also creates difficulties with its emphasis on spiritual entities. The New Age downplays rational knowledge in favor of intuition and feelings. But in the quest for knowledge, New Agers go beyond the mystical or intuitive experience and contact spirits who presumably have an advanced knowledge. These spiritual entities communicate to humanity through channels. But the belief in real spirit beings existing beyond humanity is hard to reconcile with the New Age belief that reality resides within each person.[47]

In respect to the universality of religion, the New Age is inconsistent with itself. The New Age staunchly condemns Christianity for its exclusive claims to truth. Because of its universal vision, the New Age claims a moral advantage over Christianity. But as Peters notes, the New Age assertion of "universal unity is more apparent than real. It has a built-in hierarchy" which clearly discriminates "between those who have attained higher consciousness and those who operate strictly at the level of the lower self."[48]

Practical Problems

A number of criticisms can be leveled at the New Age on practical issues. Many New Age claims do not jibe with the record of history. Others have been contradicted by science or are at best unproven hypotheses. Still, some New Age practices are outright frauds.

As noted in chapter four, the New Age movement views Eastern cultures through rose-colored spectacles, thus creating an idealized image of Eastern spirituality. They also tend to idealize the premodern world in the West, especially the classical civilizations of Greece and Rome and mythological Atlantis. They then use this idealized vision as a standard for criticizing what they perceive to be the deficiencies of modern Western society.[49]

Such a picture of Eastern spirituality, especially Hinduism, developed in nineteenth-century America. It gradually filtered out into American culture. And as Diem and Lewis note, such an image was "readily available to the fifties Beats, the sixties counterculture, and the New Age movement of the seventies and eighties."[50]

However, this idealized image of the East and the premodern world does not mesh with historical realities. The holistic worldview, which has dominated India for thousands of years, has not helped that land to eliminate hunger, poverty, violence, the institutionalized racism of the caste system, gender discrimination, and overpopulation. In fact, some of these problems have reached critical proportions in India. The Christianized West has dealt with these issues better than has India.[51] Moreover, the premodern West was no utopia. Incessant wars and violence predate the rise of the modern state. Hunger, poverty, and social and gender inequalities were more prevalent in the premodern West than they are today.

At a number of points, the New Age either stretches a scientific point or lacks adequate scientific evidence for its claims. In chapter six, the critical mass theory, also called the Hundredth Monkey theory, has been noted. In a study, when a hundred monkeys did a particular task, all the other monkeys followed. New Agers insist that when a certain number of people--a critical mass--participate in a process, a threshold will be crossed. Change will then come. A paradigm shift will take place. Such a theory is regarded as bogus science. Modern science has not verified any such process of whole-making or paradigm shifts.[52]

Moreover, if paradigm shifts do occur, they apparently have no effect on human nature. As Russell Chandler says, "they change only values and perceptions." There is "little connection between social evolution and biological evolution." If a paradigm shift took place at the time of Christ, or if such is occurring now, there is little evidence that human nature or behavior has changed significantly.[53]

New Agers have also stretched a scientific point in their use of Heisenberg's Uncertainty Principle. As noted in chapter seven, this theory contends that events in the subatomic world cannot be measured adequately because various forces at that level are not discoverable. Science concedes an element of subjectivity in the observation process. But New Age physicist Fritjof Capra goes one step further: "The human observer constitutes the final link in the chain of observation processes . . . ." He concludes that the quantum theory is evidence for the monistic unity of all reality, revealing "the basic oneness of the universe."[54]

New Agers also draw unwarranted conclusions from the work of Belgian physical chemist Ilya Prigogine. Prigogine's theory of dissipate structures says that the Second Law of Thermodynamics, which contends that all systems inherently run down or move toward disorganization, is countered by another law. He calls this other law syntropy and insists that it accounts for the evolution of higher levels of organization.[55]

Marilyn Ferguson says that Prigogine's theory "helps to account for the dramatic effects sometimes seen in meditation, hypnosis, or guided imagery." The evolution to a higher structure is analogous to "the shift to a new paradigm."[56] New Age psychologist M. Scott Peck builds on this social evolution model and applies Prigogine's theory to the spiritual evolution of humanity. He suggests that "the human race is spiritually progressing."[57]

New Agers peddle many occult practices, health remedies, and psychotechnologies that can be regarded as either unproven scientific assumptions, fraud, or some combination thereof. In America there is little control over such matters. There are few government regulations regarding the vast array of alternative medical practices and health foods. Such activities also come in the context of much religious fraud. Unscrupulous evangelists and faith healers engage in fraudulent activities, including "miracle mongering."[58]

In any encounter with holistic health practices, discernment must be exercised. Responsible New Age spokespersons such as Ken Wilber and Marilyn Ferguson acknowledge that the holistic health field provides "abundant opportunity for fraud and overpromise." Ferguson suggests several guidelines for dealing with alternative medical practices, including "making sure that the unorthodox procedures are used only to complement proven conventional treatments rather than subjecting consumers to needless risk."[59]

Many techniques in holistic medicine--kinesiology, acupuncture, psychic healing, "Therapeutic Touch," massage therapies, rolfing, orgonomy, acupressure, and zone therapy--operate on the assumption that invisible energy flows through or around the body and affects one's health. Crystal and pyramid power plus a number of psychotechnologies are also based on the premise of the flow of spiritual or divine energy. However, there is no objective scientific proof for the invisible flow of energy in or around people.[60]

Psychic surgery also appears to operate on some combination of unknown powers, psychological elements, and fraud. At times success is achieved and there is no apparent explanation for it. Yet, there have been cases of deception. Psychic surgeons have faked operations by storing phony tumors and blood in fake plastic thumbs. They also simulate the penetration of the human flesh by folding their fingers in a particular way.[61]

Astrology has also been proven wrong in a number of ways. There is no evidence that the position of the planets and stars influence human events. Moreover, since the astrological system was established in ancient times, the earth's position has shifted several times. The signs that modern astrologers read are not the same that the ancients established. Also, studies indicate that astrological predictions are highly inaccurate--in some cases they are correct about ten percent of the time.[62]

Channeling probably has several sources. But one of them is deception. Channeling has become a lucrative business and has thus attracted many fortune seekers. For example, about 300 mediums have claimed to have channeled Seth. Whatever one's position on spirit beings, mediumship must be viewed as at least a suspect activity.[63]

Where Do We Go From Here?

How should people of various religious traditions--especially Christianity--respond to the New Age? Two extremes must be avoided. On one hand, the hysterical over-reaction that many evangelical Christians have taken is counterproductive. To link the New Age with Nazism, Jim Jones, cannibalism, and ritual sacrifices is worse than irresponsible. It is an embarrassment to the evangelical community. The New Age is not even a conspiracy. As Irving Hexham notes, the failure of evangelicals to responsibly address the New Age issue "could spell the death knell of Evangelical Christianity as an intellectually respectable force. . . ."[64]

On the other hand, to view the New Age as somehow compatible with the Christian faith is a mistake. Except for a few lifestyle issues, which have been noted, Christianity and the New Age are totally at odds with each other. Yet a mystical subjectivity has penetrated much of American Christianity, making the church vulnerable to aspects of the New age. As Brooks Alexander notes, the New Age "doesn't wish to reject the church, but to absorb it."[65]

Instead, the New Age must be viewed as an aspect of a tremendous cultural shift--the convergence of East and West and the rampant pluralism that has accompanied this development. While the Age of Aquarius may not be dawning, the world is experiencing unprecedented change. Alvin Toffler is correct in describing the years from the mid-1950s to 2025 as "the hinge of history."[66] Lance Morrow refers to the coming millenium as a "cosmic divide," the "transforming boundary between one age and another. . . ."[67]

An important segment of this cultural shift is a major change in worldviews. "A massive intellectual revolution is taking place that is perhaps as great as that which marked off the modern world from the Middle Ages," writes Diogenes Allen.[68] At that time, natural humanism challenged Christian theism. Now both of these worldviews must share center stage with monistic pantheism.

The current situation is much like that which the early church faced during the Hellenistic era. Cultural and religious pluralism ran rampant. Various worldviews competed for the minds of people. According to Tim Stafford, "Now, as then, Christianity competes with a hundred religions on a spectrum from Krishna to Christ."[69] For centuries, the Judeo-Christian tradition has provided the moral guideposts for Western civilization. Today, as Carl Henry says, "The West has lost its moral compass" and is "now wallowing in a swamp of neopaganism."[70]

The New Age represents a leap into mindless relativism. The New Age makes a basic error in its assumption that there is no absolute truth out there. The only truth is personal truth, the truth within you. Morality and all other guidelines come from the inner self. However, according to Christianity, no church, no religion, and no society can function on absolute relativity. Society and religion must have a moral backbone. Absolute relativity is absurd.[71]

What is the Christian community to do about the New Age? If, as this study has argued, the New Age is an aspect of a massive cultural shift, it will not go away. America has never been "Christian" in any biblical sense.[72] However, its values and worldview have been shaped by the Judeo-Christian tradition. We now live in the post-Christian era when Christianity is no longer the definer of cultural values in America. Moreover, the clock will not be turned back to some bygone era when the dominance of the Judeo-Christian tradition went unchallenged. Christians must adjust to an environment in which rampant religious pluralism prevents any religion or worldview from dominating. In such a context, Christians can cope with the New Age in two ways. First, they can learn to detect New Age characteristics. Second, they must have a firm grasp of their own worldview.

The Christian should be aware of New Age characteristics. Notice! I did not say the New Age itself. The New Age as a self-conscious movement will probably fade, but its cultural influence will remain. Also, I did not say, New Agers. Not everyone who participates in one activity or another is a New Ager. Moreover, not everyone who uses New Age terminology is a New Ager. The use of words such as *personal growth, unity, oneness, holistic, transformation, networking, energy, synergistic,* and *consciousness* do not necessarily entail a commitment to the New Age.[73]

Be skeptical if a workshop, seminar, therapy, course, or teaching exhibits certain characteristics. Robert Burrows and Russell Chandler provide two similar lists. First, be aware of anything "explained in terms of harmonizing, manipulation, integrating, or balancing energies or polarities." Next, if a course or teaching "denigrates the value of the mind or belief," be careful. Third, if a program or therapy "makes extravagant claims--if it seems too good to be true, it probably is." Next, any therapy or teaching "supported only by testimonial anecdotes of the committed rather than by solid evidence . . ."is suspect. Finally, be aware of any teaching or practice "based on 'secret' esoteric knowledge revealed only to an inner elite."[74]

On the other side of the coin, the Christian community must develop a better understanding of its own worldview. To detect another worldview, one must have a solid grasp of one's own. *In The Universe Next Door,* James Sire says that Christians must become "world-view watchers." The same problems that have helped to give rise to the New Age--subjectivity, relativism, experience rather than belief--have infested the Christian church.[75] Sunday school classes are more like group therapy sessions. Sermons are shallow. Doctrine is regarded as dull and irrelevant. To deal with the New Age in whatever form it takes, Christians must take a more rational approach to religion. They must acquire a firm understanding of the Christian worldview and the great doctrines of their faith.

ENDNOTES

Chapter 1: The New Age Has Arrived

1. Ted Peters, *The Cosmic Self* (San Francisco: Harper San Francisco, 1991), vii.

2. Russell Chandler, *Understanding the New Age* (Dallas: Word Publishing, 1988), 34; Martin E. Marty, "An Old New Age in Publishing," *The Christian Century* November 18, 1987, p. 1019; Tom Spain, "New Media for a New Age," *Publishers Weekly* September 25, 1987, pp. 60, 61.

3. Peters, *The Cosmic Self*, viii; Chandler, *Understanding the New Age*, 24, 25.

4. Chandler, *Understanding the New Age*, 24. See also Jeffrey A. Trachtenberg, "Mainstream Metaphysics," *Forbes Magazine* June 1, 1987, pp. 156-158; Art Levine, "Mystics on Main Street," *U.S. News and World Report* February 9, 1987, pp. 67-69.

5. Annetta Miller, "Corporate Mind Control," *Newsweek* May 4, 1987, pp. 38, 39; Richard Watring, "New Age Training in Business: Mind Control in Upper Management," *Eternity* February 1988, pp. 30-32; Chandler, *Understanding the New Age*, 23, 24.

6. Otto Friedrich, "New Age Harmonies," *Time*, December 7, 1987, pp. 65, 66; Chandler, *Understanding the New Age*, 21, 22.

7. James R. Lewis and J. Gordon Melton, "Introduction," in *Perspectives on the New Age* eds. James R. Lewis and J. Gordon Melton (Albany, NY: State University of New York Press, 1992), ix; Friedrich, "New Age Harmonies," 62-72; Marty, "An Old New Age in Publishing," 1019.

8. Peters, *The Cosmic Self*, vii, viii; Newswatch, "Weapons, Arrests and Doomsday Talk Shrouds Church Universal and Triumphant," *Christian Research Journal* 12, no. 3 (1990): 27.

9. Elliot Miller, *A Crash Course on the New Age Movement* (Grand Rapids: Baker Book House, 1989), 13; Peters, *The Cosmic Self*, 4.

10. James R. Lewis, "Approaches to the Study of the New Age Movement," in *Perspectives on the New Age*, 1.

11. Lewis, "Approaches to the Study of the New Age," 3.

12. Mary Farrell Bednarowski, "The New Age Movement and Feminist Spirituality: Overlapping Conversations at the End of the Century," in *Perspectives on the New Age*, 167-178; Shoshanah Feher, "Who Holds the Cards? Women and New Age Astrology," in *Perspectives on the New Age*, 179-188; Aidan A. Kelly, "An Update on Neopagan Witchcraft in America," in *Perspectives on the New Age*, 136-151. See also Margot Adler, *Drawing Down the Moon* (Boston: Beacon Press, 1979); Noami R. Goldenberg, *Changing of the Gods* (Boston: Beacon Press, 1979); Charlene Spretnak ed. *The Politics of Woman's Spirituality* (Garden City, NY: Anchor Books, 1982).

13. Lewis, "Introduction," in *Perspectives on the New Age*, x, xi.

14. Lewis, "Introduction," in *Perspectives on the New Age*, ix-xi. With the publication of *Time's* feature article on the New Age, many New Agers became reluctant to use the term. See Friedrich, "New Age Harmonies," 62-72; David Spangler, *Emergence: The Rebirth of the Sacred* (New York: Delta, 1984), 38.

15. Randall Balmer, "Death of New Age a new era for U.S.," *The Wichita Eagle* June 3, 1991, p. 11A; "Americans still want old-time religion," *The Wichita Eagle* April 11, 1991, p. 5A; Catherine Albanese, *America: Religions and Religion* 2nd ed. (Belmont, CA: Wadsworth, 1992), 368; Mark Albrecht, "Reincarnation and the Early Church," *Update*, 7, no. 2 (1983): 34.

16. Spangler, *Emergence*, 78, 79.

17. Spangler, *Emergence*, 80, 81. See also Bednarowski, "The New Age Movement and Feminist Spirituality," 167.

18. Jonathan Adolph, "What is New Age," *The Guide to New Age Living* (1988): 6.

19. Eileen Barker, *New Religious Movements* (London: Her Majesty's Stationery, 1989), 189; Lewis, "Approaches to the Study of the New Age," 6.

20. Miller, *A Crash Course on the New Age Movement*, 14. See also Norman L. Geisler, "The New Age Movement," *Bibliotheca Sacra* 144, no. 573 (1987): 82.

21. Marilyn Ferguson, *The Aquarian Conspiracy* (Los Angeles: J. P. Tarcher, 1980), 1; Jessica Lipnack and Jeffrey Stamps, *Networking* (Garden City, NY: Doubleday, 1982), 6, 7.

22. Gordon Melton, *Encyclopedic Handbook of Cults in America* (New York: Garland Publishing, 1986), 107.

23. Ferguson, *Aquarian Conspiracy*, 23.

24. Adolph, "What is New Age?" 9; Peggy Taylor and Rick Ingrasci, "Synthesizing East and West," *New Age Journal* September/October, 1987, pp. 70, 71.

25. Geisler, "The New Age Movement," 79, 80; Steve Scott, "East Meets West: How Much Dialogue is Possible?" *Update* 6, no. 1 (1982): 66-75.

26. Robert J. L. Burrows, "Americans Get Religion in the New Age," *Christianity Today*, May 16, 1986, p. 17.

27. Diagenes Allen, "The End of the Modern World: A New Openness for Faith," *Princeton Seminary Bulletin* 11, no. 1 (1990): 12, 13; Os Guinness, *The American Hour* (New York: Free Press, 1993), 129.

28. William G. McLoughlin, *Revivals, Awakenings, and Reform* (Chicago: University of Chicago Press, 1978).

29. Ted Peters, "Post Modern Religion," *Update* 8, no. 1 (1984): 23. See also Richard Kyle, "Is There a New Age Coming?" *Christian Leader* January 17, 1989, p. 4; Richard Kyle, *The Religious Fringe* (Downers Grove, IL: InterVarsity Press, 1993), 286.

30. Gordon Melton *et al*, *New Age Almanac* (Detroit: Visible Ink Press, 1991), 3.

31. Brooks Alexander, "The New Age Movement is Nothing New," *Eternity* February 1988, p. 34. See also Kyle, "Is There a New Age Coming?" 4.

32. Robert Ellwood, "How New is the New Age?" in *Perspectives on the New Age*, 59.

33. Barbara Hargrove, "New Religious Movements and the End of the Age," *The Iliff Review* (Spring, 1982): 47; Peters, "Post Modern Religion," 23; Alexander, "The New Age Movement is Nothing New," 34; Bill Barol, *et al*, "The End of the World (Again)," *Newsweek* August 17, 1987, pp. 70, 71; Kyle, "Is There a New Age Coming?" 4.

34. Richard Woods, *The Occult Revolution* (New York: Herder and Herder, 1971), 15, 16; Ruth Tucker, *Another Gospel* (Grand Rapids: Zondervan, 1989), 319; Kyle, *The Religious Fringe*, 257.

35. Woods, *The Occult Revolution*, 15, 16; Tucker, *Another Gospel*, 319; Peter Russell, *The Global Brain* (Los Angeles: J. P. Tarcher, 1983).

36. Richard Blow, "Moronic Convergence," *New Republic* January 25, pp. 24-26; Friedrich, "New Age Harmonies," 64.

37. Friedrich, "New Age Harmonies," 34.

38. Roy Wallis, *The Elementary Forms of the New Religious Life* (Boston: Routledge and Kegan Paul, 1984), 9-37; Roy Wallis, *The Rebirth of the Gods: Reflections on the New Religions in the West* (Belfast: University of Belfast, 1978), 6-10.

39. James R. Lewis, "International Dimensions," in *Perspectives on the New Age*, 213, 214.

40. Rodney Stark and William Sims Bainbridge, *The Future of Religion* (Berkeley: University of California Press, 1985), 190-194.

41. Feher, "Who Holds the Cards?" 182; John Naisbitt and Patricia Aburdene, *Megatrends 2000* (New York: Wm. Morrow Co., 1980), 283. Albanese gives a slightly different geographic distribution. See Catherine Albanese, *America: Religions and Religion* 2nd ed. (Belmont, CA: Wadsworth Co., 1992), 368.

42. Ferguson, *Aquarian Conspiracy,* 23, 24.

43. Tucker, *Another Gospel,* 320. See also Barbara Hargrove, *Religion for a Dislocated Generation* (Valley Forge, PA: Judson Press, 1980); Barbara Hargrove, *The Emerging New Class* (New York: Pilgrim Press), 1986; Albanese, *America* (2nd ed)., 368.

44. Susan Love Brown, "Baby Boomers, American Character, and the New Age: A Synthesis," in *Perspectives on the New Age,* 90; Tucker, *Another Gospel,* 320.

45. Feher, "Who Holds the Cards?" 183.

Chapter 2: The New Age and the Occult Tradition

1. J. Gordon Melton, *Encyclopedic Handbook of Cults in America* (New York: Garland, 1985), 108.

2. J. Gordon Melton *et al, New Age Almanac* (Detroit: Visible Ink Press, 1991), 3.

3. Douglas R. Groothuis, *Unmasking the New Age* (Downers Grove, IL: InterVarsity, 1986), 131.

4. Robert Ellwood, "How New is the New Age?" in *Perspectives on the New Age* eds. James R. Lewis and J. Gordon Melton (Albany, NY: State University of New York Press, 1992), 59.

5. Marvello Truzzi, "Definitions and Dimensions of the Occult," in *On the Margin of the Visible* ed. Edward A. Tiryakian (New York: John Wiley, 1974), 243, 244; Robert Galbreath, "The History of Modern Occultism," *Journal of Popular Culture* 5 (Winter, 1971): 726-754.

6. J. Stillson Judah, *The History and Philosophy of Metaphysical Movements in America* (Philadelphia: Westminster Press, 1957), 11, 12.

7. Arthur F. Holmes, *Contours of a World View* (Grand Rapids: Eerdmans, 1983), 8; Robert Ellwood, *Religious and Spiritual Groups in Modern America* (Englewood Cliffs, NJ: Prentice Hall, 1973), 42, 43; James W. Sire, *The Universe Next Door* (Downers Grove, IL: InterVarsity Press, 1976), 22-30; Richard Kyle, *The Religious Fringe* (Downers Grove, IL: InterVarsity Press, 1993), 31.

8. Ellwood, *Religious and Spiritual Groups,* 42, 43; Kyle, *The Religious Fringe,* 31; Holmes, *Contours of a World View,* 8.

9. H. B. Kuhn, "Dualism," in *Evangelical Dictionary of Theology* ed. Walter A. Elwell (Grand Rapids: Baker Book House, 1984), 334; Kyle, *The Religious Fringe,* 31, 32; Holmes, *Contours of a World View,* 8.

10. Robert S. Ellwood, *Alternative Altars* (Chicago: University of Chicago Press, 1979), 7: Ellwood, *Religious and Spiritual Groups*, 42, 43; Philip J. Lee, *Against the Protestant Gnostics* (New York: Oxford University Press, 1987).

11. P. D. Feinberg, "Pantheism," in *Evangelical Dictionary of Theology*, 820; George A. Mather and Larry A. Nichols, *Dictionary of Cults, Sects, Religions and the Occult* (Grand Rapids: Zondervan, 1993) 22; Sire, *The Universe Next Door*, 160; Kerry D. McRoberts, *New Age or Old Lie?* (Peabody, MA: Hendrickson Publishers, 1989), 4, 5.

12. Holmes, *Contours of a World View*, 16-20. See also W. Warren Wagar, *World Views: A Study in Comparative History* (Hillsdale, IL: Dryden Press, 1977), 15-51; Crane Brinton, *The Shaping of Modern Thought* (Englewood Cliffs, NJ: Prentice-Hall, 1963), 22-53.

13. F. E. Peters, *The Harvest of Hellenism* (New York: Simon and Schuster, 1970), 196-221, 408-445; Robert M. Grant, *Augustus to Constantine* (New York: Harper and Row, 1970), 3-20.

14. Grant, *Hellenistic Religions*, xvii, xxxii-xxxv, Paul Johnson, *A History of Christianity* (New York: Atheneum, 1977), 5-8, 28, 43; Harold Mattingly, *Christianity in the Roman Empire* (New York: Norton, 1967), 17-23; Hans Lietzmann, *A History of the Early Church* 2 vols. (Cleveland: Meridan Books, 1961), 1:154-176; Kyle, *The Religious Fringe*, 33.

15. Johnson, *History of Christianity*, 5-8; 28, 43; Kyle, *The Religious Fringe*, 33, 34; Grant, *Hellenistic Religions*, xvii, xxxii-xxxv; Mattingly, *Christianity in the Roman Empire*, 17-23.

16. J. N. D. Kelly, *Early Christian Doctrines* (New York: Harper and Row, 1978), 20-22; Kyle, *The Religious Fringe*, 34; Ellwood, *Religious and Spiritual Groups*, 53; M. L. W. Laister, *Christianity and Pagan Culture in the Later Roman Empire* (Ithaca, NY: Cornell University Press, 1951), 22-24.

17. G. K. Nelson, *Spiritualism and Society* (New York: Schocken Books, 1969), 44; Mircea Eliade, *Occultism, Witchcraft and Cultural Fashions* (Chicago: University of Chicago Press, 1976), 56; Kyle, *The Religious Fringe*, 34; Mircea Eliade, *Shamanism, Archaic Techniques of Ecstasy* (Princeton: Princeton University Press, 1964), 4; Ellwood, *Religious and Spiritual Groups*, 11-18, 49-52; Irving Hexham and Karla Poewe, *Understanding Cults and New Religions* (Grand Rapids: Eerdmans, 1986), 79, 80; Michael Harner, *The Way of the Shaman* (San Francisco: Harper and Row, 1990).

18. Ellwood, *Religious and Spiritual Groups*, 52, 53; Arthur Darby Nock, *Early Gentile Christianity and its Hellenistic Background* (New York: Harper and Row, 1964), 97-99.

19. John Stevens Kerr, *The Mystery and Magic of the Occult* (Philadelphia: Fortress Press, 1971), 16-19; W. B. Crow, *A History of Magic, Witchcraft and Occultism* (North Hollywood, CA: Wilshire Book Co., 1968),

222   The New Age Movement in American Culture

179; Lawrence E. Jerome, *Astrology Disproved* (Buffalo: Prometheus Books, 1977), 20-22.

20. Carl A. Raschke, *The Interruption of Eternity* (Chicago: Nelson-Hall, 1980); W. H. C. Frend, *The Rise of Christianity* (Philadelphia: Fortress Press, 1984), 195-200; Grant, *Augustus to Constantine*, 120-130.

21. Peters, *Harvest of Hellenism*, 656; Grant, *Hellenistic Religions*, xxxiv; Harold O. J. Brown, *Heresies* (Garden City, NY: Doubleday, 1984), 46-50.

22. Pheme Perkins, *The Gnostic Dialogue* (New York: Paulist Press, 1980), 10-19; Peters, *Harvest of Hellenism*, 649; Edwin M. Yamauchi, "The Gnostics," in *Eerdmans' Handbook to the History of Christianity* ed. Tim Dowley (Grand Rapids: Eerdmans, 1977), 98, 99; Kyle, *The Religious Fringe*, 36; Kelly, *Early Christian Doctrines*, 22-28; Jaroslav Pelikan, *The Emergence of the Catholic Tradition (100-600)* (Chicago: University of Chicago Press, 1971), 85-97.

23. Harold Bloom, *The American Religion: The Emergence of the Post-Christian Nation* (New York: Simon and Schuster, 1992).

24. Lee, *Against the Protestant Gnostics*, 3-12.

25. Christopher Lasch, "The Infantile Illusion of Omnipotence and the Modern Ideology of Science," *New Oxford Review* (October 1986): 18.

26. Raschke, *Interruption of Eternity*, xi.

27. Andrew M. Greeley, "Religion's Oldest Scoop," *Psychology Today* April 13, 1980, p. 88.

28. Peter Jones, *The Gnostic Empire Strikes Back* (Phillsburg, NJ: Presbyterian and Reformed Publishing Co., 1992), 44-61. See also McRoberts, *New Age or Old Lie?*, 55-59.

29. Ted Peters, "Post-Modern Religion," *Update* 8, no. 1 (1984): 16.

30. Jacob Needleman, "Foreward," in *The Sword of Gnosis* ed. Jacob Needleman (London: Routledge and Kegan Paul, 1974), 3.

31. Marilyn Ferguson, *The Aquarian Conspiracy* (Los Angeles: J. P. Tarcher, 1980), 371, 372; Ted Peters, *The Cosmic Self* (San Francisco: Harper and Row, 1991), 83.

32. Robert I. Moore, *The Origins of European Dissent* (New York: St. Martin's 1977), iix; Rodney Stark and William Sims Bainbridge, *The Future of Religion* (Berkeley, CA: University of California Press, 1985), 108.

33. Edward Peters, ed. *Heresy and Authority in Medieval Europe* (Philadelphia: University of Pennsylvania Press, 1980), 25; Eleanor Shipley Duckett, *The Gateway to the Middle Ages: Monasticism* (Ann Arbor, MI: University of Michigan Press, 1961), 62-121; Johnson, *History of Christianity*, 128, 145, 177, 191, 192; David Knowles, *Christian Monasticism* (New York: McGraw Hill, 1969), 25-36; Eleanor Duckett, *The Wandering Saints of the Early Middle Ages* (New York: Norton, 1959), 15-79.

34. Moore, *European Dissent*, 7, 8; Johnson, *History of Christianity*, 177, 191, 192, 204-207, 214-221; Jaroslav Pelikan, *The Growth of Medieval Theology (600-1300)* (Chicago: University of Chicago Press, 1978), 213-215;

Kyle, *The Religious Fringe*, 37; Malcolm Lambert, *Medieval Heresy* (New York: Holmes and Meier, 1977), 89, 90; Jeffrey Russell, ed. *Religious Dissent in the Middle Ages* (New York: Wiley, 1971), 7, 8.

35. Gordon Leff, *The Dissolution of the Medieval Outlook* (New York: New York University Press, 1976), 91-144; J. Huizinga, *The Waning of the Middle Ages* (Garden City, NY: Doubleday, 1954), 17-28, 27-41, 177-189; Barbara W. Tuchman, *A Distant Mirror* (New York: Ballantine Books, 1978); Philip Ziegler, *The Black Death* (New York: Harper and Row, 1971), 232-279.

36. Lambert, *Medieval Heresy*, 42-66; Peters, *Heresy and Authority*, 103-107; Russell, *Religious Dissent*, 57-59; Pelikan, *Medieval Theology*, 229-235; 238-242; Brown, *Heresies*, 253-261.

37. Marjorie Reeves, *Joachim of Fiore and the Prophetic Future* (New York: Harper and Row, 1976), 1-3, 59-82; Pelikan, *Medieval Theology*, 301-303; Lambert, *Medieval Heresy*, 182-196; Gordon Leff, *Heresy in the Middle Ages* (Manchester, UK: Manchester University Press, 1967), 72-74; Kyle, *The Religious Fringe*, 38; Normon Cohn, *The Pursuit of the Millennium* (New York: Oxford University Press, 1974), 108-118.

38. Robert S. Ellwood, *Mysticism and Religion* (Englewood Cliffs, NJ: Prentice-Hall, 1980), 110-113; Steven Ozment, *The Age of Reform 1250-1550* (New Haven, CN: Yale University Press, 1980), 125-134; Georgia Harkness, *Mysticism* (Nashville: Abingdon Press, 1973), 103-116; Raymond Blakney trans. *Meister Eckhart* (New York: Harper and Row, 1941), xx-xxvii; Brown, *Heresies*, 266-268.

39. Jeffrey B. Russell, *A History of Witchcraft* (London: Thames and Hudson Ltd., 1980), 172; Christina Larner, ed. *Witchcraft and Religion* (Oxford: Basel Blackwell, 1984), 77-88.

40. Ellwood, *Religious and Spiritual Groups*, 55, 56; Leo Schaya, *The Universal Meaning of the Kabbalah* (Baltimore: Penguin Books, 1973), 15-20; Francis A. Yates, *The Occult Philosophy in the Elizabethan Age* (London: Routledge and Kegan, 1979), 2, 3.

41. Henry Kamen, *The Rise of Toleration* (New York: McGraw-Hill, 1967), 7, 8, 22, 54-56; Michael Mullett, *Radical Religious Movements in Early Modern Europe* (Boston: Allen and Unwin, 1980), 75, 78, 79; Peter J. Klassen, *Church and State in Reformation Europe* (St. Louis: Forum Press, 1975), 10-14; Kyle, *The Religious Fringe*, 40.

42. Philip Lee Ralph, *The Renaissance in Perspective* (New York: St. Martin's Press, 1973), 214-218; Ellwood, *Religious and Spiritual Groups*, 57.

43. Hugh Kearney, *Science and Change 1500-1700* (New York: McGraw-Hill, 1971), 52, 53; Ellwood, *Religious and Spiritual Groups*, 57; A. B. Hall, *The Scientific Revolution 1500-1800* (Boston: Beacon Press, 1966), 305, 306; David Bokan, *Sigmund Freud and the Jewish Mystical Tradition* (New York: Schocken Books, 1965); Herbert Butterfield, *The Origins of*

Modern Science (New York: Macmillan, 1957), 46, 47; Kyle, *The Religious Fringe*, 42.

44. John Warwick Montgomery, *Principalities and Powers* (Minneapolis: Bethany Fellowship, 1973), 104, 105; Kyle, *The Religious Fringe*, 43.

45. Keith Thomas, *Religion and the Decline of Magic* (New York: Charles Scribner's, 1971), 661-664; Roland H. Bainton, *The Reformation of the Sixteenth Century* (Boston: Beacon Press, 1952), 3-6; Kyle, *The Religious Fringe*, 45; Steven E. Ozment, ed., *The Reformation in Medieval Perspective* (Chicago: Quandrangle Books, 1971); William Cook and Ronald B. Herzman, *The Medieval World View* (New York: Oxford University Press, 1983).

46. Jeffrey Russell, *Mephistopheles* (Ithaca, NY: Cornell University Press, 1986); Catherine Albanese, *American: Religions and Religion* (Belmont, CA: Wadsworth, 1981), 164; Howard Kerr and Charles L. Crow, "Introduction," in *The Occult in America* (Urbana: University of Illinois Press, 1983), 5.

47. Albanese, *America*, 64.

48. Herbert Leventhal, *In the Shadow of the Enlightenment* (New York: New York University Press, 1976), 265-268; Kyle, *The Religious Fringe*, 47; Albanese, *America*, 164, 165.

49. Albanese, *America*, 164, 165; Kyle, *The Religious Fringe*, 47.

50. James Webb, *The Occult Underground* (LaSalle, IL: Open Court, 1974), 224; Ellwood, *Religious and Spiritual Groups*, 62, 63.

51. Webb, *Occult Underground*, 225, 226.

52. Webb, *Occult Underground*, 225, 226.

53. Justo L. Gonzalez, *The Story of Christianity* 2 vols. (San Francisco: Harper and Row, 1984), 2: 203, 204; Ruth Tucker, *Another Gospel* (Grand Rapids: Zondervan, 1989), 381-383; Ellwood, *Religious and Spiritual Groups*, 64, 65.

54. Ellwood, *Religious and Spiritual Groups*, 66; Gonzales, *Story of Christianity* 2: 203; Kyle, *The Religious Fringe*, 49.

55. Gonzales, *Story of Christianity*, 2: 203; Ellwood, *Religious and Spiritual Groups*, 66. See also Emanuel Swedenborg, *The True Christian Religion* (London: Everyman's Library, 1936); Kyle, *The Religious Fringe*, 49.

56. Kay Alexander, "Roots of the New Age," in *Perspectives on the New Age*, 33, 34.

57. Robert C. Fuller, *Mesmerism and the Cure of American Souls* (Philadelphia: University of Pennsylvania Press, 1982), 1-47; Kyle, *The Religious Fringe*, 49; Webb, *Occult Underground*, 228; Ellwood, *Religious and Spiritual Groups*, 68.

Chapter 3: Precursors of the New Age in America

1. Robert Wuthnow, "World Order and Religious Movements," in *New Religious Movements: A Perspective for Understanding Society* ed. Eileen Barker (New York: Edwin Mellen Press, 1982), 48, 49; Sidney Ahlstrom, "From Sinai to the Golden Gate," in *Understanding the New Religions* eds. Jacob Needleman and George Baker (New York: Seabury Press, 1978), 15, 16.

2. Richard Kyle, *The Religious Fringe* (Downers Grove, IL: InterVarsity Press, 1993), 54.

3. Catherine Albanese, *America: Religions and Religion* 2nd ed. (Belmont, CA: Wadsworth, 1992), 355; J. Gordon Melton *et al, New Age Almanac* (Detroit: Visible Ink Press, 1991), 5.

4. J. Stillson Judah, *The History and Philosophy of the Metaphysical Movements in America* (Philadelphia: Westminster Press, 1957), 22-46.

5. Alice Felt Tyler, *Freedom's Ferment* (New York: Harper and Row, 1944), 47; Russel Blaine Nye, *Society and Culture in America, 1830-1860* (New York: Harper and Row, 1974), 300.

6. Melton, *New Age Almanac*, 5.

7. Albanese, *America*, 171, 173. See also James C. Moseley, *A Cultural History of Religion in America* (Westport, CN: Greenwood Press, 1981), 68-71; Sidney E. Ahlstrom, *A Religious History of the American People* (New Haven, CN: Yale University Press, 1972), 600-606; Catherine Albanese, "Religion and the American Experience: A Century After," *Church History* 57, no. 3 (1988): 345.

8. Tyler, *Freedom's Ferment*, 48; Albanese, *America*, 173. See also Catherine L. Albanese, *Corresponding Motion: Transcendental Religion and the New America* (Philadelphia: Temple University Press, 1977).

9. Albanese, *America*, 173; Tyler, *Freedom's Ferment*, 48, 49; Nye, *Society and Culture*, 301; Ahlstrom, *Religious History*, 605-608.

10. Robert Ellwood, *Alternative Altars: Unconventional and Eastern Spirituality in America* (Chicago: University of Chicago Press, 1979), 94; Kyle, *The Religious Fringe*, 66; Robert Lunden, "Transcendentalism," in *Evangelical Dictionary of Theology* ed. Walter A. Elwell (Grand Rapids, MI: Baker Book House, 1984), 1107.

11. J. Gordon Melton, "New Thought and the New Age," in *Perspectives on the New Age* eds. James R. Lewis and J. Gordon Melton (Albany, NY: State University of New York Press, 1992), 21; Elliot Miller, "Channeling: Spiritistic Revelations for the New Age," *Christian Research Journal* 10, no. 2 (1987): 9.

12. Ernest Isaacs, "The Fox Sisters and American Spiritualism," in *The Occult in America* eds. Howard Kerr and Charles L. Crow (Urbana, IL: University of Illinois Press, 1983), 79, 80; Judah, *Metaphysical Movements* 50, 51.

13. Judah, *Metaphysical Movements*, 51; Ellwood, *Alternative Altars*, 91, 92; R. Laurence Moore, *In Search of White Crows* (New York: Oxford University Press), 9; Robert C. Fuller, *Mesmerism and the American Cure of Souls* (Philadelphia: University of Pennsylvania Press, 1982), 1-15.

14. Moore, *In Search of White Crows*, 9, 10.

15. Ellwood, *Alternative Altars*, 84-90, 92-94; Moore, *In Search of White Crows*, 25, 26.

16. Ellwood, *Alternative Altars* 95-98; Judah, *Metaphysical Movements*, 52-56.

17. Albanese, *America*, 175; Ellwood, *Alternative Altars*, 89-91.

18. Moore, *In Search of White Crows*, 64. Other histories of nineteenth-century Spiritualism include Geoffrey K. Nelson, *Spiritualism and Society* (London: Routledge and Kegan Paul, 1969); Howard Kerr, *Mediums and Spirit Rappers and Roaring Radicals* (Urbana, IL: University of Illinois Press, 1972); Katherine H. Porter, *Through A Glass Darkly* (Lawrence, KS: University of Kansas Press, 1958); Burton Gates, Jr., "Spiritualism in Nineteenth-Century America," Ph.D. dissertation, Boston University, 1973; Mary Farrell Bednarowski, "Nineteenth Century American Spiritualism," Ph.D. dissertation, University of Minnesota, 1973.

19. J. Gordon Melton, "New Churches of the 1920s and 1930s," in *Christianity in America* ed. Mark Noll *et al* (Grand Rapids: Eerdmans, 1983), 412; William J. Peterson, *Those Curious New Cults in the 80s* (New Canaan, CN: Keats Publishing, 1982), 58; John Kerr, *The Mystery and Magic of the Occult* (Philadelphia: Fortress Press, 1971), 94, 95.

20. Robert Ellwood, "How New is the New Age?" in *Perspectives on the New Age*, 61-65.

21. Charles S. Braden, *Spirits in Rebellion: The Rise and Development of New Thought* (Dallas: Southern Methodist University Press, 1963), 9-25; Robert Ellwood, *Religious and Spiritual Groups in Modern America* (Englewood Cliffs, NJ: Prentice-Hall, 1973), 79; Judah, *Metaphysical Groups*, 176-186. See Horatio W. Dresser, *A History of the New Thought Movement* (New York: Thomas Y. Crowell Co., 1919).

22. Braden, *Spirits in Rebellion*, 14-19; Ellwood, *Religious and Spiritual Groups*, 79, 80; Gordon Melton, *The Encyclopedia of American Religions* 2 vols. (Wilmington, NC: McGrath Publishing Co., 1978), 2:56-58.

23. Melton, *Encyclopedia of American Religions*, 2: 56-58; Ellwood, *Religious and Spiritual Groups*, 79, 80; Braden, *Spirits in Rebellion*, 14-19.

24. Albanese, *America*, 179, 180; Judah, *Metaphysical Movements*, 149-154; Braden, *Spirits in Rebellion*, 47-88; Catherine Albanese, "Physic and Metaphysic in Nineteenth-Century America: Medical Sectarians and Religious Healing," *Church History 55*, no. 4 (1986): 499-501. See also Frank Polmore, *Mesmerism and Christian Science* (London: Methuen, 1909); Robert C. Fuller, *Alternative Medicine and American Religious Life* (New York: Oxford University Press, 1989), 50, 60.

25. John F. Teahan, "Warren Felt Evans and Mental Healing: Romantic Idealism and Practical Mysticism in Nineteenth-Century America," *Church History* 48, no. 1 (1979): 63-80; Braden, *Spirits in Rebellion*, 89-128; Albanese, *America*, 180, 181; Judah, *Metaphysical Movements*, 160, 167.

26. Braden, *Spirits in Rebellion*, 89-128; Albanese, *America*, 180, 181; Teahan, "Warren Felt Evans," 63-80; Judah, *Metaphysical Movements*, 160-167.

27. Judah, *Metaphysical Movements*, 192, 193; Albanese, *America*, 182; Braden, *Spirits in Rebellion*, 323-405.

28. Melton, "New Thought and the New Age," 26. See also Donald Meyer, *Positive Thinkers* 2nd ed (New York: Pantheon Books, 1980).

29. Melton, "New Thought and the New Age," 26, 27.

30. Ellwood, *Religious and Spiritual Groups*, 97; Charles S. Braden, *These Also Believe* (New York: Macmillan Co., 1957), 225; Melton, *New Age Almanac*, 6.

31. G. Baseden Butt, *Madame Blavatsky* (London: Rider and Co., 1925), 2-54; Ellwood, *Alternative Altars*, 107-111; Judah, *Metaphysical Movements*, 92, 93; Melton, *New Age Almanac*, 16. See also Marion Meade, *Madame Blavatsky* (New York: Putnam, 1980); Alvin B. Kuhn, *Theosophy: A Modern Revival of Ancient Wisdom* (New York: Henry Holt and Co., 1930).

32. Ellwood, *Alternative Altars*, 111-112; Ellwood, *Religious and Spiritual Groups*, 76; Braden, *These Also Believe*, 222-226; Melton, *Encyclopedia of American Relgions*, 2:135-175.

33. Braden, *These Also Believe*, 243-246.

34. Judah, *Metaphysical Movements*, 103-108; Braden, *These Also Believe*, 246-250.

35. Judah, *Metaphysical Movements*, 104, 105; Melton, *New Age Almanac*, 16.

36. Melton, *New Age Almanac*, 16.

37. Albanese, *America* (2nd ed), 356.

38. Albanese, *America* (2nd ed), 356.

39. Mary Farrell Bednarowski, *New Religions and the Theological Imagination in America* (Bloomington, IN: Indiana University Press, 1989), 18.

40. Albanese, *America* (2nd ed), 356, 357.

41. Ruth Tucker, *Another Gospel* (Grand Rapids: Zondervan, 1989), 322. Bednarowski, *New Religions and the Theological Imagination in America*, 14, 15.

42. For more on Eastern contacts with the West and the United States specifically see Carl T. Jackson, *The Oriental Religions and American Thought: Nineteenth Century Explorations* (Westport, CN: Greenwood Press, 1981), 3; William McNeill, *The Rise of the West* (Chicago: University of

Chicago Press, 1963); S. Radhakrishman, *Eastern Religions and Western Thought* (New York: A Galaxy Book, 1959).

43. Andrea Grace Diem and James B. Lewis, "Imaging India: The Influence of Hinduism on the New Age Movement," in *Perspectives on the New Age*, 48, 49; Jackson *Oriental Releigions*, 25, 32, 45, 46, 63, 64, 157, 158; J. Gordon Melton, "How New Is New: The Flowering of the 'New' Religious Consciousness since 1965," in *The Future of New Religious Movements* eds. David G. Bromley and Phillip E. Hammond (Macon, GA: Mercer University Press, 1987), 49; Ronald Enroth and J. Gordon Melton, *Why Cults Succeed Where the Church Fails* (Elgin, IL: Brethren Press, 1985), 120-123.

44. Jackson, *Oriental Religions*, 265; Diem and Lewis, "Imaging India," 49.

45. David M. Reimers, *Still the Golden Door: The Third World Comes to America* (New York: Columbia University Press, 1985), 1-10.

46. Enroth and Melton, *Why Cults Succeed*, 122, 123; Melton, "How New Is New?" 50, 51.

47. Diem and Lewis, "Imaging India," 49.

48. Roland N. Stromberg, *An Intellectual History of Modern Europe* 2nd ed. (Englewood Cliffs, NJ: Prentice-Hall, 1975), 375-378; Fritjof Capra, *The Turning Point* (New York: Bantam Books, 1982) 164, 165.

49. Melton, "How New is New?" 55; Carl A. Raschke, "The Human Potential Movement," *Theology Today* 33, no 3 (1976): 253, 254; Capra, *The Turning Point*, 359-363. See also Paul C. Vitz, *Psychology as Religion* (Grand Rapids: Wm. Eerdmans, 1977); C. G. Jung, *Modern Man in Search of a Soul* (New York: Harcourt, Brace, 1933); Carl Gustav Jung, *Psychology and Religion* (New Haven, CN: Yale University Press, 1938).

50. Moore, *In Search of White Crows*, 134-138; J. B. Rhine, "Parapsychology,"in *Encyclopedia of the Unexplained* ed. Richard Cavendish (New York: McGraw-Hill, 1974), 178, 180-182.

51. Moore, *In Search of White Crows*, 185, 198, 204, 210, 213, 219, 221, 235.

52. Melton, *New Age Almanac*, 8; Moore, *In Search of White Crows*, 185, 198, 204, 210, 213, 219, 221, 235.

Chapter 4: American Society and the New Age

1. Robert Wuthnow, "World Order and Religious Movements," in *New Relgious Movements: A Perspective for Understanding Society* ed. Eileen Barker (Edwin Mellen Press, 1982), 48.

2. Theodore Roszak, *The Making of a Counter Culture* (Garden City, NY: Doubleday and Co., 1969), 141; Wuthnow, "World Order and Religious Movements, 48; Allan W. Eister, "Cultural Crises and New Religious Movements: A Paradigmatic Statement of a Theory of Cults," in

Religious Movements in Contemporary America eds. Irving I. Zaretsky and Mark P. Leone (Princeton: Princeton University Press, 1974), 623.

3. Robert S. Ellwood, Jr., *The Eagle and the Rising Sun* (Philadelphia: Westminster Press, 1974), 13, 14; J. Gordon Melton, "The Flowering of the New Religious Consciousness," in *Why Cults Succeed Where the Church Fails* Ronald M. Enroth and J. Gordon Melton (Elgin, IL: Brethren Press, 1985), 124; Richard Kyle, "The Cults: Why Now and Who Gets Caught," *Journal of the American Scientific Affiliation* 33, no. 2 (1981): 95.

4. Melton, "Flowering of the New Religious Consciousness," 124; J. Gordon Melton and Robert L. Moore, *The Cult Experience* (New York: Pilgrim Press, 1982), 26. See Richard Polenburg, *One Nation Divisible* (New York: Pelican Books, 1980), 205-208; David M. Reimers, *Still the Golden Door* (New York: Columbia University Press, 1985), 63-90.

5. Andrea Grace Diem and James R. Lewis, "Imagining India: The Influence of Hinduism on the New Age Movement," in *Perspectives on the New Age* eds. James R. Lewis and J. Gordon Melton (Albany, NY: State University of New York Press, 1992), 49-51.

6. Fritjof Capra, *The Tao of Physics* 3rd ed. (Boston: Shambhala, 1991). Such an approach is found in many places in the above book. See page 25 for one example.

7. Diem and Lewis, "Imagining India," 51.

8. Wade Clark Roof and William McKinney, *American Mainline Religion* (New Brunswick, NJ: Rutgers University Press, 1988), 31, 35.

9. Roof and McKinney, *American Mainline Religion*, 35.

10. William G. McLoughlin, *Revivals, Awakenings, and Reform* (Chicago: University of Chicago Press, 1978), 150-178.

11. Roof and McKinney, *American Mainline Religion*, 29-32, 35.

12. Sydney Ahlstrom, *A Religious History of the American People* (New Haven, CN: Yale University Press, 1972), 1093-1096; Kyle, "The Cults," 95.

13. Roy Wallis, *The Rebirth of the Gods: Reflections on the New Religions in the West* (Belfast: University of Belfast, 1978), 16, 17.

14. Erling Jorstad, *Holding Fast/Pressing On: Religion in American in the 1980s* (New York: Praeger Publishers, 1990), 129, 130.

15. Gordon Melton, *Encyclopedic Handbook of Cults in America* (New York: Garland Publishing, 1986), 113. See also Marilyn Ferguson, *The Aquarian Conspiracy* (Los Angeles: J. P. Tarcher, 1980), 45; Richard Blow, "Moronic Convergence," *New Republic* January 25, 1988, 24.

16. Robert N. Bellah, *et al*, *Habits of the Heart* (New York: Harper and Row, 1985), 220-225.

17. Roof and McKinney, *American Mainline Religion*, 45-47; Daniel Yankelovich, "A Crisis of Moral Legitimacy?" *Dissent* 21 (Fall 1974): 526, 527. See Edwin Schur, *The Awareness Trap* (New York: McGraw-Hill, 1976).

18. Thomas Luckmann, *The Invisible Religion* (New York: Macmillan, 1967).

19. Bellah, *Habits of the Heart*; Jorstad, *Holding Fast*, 129, 130.

20. Jorstad, *Holding Fast*, 153.

21. Roof and McKinney, *American Mainline Religion*, 49, 50, 62.

22. Wade Clark Roof, "America's Voluntary Establishment: Mainline Religion in Transition," in *Religion and America* eds. Mary Douglas and Steven Tipton (Boston: Beacon Press, 1983), 132, 133.

23. Roof and McKinney, *American Mainline Religion*, 49, 50; Roof, "America's Voluntary Establishment," 132. See also Randall Balmer, "Death of New Age a New Era for U.S.," *Wichita Eagle* June 3, 1991, p. 11A; Carl A. Raschke, *The Bursting of New Wineskins* (Pittsburgh: Pickwick Press, 1978), 69-81.

24. Editorial in *The 1989 Guide to New Age Living* (Farmingdale, NY: N.P.), 103. For quote see Jorstad, *Holding Fast*, 168.

25. Barbara Hargrove, *The Emerging New Class* (New York: Pilgrim Press, 1986), 165; Jorstad, *Holding Fast*, 167.

26. Robert Galbreath, *The Occult in America* (Urbana, IL: University of Illinois Press, 1983), 21. See also Michael Brown, "Getting Serious About the Occult," *Atlantic Monthly* October 1978, pp. 95-104.

27. Richard Kyle, *The Religious Fringe* (Downers Grove, IL: InterVarsity Press, 1993), 259.

28. Martin Marty, "The Occult Establishment," *Social Research* 37 (1970): 228; Martin Marty, *A Nation of Behavers* (Chicago: University of Chicago Press, 1976), 135, 139, 140.

29. Melton, *Cults in America*, 116; Robert Burrows, "Corporate Management Cautioned on New Age," *Eternity* February 1988, p. 33; Carl A. Raschke, *The Interruption of Eternity* (Chicago: Nelson-Hall, 1980) 105 ff.; Carl A. Raschke, "The Human Potential Movement," *Theology Today* 33, no. 3 (1976): 254.

30. Ronald Enroth, "The Occult," in *Evangelical Dictionary of Theology* ed. Walter Elwell (Grand Rapids, MI: Baker Book House, 1984), 788. See also John Cooper, *Religion in the Age of Aquarius* (Philadelphia: Westminster Press, 1971), 28-31.

31. Mircea Eliade, *Occultism, Witchcraft, and Cultural Fashions* (Chicago: University of Chicago Press, 1976), 67; Nat Freedland, (New York: Putnam's, 1972), 17; Marty, *Nation of Behavers*, 135, 136.

32. Richard Watring, "New Age Training in Business: Mind Control in Upper Management?" *Eternity* February 1988, pp. 30-32; Raschke, "Human Potential Movement," 254-257; Freedland, *Occult Explosion*, 19. See also Colin Campbell, "The Secret Religion of the Educated Classes," *Sociological Analyses* 39, no 2 (1978): 146-156.

33. Ronald Enroth, *The Lure of the Cults* (Chappaqua, NY: Christian Herald Books, 1979), 43, 44. See also Robert Wuthnow and Charles Y.

Glock, "God in the Gut," *Psychology Today* (November 1974), pp. 131-136; Jacob Needleman, "Winds from the East," *Commonweal* April 30, 1971, 188-199.

34. Theodore Roszak, "Ethics, Ecstasy, and the Study of New Religions," in *Understanding the New Religions* eds. Jacob Needleman and George Baker (New York: Seabury Press, 1978), 52.

35. Michael Schaller, Virginia Schraff, and Robert D. Schulzinger, *Present Tense* (Boston: Houghton Mifflin, 1992), 325.

36. Sydney E. Ahlstrom, "The Traumatic Years: American Religion and Culture in the '60s and '70s,"*Theology Today* 36, no. 4 (1980): 510, 511. See also Milton Viorst, *Fire in the Streets* (New York: Simon and Schuster, 1979); Steven M. Tipton, *Getting Saved from the Sixties* (Berkeley: University of California Press, 1982), 2.

37. Kyle, The Cults," 95; Ahlstrom, *Religious History of the American People*, 1091. See also Barbara Hargrove, *Religion for a Dislocated Generation* (Valley Forge, PA: Judson Press, 1980), 16-22. See also Daniel Bell, "Religion in the Sixties," *Social Research* 38, no. 3 (1971): 447-497.

38. See Sydney E. Ahlstrom, "The Radical Turn in Theology and Ethics: Why It Occurred in the 1960s," *The Annuals of the American Academy of Political and Social Sciences* 387 (January 1970): 9, 12; Roszak, *Making of a Counter Culture*, 1-41.

39. Theodore Roszak, *Unfinished Animal* (New York: Harper and Row, 1975), 7, 8, 14, 16, 19, 20; William Braden, *The Age of Aquarius: Technology and the Cultural Revolution* (Chicago: Quadrangle Books, 1970); Charles Reich, *The Greening of America* (New York: Random House, 1970), 17-19; Hargrove, *Dislocated Generation*, 44-65.

40. Gordon Melton, "How New is New?" in *The Future of New Religious Movements* eds. David G. Bromley and Phillip E. Hammond (Macon, GA: Mercer University Press, 1987), 54, 55.

41. Melton, "How New is New?" 55; Raschke, "Human Potential Movement," 253, 254. See also Paul C. Vitz, *Psychology as Religion* (Grand Rapids: Wm. Eerdmans, 1977).

42. Ahlstrom, "The Radical Turn in Theology and Ethics," 11; Kyle, "The Cults," 95.

43. Ahlstrom, "The Traumatic Years," 513; Ahlstrom, "The Radical Turn," 11, 12.

44. Ahlstrom, "The Radical Turn," 12; Ahlstrom, "The Traumatic Years," 512, 513.

45. Ronald Enroth, Edward E. Ericson, Jr. and C. Breckenridge Peters, *The Jesus People* (Grand Rapids: Wm. Eerdmans, 1972), 182.

46. Martin E. Marty, "Foreward,"in *Understanding Church Growth and Decline, 1950-1978* eds. Dean R. Hoge and David A. Roozen (New York: Pilgrim Press, 1979), 10. See also Os Guinness, *The American Hour* (New York: The Free Press, 1993), 91-101.

47. Ahlstrom, *Religious History of the American People*, 1080.

48. Ferguson, *Aquarian Conspiracy*, 8, 9; Douglas R. Groothuis, *Unmasking the New Age* (Downers Grove, IL: InterVarsity Press, 1986), 38, 39.

49. Groothuis, *Unmasking the New Age*, 38, 39.

50. Ferguson, *Aquarian Conspiracy*, 89, 90.

51. Elliot Miller, *A Crash Course on the New Age Movement*, 24.

52. Martin Marty, "As the 'New Religions' Grow Older," in *Encyclopedia Britannica, 1986 Book of the Year*, eds. Daphne Daume and J. E. Davis (Chicago: Encyclopedia Britannica, 1986), 370; Marty, *A Nation of Behavers*, 135; Hargrove, *Dislocated Generation*, 44-47.

53. Kyle, *The Religious Fringe*, 187.

54. Marty, "New Religions Grow Older," 371; Mary Ann Groves, "Marginal Religious Movements as Precursors of a Sociological Revolution," *Thought* 61, no. 241 (1986): 267, 268; Daniel Yankelovich, *New Rules* (New York: Bantam Books, 1982), 1-4; Daniel Yankelovich, "New Rules in American Life: Searching for Self-Fulfillment in a World Turned Upside Down," *Psychology Today* April 1981, 39-43; Henry Fairlie, "A Decade of Reaction" Part I, *The New Republic* January 6, 1979, p. 17; Daniel A. Foss and Ralph W. Larkin, "From 'Gates of Eden' to 'Day of the Locust': An Analysis of the Youth Movement of the 1960s and the Heirs of the Early 1970s--the Post-movement Groups," *Theory and Society* 3, (1976): 56; Arthur M. Schlesinger, Jr. *The Cycles of American History* (Boston: Houghlin Mifflin, 1986); Morris Dickstein, "Winding Down the 60s," *The Nation* May 21, 1977, pp. 632, 633.

55. Yankelovich, *New Rules*, 1-4; Yankelovich, "New Rules in American Life," 39-43; Fairlie, "A Decade of Reaction," 17; Foss, "From Gates of Eden," 56; Christopher Lasch, *The Culture of Narcissism* (New York: Norton, 1979), 4, 5. See also Peter Marin, "The New Narcissism, " *Harper's* October 1975, pp. 45-56; Christopher Lasch, "The Narcissistic Personality of Our Time," *Partisan Review* (1977): 9-19; Bill Barol, "The Eighties are Over," *Newsweek* January 4, 1988, pp. 40-48; Christopher Lasch, "Soul of a New Age," *Omni* October 1987, pp. 78-84.

56. Balmer, "Death of New Age a New Era for U.S.," 11A; Richard Blow, "Moronic Convergence," *New Republic* January 25, 1988, 26.

57. Peter Clecak argues that there is more continuity between the sixties and seventies than meets the eye. See Peter Clecak, *America's Quest for the Ideal Self* (New York: Oxford University Press, 1983), 5, 6; Peter Clecak, "Culture and Politics in the Sixties," *Dissent* 24 (Fall 1977): 439-443.

58. Groothuis, *Unmasking the New Age*, 39, 40. See also Jerry Adler, *et al*, "The Graying of Aquarius," *Newsweek* March 30, 1987, pp. 56-58; Clecak, *America's Quest*, 4-8.

59. Groothuis, *Unmasking the New Age*, 45, 46.

60. The New Age could be regarded as a world-affirming movement. It has not rejected society as did many of the counterculture groups. See Wallis, *Rebirth of the Gods*, 8, 9; Groothuis, *Unmasking the New Age*, 45, 46; Robert Burrows, "Americans Get Religion in the New Age," *Christianity Today* May 16, 1986, p. 17; Richard Kyle, "Is There a New Age Coming?" *Christian Leader* January 17, 1989, p. 6.

Chapter 5: The Modern New Age

1. Robert Ellwood, *Religious and Spiritual Groups in Modern America* (Englewood Cliffs, NJ: Prentice Hall, 1973), 258; Robert Ellwood, *Alternative Altars* (Chicago: University of Chicago Press, 1979), 139, 147, 158; Christmas Humphreys, *Zen Buddhism* (New York: Macmillan Co., 1962), 158-160; Alan W. Watts, *The Way of Zen* (New York: Pantheon, 1957), 174, 201; Steven M. Tipton, *Getting Saved from the Sixties* (Berkeley, CA: University of California Press, 1982), 153.

2. Humphreys, *Zen Buddhism*, 12-14; Ellwood, *Religious and Spiritual Groups*, 258.

3. George Braswell, *Understanding Sectarian Groups in America* (Nashville: Broadman Press, 1986), 316.

4. Gordon Melton, *The Encyclopedia of American Religions* 2 vols. (Wilmington, NC: McGrath Publishing Co., 1978), 2: 360; Ellwood, *Religious and Spiritual Groups*, 220-224; Catherine Albanese, *America: Religions and Religion* (Belmont, CA: Wadsworth, 1981), 205, 206.

5. Ellwood, *Religious and Spiritual Groups*, 225-229; Albanese, *America*, 206, 207; Melton, *Encyclopedia of American Religions*, 2:361,362. See also Paramathansa Yogananda, *Autobiography of a Yogi* (Los Angeles: Self-Realization Fellowship, 1959).

6. John Newport, *Christ and the New Consciousness* (Nashville, TN: Broadman Press, 1978), 21, 22; Braswell, *Understanding Sectarian Groups*, 283, 284; "TM Continues to Flourish, Despite Legal Battles," *Christian Research Journal* 12, no. 2 (1989): 5.

7. David G. Bromley and Anson D. Shupe, Jr. *Strange Gods: The Great American Cult Scare* (Boston: Beacon Press, 1981), 62; Jeanne Messer, "Guru Maharj Ji and the Divine Light Mission," in *The New Religious Consciousness* eds. Charles Glock and Robert Bellah (Berkeley, CA: University of California Press, 1976), 53, 54; James V. Downton, *Sacred Journeys: Conversion of Young Americans to Divine Light Mission* (New York: Columbia University Press, 1979), 223.

8. J. Gordon Melton, *Encyclopedic Handbook of Cults in America* (New York: Garland Publishing, 1986), 182-185,

9. Robert Ellwood, "Introduction," in *New Religious Movements in the United States and Canada* comp. Diane Choquette (Greenwood Press, 1985), 11, 12; Newport, *Christ and the New Consciousness*, 66-81.

10. Newport, *Christ and the New Consciousness*, 79, 80.

11. Albanese, *America*, 201, 202; William McElwee Miller, *The Baha'i Faith: Its History and Teachings* (South Pasadena, CA: William Carey Library, 1974), 138-165; Ruth Tucker, *Another Gospel* (Grand Rapids: Zondervan, 1989), 286.

12. Gordon Melton, "How New is New?" in *The Future of New Religious Movements* eds. David G. Bromley and Phillip E. Hammond (Macon, GA: Macon University Press, 1987), 52.

13. Marcello Truzzi, "The Occult Revival as Popular Culture," *The Sociological Quarterly* 13 (Winter 1972): 18, 19; Nat Freedland, *The Occult Explosion* (New York: Putnam's, 1972), 111, 119; Martin Marty, "The Occult Establishment," *Social Research* 37 (1970): 223.

14. Richard Woods, *The Occult Revolution* (New York: Herder and Herder, 1971), 149.

15. Woods, *Occult Revolution*, 160-165; James Bjornstad, *Twentieth Century Prophecy* (Minneapolis: Bethany Fellowship, 1969), 84-89; John Godwin, *Occult America* (Garden City, NY: Doubleday, 1972), 100-111. See Jess Stern, *Edgar Cayce: The Sleeping Prophet* (New York: New American Library, 1969).

16. Ruth Montgomery, *A Gift of Prophecy* (New York: Bantam Books, 1965), 103, 155, 164, 176; Woods, *Occult Revolution*, 165-167; Jeane Dixon, *The Call to Glory* (New York: Bantam Books, 1971), 160-184.

17. Jeffrey B. Russell, *A History of Witchcraft* (London: Thames and Hudson, 1980), 148, 149, 157-159; Marcello Truzzi, "Witchcraft and Satanism," in *On the Margin of the Visible* (New York: John Wiley, 1974), 215; Truzzi, "The Occult Revival as Popular Culture," 22, 23; Margot Adler, *Drawing Down the Moon* (Boston: Beacon Press, 1979), 150-170; Gordon Fleming, "Black Magic Against White," in *Witchcraft Today* ed. Martin Ebon (New York: New American Library, 1971), 53-68.

18. James A. Pike, *The Other Side* (Garden City, NY: Doubleday, 1968); William Petersen, *Those Curious New Cults in the 80s* (New Canaan, CN: Keats Publishing, 1982), 53; John Kerr, *The Mystery and Magic of the Occult* (Philadelphia: Fortress Press, 1971), 102-105.

19. Richard H. Neff, *Psychic Phenomena and Religion* (Philadelphia: Westminster Press, 1971), 144, 145; Braswell, *Understanding Sectarian Groups*, 253; Morey Bernstein, *The Search for Bridley Murphy* (New York: Doubleday, 1956).

20. Rodney Stark and William Sims Bainbridge, *The Future of Religion* (Berkeley, CA: University of California Press, 1985), 197-199, 205; David M. Jacobs, "UFOs and Scientific Legitimacy," in *The Occult in America* eds. Howard Kerr and Charles L. Crow (Urbana, IL: University of Illinois Press, 1983), 218; Albanese, *America* (2nd ed.), 357. See also Irving Hexham, "Yoga, UFOs, and Cult Membership," *Update* 10, no. 3 (1986): 3-17; Robert W. Balch and David Taylor, "Seekers and Saucers," *American Behavioral Scientist* 40, no. 6 (1977): 839-861; Mark Albrecht and Brooks

Alexander, "UFOs: Is Science Fiction Coming True?" *SCP Journal* 1, no. 1 (1977): 12-23; Whitley Streiber, "UFO Cults are Flourishing in New Age Circles," *Christian Research Journal* 13, no. 1 (1990): 5, 6; Margaret Mead, "UFOs--Visitors From Outer Space?" *Redbook Magazine* September 1974, pp. 57-59.

21. Albanese, *America* (2nd ed.), 359; Catherine Albanese, *Nature Religion in America* (Chicago: University of Chicago Press, 1900), 153ff.

22. Robert Burrows, "The Coming of the New Age," in *The New Age Rage* ed. Karen Hoyt (Old Tappan, NJ: Revell, 1987), 29; Russell Chandler, *Understanding the New Age* (Waco, TX: Word, 1988), 49; Carlos Castaneda, *The Teachings of Don Juan* (Berkeley, CA: University of California Press, 1968).

23. Burrows, "The Coming of the New Age," 29; Kay Alexander, "Roots of the New Age," in *Perspectives on the New Age* eds. James Lewis and J. Gordon Melton (Albany, NY: State University of New York Press, 1992), 36-38. See also B. F. Skinner, *About Behaviorism* (New York: Alfred Knopf, 1974); B. F. Skinner, *The Behavior of Organisms* (New York: Appleton-Century, 1938); A. H. Maslow, *Toward a Psychology of Being* (Princeton, NJ: Van Nostrand, 1962); Carl R. Rogers, *On Becoming a Person* (Cambridge, MA: Riverside Press, 1961).

24. John Allan, *Shopping for a God* (Leicester, UK: InterVarsity Press, 1986), 96; Carl A. Raschke, "The Human Potential Movement," *Theology Today* 33, no. 3 (1976): 255, 256; Francis Adeney, "The Flowering of the Human Potential Movement," *SCP Journal* 5, no. 1 (Winter 1981-82): 11, 13; Fritjof Capra, *The Turning Point* (New York: Bantam Books, 1982), 364, 365. See also Frank G. Goble, *The Third Force* (New York: Grossman, 1970).

25. Quoted in Alexander, "Roots of the New Age," 42. See also A. H. Maslow, *The Farther Reaches of Human Nature* (New York: Penguin Books, 1971); Capra, *The Turning Point*, 365.

26. Ted Peters, *The Cosmic Self* (San Francisco: Harper San Francisco, 1991), 12-14; Alexander, "Roots of the New Age," 36-38; Capra, *The Turning Point*, 365.

27. Burrows, "The Coming of the New Age," 30; Allan, *Shopping for a God*, 96, 97.

28. Alexander, "Roots of the New Age," 44; Allan, *Shopping for a God*, 97, 98.

29. Paul C. Reisser, Teri K. Reisser and John Weldon, *New Age Medicine* (Downers Grove, IL: InterVarsity Press, 1987), 11; Paul C. Reisser, "Holistic Health," in *The New Age Rage*, 55-73; Capra, *The Turning Point*, 305-322.

30. Melton, *New Age Almanac*, 172; Brooks Alexander, "Holistic Health from the Inside," *SCP Journal* 2, no. 1 (1978): 6. See also Robert C. Fuller, *Alternative Medicine and American Religious Life* (New York:

Oxford University Press, 1989; Catherine L. Albanese, "Physic and Metaphysic in Nineteenth-Century America," *Church History* 55, no. 4 (1986): 489-502.

31. Melton, *New Age Almanac*, 35; J. Gordon Melton, "New Thought and the New Age," in *Perspectives on the New Age*, 20.

32. Melton, *New Age Almanac*, 381, 401. See also David Spangler, *Revelation: The Birth of a New Age* (San Francisco: The Rainbow Bridge, 1976).

33. Melton, "New Thought and the New Age," 18.

34. Melton, "New Thought and the New Age," 21.

35. James Bjornstad, "America's Spiritual, Sometimes Satanic, Smorgasbord," *Christianity Today* October 23, 1981, pp. 1377, 1378; Jorstad, *Holding Fast*, 170.

36. Jerry Adler, "The Graying of Aquarius," *Newsweek* March 30, 1987, pp. 56-58; Jorstad, *Holding Fast*, 170.

37. Jorstad, *Holding Fast*, 170, 171; Otto Friedrich, "New Age Harmonies," *Time* December 7, 1987, pp. 62-69.

38. Robert Bezilla, ed. *Religion in America 1992-1993* (Princeton, NJ: Princeton Research Center, 1993), 30-34; George Barna, *The Barna Report 1992-93* (Ventura, CA: Regal Books, 1992), 84-86.

39. J. Gordon Melton, "A History of the New Age Movement," in *Not Necessarily the New Age* ed. Robert Basil (Buffalo: Prometheus Books, 1988), 43, 44; Melton, *New Age Almanac*, 418. See also Tom Spain, "New Media for a New Age," *Publishers Weekly* September 25, 1987, pp. 60-61; Martin E. Marty, "An Old New Age in Publishing," *The Christian Century* November 18, 1987, p. 1019.

40. Jorstad, *Holding Fast*, 169, 170; Melton, *Cults in America*, 108; Melton, "A History of the New Age Movement," 36, 43.

41. Chandler, *Understanding the New Age*, 63; Melton, *Cults in America*, 108; Jorstad, *Holding Fast*, 169.

42. Melton, "A History of the New Age Movement," 44. See also Baba Ram Dass, *Be Here and Now* (Christobal, NM: Lama Foundation, 1972); Baba Ram Dass and Stephen Levine, *Grist for the Mill* (Castro Valley, CA: Unity Press, 1977); Baba Ram Dass and Daniel Goleman, *Journey of Awakening* (New York: Bantam, 1978); Baba Ram Dass, *Miracle of Love* (New York: Dutton, 1979).

43. Quoted in Melton, *New Age Almanac*, 53. See also Richard Smoley, "Pitfalls of a Course in Miracles," *Gnosis Magazine* (Fall 1987): 17-19; *A Course in Miracles* (Tiburon, CA: Foundation for Inner Peace, 1975).

44. Melton, *New Age Almanac*, 435. See David Spangler, *Revelation: The Birth of a New Age* (Middletown, WI: Lorean Press, 1976); David Spangler, *Reflections on the Christ* (Forres, Scotland: Findhorn Publications, 1978); David Spangler, *Emergence: The Rebirth of the Sacred* (New York: Dell Publishing Co., 1984).

45. Marilyn Ferguson, *The Aquarian Conspiracy* (Los Angeles: J. P. Tarcher, 1980); Chandler, *Understanding the New Age*, 56, 57.

46. See Mark Satin, *New Age Politics* (New York: Delta Books, 1978); Mark Satin, *New Options for America* (Fresno, CA: California State University Press, 1991).

47. Donald Keys, *Earth at Omega* (Boston: Branden Press, 1985); Douglas Groothuis, "Politics: Building an International Platform," in *The New Age Rage*, 93, 94.

48. Benjamin Creme, *The Reappearance of the Christ and the Masters of Wisdom* (Los Angeles: Tara Center, 1980); Benjamin Creme, *Messages from Maitreya the Christ* (London: Tara Center, 1980); Melton, *New Age Almanac*, 316.

49. Fritjof Capra, *The Tao of Physics* (Boston: Shambhala, 1991), 17, 18. See also Capra, *The Turning Point*; F. Capra and C. Spretnak, *Green Politics* (New York: Dutton, 1984); Fritjof Capra, *Uncommon Wisdom* (New York: Bantam Books, 1989).

50. Ken Wilbur, *The Atman Project* (Wheaton, IL: Theosophical Publishing House, 1980); Ken Wilber, *Up from Eden* (Garden City, NY: Anchor Press/Doubleday, 1981).

51. Shirley MacLaine, *Out on a Limb* (New York: Bantam Books, 1983); Shirley MacLaine, *Dancing in the Light* (New York: Bantam Books, 1985); Shirley MacLaine, *It's All in the Playing* (New York: Bantam Books, 1987); Jorstad, *Holding Fast*, 172, 173; Phyllis Battele, "Shirley MacLaine: An Interview That Will Amaze You," *Ladies Home Journal* June 1983, pp. 24-33; Nina Easton, "Shirley MacLaine's Mysticism for the Masses," *Los Angeles Times Magazine* September 6, 1987, pp. 5-10, 32.

52. Jorstad, *Holding Fast*, 173; Annetta Miller, "Corporate Mind Control," *Newsweek* May 4, 1987, pp. 38, 39.

53. Richard Watring, "New Age Training in Business: Mind Control in Upper Management?" *Eternity* February 1988, pp. 30-32; Jorstad, *Holding Fast*, 173; Robert Burrows, "Corporate Management Cautioned on New Age," *Eternity* February 1988, pp. 33, 34; Steve Rabey, "Karma for Cash: A New Age for Workers?" *Christianity Today* June 17, 1988, pp. 70-74.

54. Kenneth Woodward, *et al*, "Getting Your Head Together," *Newsweek* September 6, 1976, p. 58; Stanley Dokupil and Brooks Alexander, "Est: The Philosophy of Self-Worship," *SCP Journal* 5, no. 1 (Winter 1981-82):20; J. Yutaka Amando "Bad for Business," *Eternity* March 1986, pp. 55-57.

55. John Rudkin Clark, "Secular Salvation: Life Change Through 'est,'" *Christian Century* November 10, 1976, p. 982.

56. Mark Brewer, "We're Gonna Tear You Down and Put You Back Together," *Psychology Today* August 1975, p. 35; William Petersen, *Those Curious New Cults in the 80s* (New Canaan, CT: Keats Publishing, 1982),

206; Allan, *Shopping for a God*, 98; Peter Marin, "The New Narcissism," *Harper's* October 1975, pp. 46, 47.

57. Peterson, *Curious New Cults*, 207. See Donald Stone, "Social Consciousness in the Human Potential Movement," in *In Gods We Trust* eds. Thomas Robbins and Dick Anthony (New Brunswick, NJ: Transaction Books, 1981), 215, 227.

58. Dokupil, "Est," 20; John Weldon, "est," in *A Guide to Cults and New Religions* ed. Ron Enroth (Downers Grove, IL: InterVarsity Press, 1983), 76; Petersen, *Curious New Cults*, 206; Adam Smith, "Powers of the Mind, Part II: The est Experience," *New York Magazine* September 29, 1975, p. 35; Amano, "Bad for Business," 55.

59. Weldon, "est," 84; Brewer, "We're Gonna Tear You Down," 39; Petersen, *Curious New Cults*, 208; Tucker, *Another Gospel*, 368. For the quotation see Weldon, "est," 84.

60. Newport, *Christ and the New Consciousness*, 108-110; Kevin Garvey, "The Serpentine Serenity of Est," *Christianity Today* January 21, 1977, pp. 14, 15; Woodward, "Getting Your Head Together," 58; Brewer, "We're Gonna Tear You Down," 39, 40.

61. Chandler, *Understanding the New Age*, 73-75; Melton, *Cults in America*, 146-151.

62. Melton, *Cults in America*, 135-139; Russell and Norman B. Chandler, "Guru Ma-Leader of a Multimillion Dollar Church," *Los Angeles Times* February 11, 1980, pt. II, pp. 1, 3, 4, 5; "Weapons Arrests and 'Doomsday Talk' Shrouds Church Universal and Triumphant," *Christian Research Journal* 12, no. 3 (1990): 27.

63. Chandler, *Understanding the New Age*, 62; Melton, *Cults in America*, 137. See also Elizabeth Clare Prophet, *The Last Years of Jesus* (Livingston, MT: Summit University Press, 1987).

64. Tucker, *Another Gospel*, 310; Melton, *Cults in America*, 131; William Whalen, *Strange Gods* (Huntington, IN: Our Sunday Visitor), 62, 69.

65. Whalen, *Strange Gods*, 62, 69; Melton, *Cults in America*, 131.

66. Bryan Wilson, *Religious Sects* (New York: McGraw-Hill, 1970), 163; Brooks Alexander, "Scientology: Human Potential Bellweather," *SCP Journal* 5, no. 1 (Winter 1981-82): 27; Frank K. Flinn, "Scientology as Technological Buddhism," in *Alternatives to American Mainline Churches* ed. Joseph H. Fichter (Barrytown, NY: Unification Theological Seminary, 1983), 93, 103; Peter W. Williams, *Popular Religion in America* (Englewood Cliffs, NJ: Prentice-Hall, 1980), 218.

67. L. Ron Hubbard, *Dianetics* (Los Angeles: Bridge Publications, 1950), 51-78; Newport, *Christ and the New Consciousness*, 86, 87; Whalen, *Strange Gods*, 49, 50; Wilson, *Religious Sects*, 164.

68. Roy Wallis, *The Road to Total Freedom* (New York: Columbia University Press, 1977), 77-100; David G. Bromley and Anson D. Shupe,

Jr. *Strange Gods* (Boston: Beacon Press, 1981), 48; Wilson, *Religious Sects*, 163; "Scientology," *Newsweek* September 12, 1974, p. 84.

69. Neal Karlen and Pamela Abramson, "Bhagwan's Realm," *Newsweek* December 3, 1984, pp. 34-38; Julia Duin, "The Guru down the Road," *Christianity Today* April 23, 1982, pp. 38-40; Neal Karlen, "Busting the Bhagwan," *Newsweek* November 11, 1985, pp. 26-32; "Goodbye, Guru," *Newsweek* November 25, 1985, p. 50; Lewis F. Carter, "The 'New Renuciates' of the Bhagwan Shree Rajneesh," *Journal for the Scientific Study of Religion* 26, no. 2 (1987): 159-163.

70. Melton, *Cults in America*, 147.

71. Quoted from Eckart Ploether, "Bhajwan Shree Rajneesh," in *A Guide to Cults and New Religions*, 46, which in turn quoted from *Orange Juice*, a newsletter of the Rajneesh Meditation Center, San Francisco, September 1981.

72. Floether, "Bhagwan Shree Rajneesh," 46, 47.

73. Melton, *New Age Almanac*, 366.

74. Melton, *New Age Almanac*, 366; Melton, "A History of the New Age Movement," 45.

75. Melton, *New Age Almanac*, 172, 173, 366; Melton, "A History of the New Age Movement," 45. See also Leslie J. Kaslof, ed. *Wholistic Dimensions in Healing* (Garden City, NY: Doubleday, 1978).

76. Melton, *New Age Almanac*, 377, 378; Chandler, *Understanding the New Age*, 68-79. See also Earl D. C. Brewer, "A Religious Vision for the 21st Century," *Futurist* (July-August 1986): 14-18.

77. Melton, *New Age Almanac*, 285, 287; Chandler, *Understanding the New Age*, 113.

78. Melton, *New Age Almanac*, 55, 57, 69, 89, 106, 112, 131, 331.

Chapter 6: New Age Religious and Philosophical Assumptions

1. Douglas R. Groothuis, *Unmasking the New Age* (Downers Grove, IL: InterVarsity Press, 1986), 18.

2. Groothuis, *Unmasking the New Age*, 18.

3. Ted Peters, *The Cosmic Self* (San Francisco: Harper San Francisco, 1991), 54, 55.

4. Elliot Miller, *A Crash Course on the New Age Movement* (Grand Rapids: Baker, 1989), 207.

5. Gordon Melton, *Encyclopedic Handbook of Cults in America* (New York: Garland Publishing, 1986), 112, 113.

6. Peters, *Cosmic Self*, 57-90; Ted Peters, "Discerning the Spirits of the New Age," *The Christian Century* August 1988, pp. 763-766. In evaluating post-modern religion, Peters identifies the same themes. See Ted Peters, "Post-Modern Religion," *Update* 8, no. 1 (1984): 16-31.

7. Groothuis, *Unmasking the New Age*, 18-31. See also Douglas Groothuis, *Confronting the New Age* (Downers Grove, IL:InterVarsity Press, 1988), 20-32.

8. Miller, *A Crash Course on the New Age Movement*, 16, 17. See also Kerry D. McRoberts, *New Age or Old Lie?* (Peabody, MA: Hendrickson Publishers, 1989), 62, 63.

9. Ruth Tucker, *Another Gospel* (Grand Rapids: Zondervan Books, 1989), 335; Robert Burrows, "A Vision for a New Humanity," in *The New Age Rage* ed. Karen Hoyt (Old Tappan, NJ: Fleming H. Revell, 1987), 33.

10. Some examples include Marilyn Ferguson, *The Aquarian Conspiracy* (Los Angeles: J. P. Tarcher, 1980); Fritjof Capra, *The Turning Point* (New York: Bantam Books, 1982); Donald Keys, *Earth at Omega* (Boston: Branden Press, 1985); Frank Palmeri, "Apocalypse: Then and Now," *The Humanist* 43, no. 1 (1983): 26-28.

11. David Spangler, *Revelation: The Birth of a New Age* (Middletown, WI: Lorian Press, 1976); David Spangler, *Towards a Planetary Vision* 2nd ed (Forres, Scotland: Finhorn Publication, 1977); Benjamin Creme, *The Reappearance of the Christ and the Masters of Wisdom* (Los Angeles: Tara Center, 1980); George Trevelyan, *Vision of the Aquarian Age* (Walpole, NH: Stillpoint Publishing, 1984); Alice Bailey, *The Reappearance of the Christ* (New York: Lucis Publishing Co., 1979).

12. Catherine Albanese, *America: Religion and Religions* 2nd ed (Belmont, CA: Wadsworth, 1992), 363; Robert Burrows, "New Age Movment: Self-Deification in a Secular Culture," *SCP Newsletter* 10, no. 5 (1984-85): 4; Spangler, *Towards a Planetary Vision*, 119.

13. Barbara Hargrove, "New Religious Movements and the End of the Age," *The Iliff Review* (Spring 1982): 42-46; William Martin, "Waiting for the End," *The Atlantic Monthly* (June 1982): 34-36. For an excellent study of millennialism in America see Paul Boyer, *When Time Shall Be No More* (Cambridge, MA: Harvard University Press, 1992). See also Gary DeMar, *Last Days Madness* (Brentwood, TN: Wolgemuth and Hyatt, 1991).

14. Vishal Mangalwadi, *When the New Age Gets Old* (Downers Grove, IL: InterVarsity, 1992), 26, 27.

15. David Spangler, *Reflections on the Christ* (Findhorn, Scotland: Findhorn Publications, 1978), 11, 19. See also Spangler, *Revelation*; David Spangler, *Emergence: The Rebirth of the Sacred* (New York: Delta, 1984).

16. Capra, *The Turning Point*. See also Fritjof Capra, *The Tao of Physics* 3rd ed (Boston: Shambhala, 1991).

17. Thomas Kuhn, *The Structure of Scientific Revolutions* (Chicago: University of Chicago Press, 1962); Ferguson, *Aquarian Conspiracy*, 26; Miller, *A Crash Course on the New Age Movement*, 57.

18. Ferguson, *Aquarian Conspiracy*, 26-28.

19. Capra, *The Turning Point*, 53-74, 101-122; Robert J. L. Burrows, "Americans Get Religion in the New Age," *Christianity Today* May 16,

1986, pp. 18, 19. See also Capra, *Tao of Physics*; Michael Talbot, *Beyond the Quantum* (New York: Bantam Books, 1986); Paul Davies, *God and the New Physics* (New York: Simon and Schuster, 1983).

20. Many New Age sources promote these general views. Some examples include Capra, *The Turning Point*; Ferguson, *The Aquarian Conspiracy*; Spangler, *Emergence*.

21. Spangler, *Reflections on the Christ*, 4, 6-10, 40, 41; Creme, *Reappearance of the Christ*, 28, 46-48; Shirley MacLaine, *Out on a Limb* (New York: Bantam Books, 1983), 91. For an evangelical critique of the New Age view of Christ see Ron Rhodes, *The Counterfeit Christ of the New Age Movement* (Grand Rapids: Baker, 1990); Norman Geisler, "The New Age Movement," *Bibliotheca Sacra* 144, no. 573 (1987): 91, 92; Ron Rhodes, "The Christ of the New Age Movement," *Christian Research Journal* part one 12, no. 1 (1989): 9-14; part two 12, no. 2 (1989): 15-20; Ronald Rhodes, "The New Age Christology of David Spangler," *Bibliotheca Sacra* 144, no. 576 (1987): 402-418; Douglas Groothuis, "The Shamanized Jesus," *Christianity Today* April 29, 1991, pp. 20-23.

22. Spangler, *Reflections on the Christ*, 4-10; Trevelyan, *A Vision of the Aquarian Age*, 137; Rhodes, "The Christ of the New Age Movement," 12.

23. Gordon Melton, *New Age Almanac* (Detroit: Visible Ink Press, 1991), 10; Tucker, *Another Gospel*, 335. See also Alice Bailey, *The Externalization of the Hierarchy* (New York: Lucis, 1957); Jonathan Adolph, "What is New Age?" *The Guide to New Age Living* (1988): 9.

24. Creme, *Reappearance of Christ*, 31, 32, 55, 56; Melton, *New Age Almanac*, 316; Tucker, *Another Gospel*, 336, 337; Rhodes, "The Christ of the New Age Movement," 11, 12.

25. Bill Barol, "The End of the World (Again)," *Newsweek* August 17, 1987, pp. 70, 71; Martha Smilgis, "A New Age Dawning," *Time* August 31, 1987, p. 83; Tucker, *Another Gospel*, 335, 336.

26. See Hillel Schwartz, *Century's End* (New York: Doubleday, 1990); John Naisbitt and Patricia Aburdene, *Megatrends 2000* (New York: Wm. Morrow Co., 1990), 11-17; Richard Erdoes, *A.D. 1000: Living on the Brink of Apocalypse* (New York: Harper and Row, 1988), viii-xi; Kenneth A. Myers, "Fear and Frenzy on the Eve of A.D. 2000," *Genesis* 3, no. 1 (1990): 1, 3; Curt Suplee, "Apocalypse Now," *Washington Post* December 17, 1989, pp. 131, 132.

27. Peter Russell, *The Global Brain* (Los Angeles: J. P. Tarcher, 1983), 98-100; Capra, *The Turning Point*, 286-288; Ted Peters, "Discerning the Spirits of the New Age," 764; Peters, *Cosmic Self*, 75.

28. Quotes from Miller, *Crash Course on the New Age Movement*, 53, 65. See also Capra, *The Turning Point*, 286-288.

29. Ferguson, *Aquarian Conspiracy*, 68, 71, 72.

30. Gordon Melton, "A History of the New Age Movement," in *Not Necessarily the New Age* ed. Robert Basil (Buffalo: Prometheus Books, 1988), 46; Melton, *Cults in America*, 113.

31. Ferguson, *Aquarian Conspiracy*, 85-89. See also Richard Blow, "Moronic Convergence," *New Republic* January 25, 1988, p. 24; John W. Cooper, "Testing the Spirit of the Age of Aquarius: The New Age Movement," *Calvin Theological Journal* 22, no. 2 (1987): 300; Joseph M. Hopkins, "Experts on Nontraditional Religions Try to Pin Down the New Age Movement," *Christianity Today* May 17, 1985, p. 68; Russell, *Global Brain*, 173, 174.

32. Ferguson, *Aquarian Conspiracy*, 103, 107.

33. Willis Harmon, *An Incomplete Guide to the Future* (San Francisco: San Francisco Book Company, 1976), 104; Barbara Marx Hubbard, *The Hunger of Eve* (Harrisburg, PA: Stackpole Books, 1976) 54 ff. See also Peters, "Post Modern Religion," 21.

34. Gary Zukav, *The Seat of the Soul* (New York: Simon and Schuster, 1989), 204.

35. Peters, *Cosmic Self*, 80; Groothuis, *Unmasking the New Age*, 21; Burrows, "New Age Movement," 6.

36. Theodore Roszak, *Unfinished Animal* (New York: Harper and Row, 1975), 225.

37. Burrows, "New Age Movement," 7.

38. Ferguson, *Aquarian Conspiracy*, 116, 117.

39. Trevelyan, *A Vision of the Aquarian Age*, 76.

40. Adolph, "What is New Age?" 10. See also M. Scott Peck, "A New American Revolution," *New Age Journal* (May/June 1987): 50.

41. Keys, *Earth at Omega*, 159.

42. Melton, *Cults in America*, 114. See also Mark Satin, *New Options for America* (Fresno, CA: The Press at California State University Press, 1991); Benjamin Ferencz and Ken Keyes, Jr., *Planethood* (Coos Bay, OR: Love Lane Books, 1991); Keys, *Earth at Omega*.

43. Peters, *Cosmic Self*, 77, 78; Spangler, *Emergence*, 96. See also Russell, *Global Brain*, 193-198.

44. Keys, *Earth at Omega*, iv.

45. Pierre Teilhard de Chardin, *The Phenomenon of Man* (New York: Harper and Row, 1961), 30, 181, 182, 251, 258, 259. A number of key New Age spokespersons regard Pierre Teilhard de Chardin as their forerunner. See Ferguson, *Aquarian Conspiracy*; Capra, *The Turning Point*; Keys, *Earth at Omega*.

46. Spangler, *Emergence*, 43-45; Tod Connor, "Is the Earth Alive?" *Christianity Today* January 11, 1993, pp. 22-25; Miller, *A Crash Course on the New Age Movement*, 71; Harold Gilliam, "Deep ecology vs. environmentalism," *Utne Reader* (October/November 1985): 68; Roszak, *Person Planet*, 38-45.

47. For a discussion of the parallels between the New Age and fundamentalism see Catherine Albanese, "Religion and the American Experience: A Century After," *Church History* 57, no. 3 (1988): 349, 350.

48. A number of sources present these general ideas. See Burrows, "New Age Movement," 6; Peters, "Discerning the Spirits of the New Age," 765; Peters, "Post-Modern Religion," 24, 25; Groothuis, *Unmasking the New Age*, 25, 26.

49. Peters, "Post-Modern Religion," 24; Peters, *Cosmic Self*, 81.

50. Elaine Pagels, *The Gnostic Gospels* (New York: Random House, 1981), xvii ff; Peters, *Cosmic Self*, 81; Peters, "Post-Modern Religion," 23.

51. Ferguson, *Aquarian Conspiracy*, 371, 372.

52. See Harold Bloom, *The American Religion* (New York: Simon and Schuster, 1992); Philip Lee, *Against the Protestant Gnostics* (New York: Oxford University Press, 1987); Christopher Lasch, "The Infantile Illusion of Omnipotence and the Modern Ideology of Science," *New Oxford Review* (October 1986): 18; Andrew Greeley, "Religion's Oldest Scoop," *Psychology Today* (April 13, 1980): 86-94.

53. Carl A. Raschke, *The Interruption of Eternity* (Chicago: Nelson-Hall, 1980), xi.

54. Peters, "Post-Modern Religion," 17; Peters, *Cosmic Self*, 56.

55. Fr. Stephen Fuchs, "The New Age Movement," *Areopagus* 4, no. 3 (1991): 6, 7.

56. Burrows, "New Age Movement," 6.

57. Quoted from John Weldon, "est," in *A Guide to Cults and New Religions* ed. Ron Enroth (Downers Grove, IL: InterVarsity Press, 1983), 84.

58. Capra, *The Turning Point*, 293, 294; Maxine Negri, "Age-old Problems of the New Age Movement," *Humanist* (March/April 1988): 24; Ferguson, *Aquarian Conspiracy*, 295-300. Michael S. Gazzaniga, "The Social Brain," *Psychology Today* (May 1985): 38; Jerry Levy, "Right Brain, Left Brain: Fact and Fiction," *Psychology Today* (May 1985): 43, 44; Herbert Benson and William Proctor, "Your Maximum Mind," *New Age Journal* (November/December, 1987): 19-23, 75-77.

59. Melton, *Cults in America*, 114.

60. Robert Burrows, "Americans Get Religion in the New Age," *Christianity Today* May 16, 1986, p. 18; Groothuis, *Unmasking the New Age*, 18, 19; Negri, "Age-old Problems of the New Age Movement," 23, 24.

61. Trevelyan, *A Vision of the Aquarian Age*, 7.

62. Capra, *The Turning Point*, 371.

63. Ferguson, *Aquarian Conspiracy*, 371, 372.

64. Spangler, *Towards a Planetary Vision*, xi.

65. Burrows, "New Age Movement," 5, 6. See also Creme, *The Reappearance of Christ*, 111.

66. Groothuis, *Unmasking the New Age*, 20.

67. Creme, *The Reappearance of the Christ*, 111, 115.

68. Spangler, *Reflections on the Christ*, 81, 82.

69. Bob Hunter, "Ecology as Religion," *Greenpeace Chronicles* (August 1979): 3.

70. Gilliam, "Deep ecology vs. environmentalism," 66, 67. See also Capra, *The Turning Point*, 412; William Anderson, *Green Man* (San Francisco: Harper Collins, 1990).

71. Creme, *The Reappearance of the Christ*, 25, 119. See also Mark and Elizabeth Prophet, *Climb the Highest Mountain* (Los Angeles: Summit University Press, 1974); 228.

72. Spangler, *Towards a Planetary Vision*, 86, 87; Spangler, *Reflections on the Christ*, 10.

73. Peters, *Cosmic Self*, 86.

74. Creme, *Reflections on the Christ*, 134.

75. McLaine, *Out on a Limb*, 347.

76. Peters, *Cosmic Self*, 69. See also Eric Butterworth, *Discover the Power Within You* (San Francisco: Harper and Row, 1989).

77. Peters, "Discerning the Spirits of the New Age," 764; Peters, *Cosmic Self*, 58.

78. Diogenes Allen, "The End of the Modern World: A New Openness for Faith," *Princeton Seminary Bulletin* 11, no. 1 (1990): 12, 13; Os Guinness, *The American Hour* (New York: Free Press, 1993), 69; Peters, "Discerning the Spirits of the New Age," 764.

79. Alvin Toffler, *The Third Wave* (New York: Bantam Books, 1980), 300-302.

80. Capra, *The Turning Point*, 59. See also Theodore Roszak, *Where the Wasteland Ends* (Garden City, NY: Doubleday 1972), 242-25.

81. Capra, *The Turning Point*, 59, 367, 368, 389. See also Toffler, *The Third Wave*, 301, 302; Capra, *Tao of Physics*, 130, 131; Paul Davis, *God and the New Physics* (New York: Simon and Schuster, 1983), 58-71.

82. Otto Friedrich, "New Age Harmonies," *Time* December 7, 1987, p. 69.

83. Toffler, *The Third Wave*, 302.

84. Michael Talbot, *Beyond the Quantum* (New York: Bantam Books, 1985), 4, 12; Miller, *A Crash Course on the New Age Movement*, 39.

85. Ferguson, *Aquarian Conspiracy*, 170-176. Quoted from Miller, *A Crash Course on the New Age Movement*, 39; Talbot, *Beyond the Quantum*, 4, 12.

86. Melton, *Cults in America*, 116.

87. Paul Edwards, "The Case Against Karma and Reincarnation," in *Not Necessarily the New Age* ed. Robert Basil (Buffalo: Prometheus Books, 1988), 87-89.

88. Gordon Melton, "How New Is New? The Flowering of the 'New' Religious Consciousness since 1965," in *The Future of New Religious*

Movements eds. David G. Bromley and Phillip E. Hammond (Macon, GA: Mercer University Press, 1987), 54; Peters, *Cosmic Self*, 72; Mark Albrecht, "Reincarnation and the Early Church," *Update* 7, no. 2 (1983): 34.

89. Norman L. Geisler and Yutaka Amano, *The Reincarnation Sensation* (Wheaton, IL: Tyndale, 1986), 8-14.

90. Peters, "Post-Modern Religion," 21; Peters, *Cosmic Self*, 74.

91. Melton, *Cults in America*, 113, 114; Melton, *New Age Almanac*, 89.

Chapter 7: Science and Education in the New Age

1. Theodore Roszak, *Unfinished Animal* (New York: Harper and Row, 1975), 153-156; Michael Talbot, *Beyond the Quantum* (New York: Bantam Books, 1988), 89, 90; Ted Peters, *The Cosmic Self* (San Francisco: Harper San Francisco, 1991), 133, 134.

2. Marilyn Ferguson, *The Aquarian Conspiracy* (Los Angeles: J. P. Tarcher, 1980), 146, 147.

3. Fritjof Capra, *The Turning Point* (New York: Bantam Books, 1982), 53 ff., 123 ff., 188 ff.

4. Peters, *Cosmic Self*, 133, 134.

5. Fritjof Capra, *The Tao of Physics* 3rd ed. (Boston: Shambhala, 1991), 20.

6. Capra, *Tao of Physics*, 21, 22. See also Gordon Leff, *The Dissolution of the Medieval Outlook* (New York: Harper and Row, 1976); William R. Cook and Ronald B. Herzman, *The Medieval World View* (New York: Oxford University Press, 1983); David Knowles, *The Evolution of Medieval Thought* (New York: Vintage Books, 1962).

7. See Keith Thomas, *Religion and the Decline of Magic* (New York: Scribner's Sons, 1971); Peter Burke, *Popular Culture in Early Modern Europe* (New York: Harper and Row, 1978).

8. Quote from Capra, *Tao of Physics*, 22, 23. Peters, *Cosmic Self*, 136, 137; A. R. Hall, *The Scientific Revolution 1500-1800* 2nd ed. (Boston: Beacon Press, 1962), 177-184; Herbert Butterfield, *The Origins of Modern Science* rev. ed. (New York: Free Press, 1957), 122-128; W. Warren Wagar, *World Views: A Study in Comparative History* (Hillsdale, IL: Dryden Press, 1977), 15-51.

9. Capra, *The Turning Point*, 63, 64; Alan G. R. Smith, *Science and Society* (London: Harcourt, Brace Jovanovich, 1972), 123-134; Hall, *The Scientific Revolution 1500-1800*, 244-276; Butterfield, *The Origins of Modern Science*, 164-170.

10. Alvin Toffler, *The Third Wave* (New York: Bantam Books, 1982), 10, 36.

11. Capra, *Tao of Physics*, 164 ff.; Douglas Groothuis, *Unmasking the New Age* (Downers Grove, IL: InterVarsity Press, 1986), 94; Dean C. Halverson, "Science: Quantum Physics," in *The New Age Rage* ed. Karen Hoyt (Old Tappan, NJ: Fleming Revell, 1987), 74, 75; Nathan Spielberg

and Bryon D. Anderson, *Seven Ideas that Shook the Universe* (New York: John Wiley, 1985), 193-214.

12. Quote from Halverson, "Science: Quantum Physics," 75. Capra, *The Turning Point*, 75-77; Groothuis, *Unmasking the New Age* 95; Vishal Mangalwadi, *When the New Age Gets Old* (Downers Grove, IL: InterVarsity Press, 1992), 247, 249; Spielberg and Anderson, *Seven Ideas that Shook the Universe*, 220-237.

13. Talbot, *Beyond the Quantum*, 21, 22; Groothuis, *Unmasking the New Age*, 95; Capra, *Tao of Physics*, 67.

14. Halverson, "Science: Quantum Physics and Quantum Leaps," 76; Capra, *Tao of Physics*, 132, 133; Paul Davies, *Other Worlds* (New York: Simon and Schuster, 1980), 75; Spielberg and Anderson, *Seven Ideas that Shook the Universe*, 237-240.

15. Werner Heisenberg, *Physics and Philosophy* (New York: Harper Brothers, 1958); Halverson, "Science: Quantum Physics and Quantum Leaps," 77; Groothuis, *Unmasking the New Age*, 96; Capra, *Tao of Physics*, 132, 133; Talbot, *Beyond the Quantum*, 17, 18; Spielberg and Anderson, *Seven Ideas that Shook the Universe*, 251-256.

16. Capra, *Tao of Physics*, 61, 62.

17. Halverson, "Science: Quantum Physics and Quantum Leaps," 77, 78.

18. Capra, *The Turning Point*, 95, 96; Talbot, *Beyond the Quantum*, 40-54; Halverson, "Science: Quantum Physics and Quantum Leaps," 83.

19. Peters, *Cosmic Self*, 142-145. See also Talbot, *Beyond the Quantum*, 40-56, 67, 68, 163, 164; Capra, *The Turning Point*, 95, 96; Ted Peters, "David Bohm, Post-Modernism, and the Divine," *Zygon* 20 (June 1985): 193-217; René Weber, "The Enfolding-Unfolding Universe: A Conversation with David Bohm," in *Holographic Paradigm* ed. Ken Wilber (Boulder, CO: Shambhala, 1982); Arthur Koestler, *Janus* (New York: Random House, 1978).

20. Groothuis, *Unmasking the New Age*, 96; Mangalwadi, *When the New Age Gets Old*, 262.

21. Peters, *Cosmic Self*, 133.

22. Ferguson, *Aquarian Conspiracy*, 152.

23. Paul Davies, *God and the New Physics* (New York: Simon and Schuster, 1983), 5.

24. Capra, *Tao of Physics* 19, 20.

25. Gary Zukav, *The Dancing Wu Li Masters* (New York: Morrow, 1979), 26.

26. Capra, *Tao of Physics*, 17, 18, 24, 25.

27. Capra, *Tao of Physics*, 31.

28. Capra, *The Turning Point*, 412.

29. Michael Talbot, *Mysticism and the New Physics* (New York: Bantam Books, 1981), 4, 5.

30. Ferguson, *Aquarian Conspiracy*, 167-187.

31. Quoted from Elliot Miller, *A Crash Course on the New Age Movement* (Grand Rapids: Baker Book House, 1989), 40.

32. Quoted in Miller, *A Crash Course on the New Age Movement*, 43.

33. Talbot, *Mysticism and the New Physics*, 54, 152.

34. Shirley MacLaine, *Going Within* (New York: Bantam Books, 1990), 45, 46.

35. Fred Alan Wolf, *Taking the Quantum Leap* (San Francisco: Harper and Row, 1981), 63.

36. Talbot, *Mysticism and the New Physics*, 152.

37. Capra, *The Turning Point*, 87.

38. Halverson, "Science: Quantum Physics and Quantum Leaps," 75, 76; Mangalwadi, *When the New Age Gets Old*, 7.

39. Groothuis, *Unmasking the New Age*, 93, 94; Halverson, "Science: Quantum Physics and Quantum Leaps," 85, 86.

40. Davies, *God and the New Physics*, ix.

41. Ferguson, *Aquarian Conspiracy*, 172.

42. P. A. Schlipp (ed.) *Albert Einstein: Philosopher Scientist* (Evanston, IL: The Library of Living Philosophers, 1949), 248.

43. Richard H. Bube, "Science and Pseudoscience," *The Reformed Journal* (November 1982): 11.

44. Ferguson, *Aquarian Conspiracy*, 156.

45. Davies, *God and the New Physics*, 61.

46. Capra, *Tao of Physics*, 130, 290; Capra, *The Turning Point*, 80, 81.

47. Groothuis, *Unmasking the New Age*, 99.

48. Ferguson, *Aquarian Conspiracy*, 177, 182.

49. Jonathan Adolph, "What is New Age?" *The Guide to New Age Living* (1988):6.

50. Mangalwadi, *When the New Age Gets Old*, 139.

51. Theodore Roszak, *Where the Wasteland Ends* (Garden City, NY: Anchor Books, 1972), 101, 102, 108, 109, 116-124. In particular, John Calvin, John Knox, and the subsequent Puritan tradition vociferously condemned anything resembling idolatry. See Carlos M. Eire, *War Against the Idols* (Cambridge: Cambridge University Press, 1986); Richard Kyle, *The Mind of John Knox* (Lawrence, KS: Coronado Press, 1984); Richard Kyle, "John Knox and the Purification of Religion: The Intellectual Aspects of His Crusade Against Idolatry," *Archiv für Reformationsgeschichte* 77 (1986): 265-280.

52. Roszak, *Where the Wasteland Ends*, 215, 217.

53. As mentioned in earlier chapters, many New Age spokespersons note this theme.   See Capra, *The Turning Point*; Roszak, *Where the Wasteland Ends*; Talbot, *Beyond the Quantum*; Davies, *God and the New Physics*; Toffler, *The Third Wave*.

54. Roszak, *Where the Wasteland Ends*, 114.

55. Mangalwadi, *When the New Age Gets Old*, 131; David Icke, *The Truth Vibrations* (London: The Aquarian Press, 1991), 133.

56. Roszak, *Where The Wasteland Ends*, 216.

57. Capra, *The Turning Point*, 235, 242.

58. Such a position is common in many New Age sources. See Ferguson, *Aquarian Conspiracy*, 405 ff.; David Spangler, *Emergence: The Rebirth of the Sacred* (New York: Dell Publishing), 41 ff.; Capra, *The Turning Point*, 224 ff.; George Trevelyan, *A Vision of the Aquarian Age* (Walpole, NH: Stillpoint Publishing, 1984), 114. See also Groothuis, *Unmasking the New Age*, 48.

59. Capra, *The Turning Point*, 411, 412.

60. Capra, *The Turning Point*, 412; Spangler, *Emergence*, 41, 42; Bob Hunter, "Ecology as Religion," *Greenpeace Chronicles* (August 1979): 3; Peter Russell, *The Global Brain* (Los Angeles: J. P. Tarcher, 1983), 128, 129; William Anderson, *Green Men* (London: Harper Collins, 1990).

61. Capra, *The Turning Point*, 412. For a focus on deep ecology in Western history see Anderson, *Green Men*. See also Ronald J. Sider, "Green Politics: Biblical or Buddhist?" *SCP Newsletter* (Fall 1985): 7-11.

62. Capra, *The Turning Point*, 284; Spangler, *Emergence*, 43-45; Tod Connor, "Is the Earth Alive?" *Christianity Today* January 11, 1993, pp. 22-25; Harold Gilliam, "Deep ecology vs. environmentalism," *Utne Reader* (October/November 1985):68.

63. Russell, *The Global Brain*, 23, 24.

64. Theodore Roszak, *Person/Planet* (Garden City: Anchor Press, 1979), 38, 39; Mangalwadi, *When the New Age Gets Old*, 132, 133; Margot Adler, *Drawing Down the Moon* (Boston: Beacon Press, 1979).

65. Russell, *The Global Brain*, 206, 207.

66. Toffler, *The Third Wave*, 256, 346, 347.

67. Capra, *The Turning Point*, 409.

68. Ferguson, *Aquarian Conspiracy*, 289, 290. See also Mark Satin, *New Age Politics* (New York: Delta Books, 1978), 126, 250.

69. Ferguson, *Aquarian Conspiracy*, 290, 291.

70. Ferguson, *Aquarian Conspiracy*, 290, 291.

71. Ferguson, *Aquarian Conspiracy*, 287, 288, 291, 292. See also Satin, *New Age Politics*, 251.

72. Ferguson, *Aquarian Conspiracy*, 281.

73. Gordon Melton, *New Age Almanac* (Detroit: Visible Ink Press, 1991), 384, 385.

74. Melton, *New Age Almanac*, 386.

75. Mark Satin, *New Options for America* (Fresno, CA: The Press at California State University, 1991), 119, 120.

76. Groothuis, *Unmasking the New Age*, 124; Douglas R. Groothuis, "Politics: Building on International Platform," in *New Age Rage*, 100.

77. Francis Adeney, "Educators Look East," *Spiritual Counterfeits Journal* 5, no. 1 (Winter 1981): 28; Russell Chandler, *Understanding the New Age* (Waco, TX: Word Books, 1988), 154, 155.

78. Adeney, "Educators Look East," 29.

Chapter 8: The New Age Reaches Out: Politics and Economics

1. Marilyn Ferguson, *The Aquarian Conspiracy* (Los Angeles: J. P. Tarcher, 1980), 191.

2. These general ideas can be found in a number of New Age sources. See Alvin Toffler, *The Third Wave* (New York: Bantam Books, 1980); Donald Keys, *Earth at Omega* (Boston: Branden Publishing, 1985); Mark Satin, *New Options for America* (Fresno, CA: The Press at California State University, Fresno, 1991).

3. Elliot Miller, *A Crash Course on the New Age Movement* (Grand Rapids: Baker Book House, 1989), 107, 108; Gordon Melton, *New Age Almanac* (Detroit: Visible Ink Press, 1991), 427, 428.

4. Melton, *New Age Almanac*, 428.

5. Ferguson, *Aquarian Conspiracy*, 228, 229.

6. Quote from Miller, *A Crash Course on the New Age Movement*, 111.

7. Fritjof Capra and Charlene Spretnak, *Green Politics* (New York: Dutton, 1984), xix, xx. See also Fritjof Capra and Charlene Spretnak, "Who are the Greens?" *New Age Journal* (April 1984): 90-96.

8. Mark Satin, *New Age Politics* (New York: Delta Books, 1978), 8.

9. Satin, *New Age Politics*, 235; Ferguson, *Aquarian Conspiracy*, 211.

10. Douglas Groothuis, *Unmasking the New Age* (Downers Grove, IL: InterVarsity Press, 1986), 112; Miller, *A Crash Course on the New Age Movement*, 112.

11. Groothuis, *Unmasking the New Age*, 112, 113. See also Milton Viorst, *Fire in the Streets* (New York: Simon and Schuster, 1979); Allen J. Matusow, *The Unraveling of America* (New York: Harper and Row, 1984), 275-344; Morris Dickstein, *Gates of Eden* (New York: Basic Books, 1977); Peter Clecak, "Culture and Politics in the Sixties," *Dissent* 24 (Fall 1977), 439-443.

12. Groothuis, *Unmasking the New Age*, 112, 113; Jerry Rubin, *Growing (Up) at Thirty-Seven* (New York: M. Evans, 1976), 208.

13. Such general ideas can be found in a number of New Age sources. See Satin, *New Age Politics*, 239 ff.; Satin, *New Options for America*; Benjamin Ferencz and Ken Keyes, Jr. *Planethood* (Coos Bay, OR: Love Line Books, 1991).

14. Satin, *New Age Politics*, 55, 60, 61, 246.

15. Ferencz and Keyes, *Planethood*, xviii, xix, 137; Miller, *A Crash Course on the New Age Movement*, 108, 112; Russell Chandler, *Understanding the New Age* (Dallas: Word Publishing, 1988), 195.

250   *The New Age Movement in American Culture*

16. M. Scott Peck, "A New American Revolution," *New Age Journal* (May/June 1987): 52, 53; Satin, *New Options for America*, 14, 15; Groothuis, *Unmasking the New Age*, 122; Miller, *A Crash Course on the New Age Movement*, 108; Steven D. Stark, "Clinton reflects the feminization of politics," *Wichita Eagle* May 8, 1993, p. 9A. For quote see Ferguson, *Aquarian Conspiracy*, 231.

17. Donald Keys, *Earth at Omega* (Boston: Branden Publishing, 1982), 127, 128.

18. Satin, *New Options for America*, 202, 203.

19. Ferguson, *Aquarian Conspiracy*, 210, 212; Satin, *New Age Politics*, 22, 32, 104, 137, 143, 188.

20. Ferguson, *Aquarian Conspiracy*, 210-212.

21. Satin, *New Age Politics*, 236-238; Satin, *New Options for America*, 66-68.

22. Satin, *New Age Politics*, 246-250.

23. Satin, *New Age Politics*, 250-255.

24. Satin, *New Age Politics*, 20; Melton, *New Age Almanac*, 427.

25. Douglas Groothuis, "Politics: Building An International Platform," in *The New Age Rage* (Old Tappan, NJ: Fleming Revell, 1987), 91, 92.

26. Capra and Spretnak, *Green Politics*, 33; Fritjof Capra, *The Turning Point* (New York: Bantam Books, 1982), 41, 47, 412, 413; Satin, *New Age Politics*, 242, 243.

27. Groothuis, *Unmasking the New Age*, 116, 117; Miller, *A Crash Course on the New Age Movement*, 118. While they may not always connect religion and politics, a wide range of New Age sources articulate the theme of global unity. See Ferencz and Keyes, *Planethood*; Satin, *New Age Politics*; Keys, *Earth at Omega*.

28. Charlene Spretnak, "Introduction," in *The Politics of Women's Spirituality* ed. Charlene Spretnak (Garden City, NY: Doubleday, 1982), xviii, xxiii.

29. Ferguson, *Aquarian Conspiracy*, 226.

30. Some examples include Satin, *New Options for America*; Keys, *Earth at Omega*; Ferguson, *Aquarian Conspiracy*.

31. Ferguson, *Aquarian Conspiracy*, 190.

32. David Spangler, *Reflections on the Christ* (Findhorn, Scotland: Findhorn Publications, 1977), 36-40.

33. Benjamin Creme, *The Reappearance of the Christ and the Masters of Wisdom* (North Hollywood, CA: Tara Center, 1980), 164, 165; Groothuis, "Politics: Building an International Platform," 95.

34. Groothuis, "Politics: Building an International Platform," 102, 103; Robert Ellwood, Jr., *Religious and Spiritual Groups in Modern America* (Englewood Cliffs, NJ: Prentice Hall, 1973), 78, 79.

35. H. G. Wells is an example of a proponent of a world state. See Miller, *A Crash Course on the New Age Movement*, 115; W. Warren Wagar,

H. G. Wells and the World State (New Haven, CN: Yale University Press, 1961).

36. Satin, *New Age Politics*, 148, 149; Melton, *New Age Almanac*, 425.

37. Groothuis, *Unmasking the New Age*, 117; Groothuis, "Politics: Building an International Platform," 96.

38. Ferguson, *Aquarian Conspiracy*, 191.

39. Capra and Spretnak, "Who Are the Greens?" 34; Capra and Spretnak, *Green Politics*.

40. Capra, *The Turning Point*, 234, 262.

41. Keys, *Earth at Omega*, 4.

42. Ferencz and Keyes, *Planethood*, xiv, xv.

43. Miller, *A Crash Course on the New Age Movement*, 118.

44. Ferencz and Keyes, *Planethood*, xvi.

45. Satin, *New Age Politics*, 149.

46. Alvin Toffler, *The Third Wave* (New York: Bantam Books, 1981), 437.

47. Satin, *New Age Politics*, 35.

48. Satin, *New Age Politics*, 34, 35, 146, 159, 150.

49. Ferguson, *Aquarian Conspiracy*, 196.

50. Toffler, *The Third Wave*, 434.

51. Robert Muller, *New Genesis* (Garden City, NY: Doubleday, 1982), 37, 134.

52. Muller, *New Genesis*, 45, 46, 122.

53. Keys, *Earth at Omega* iv, vi, 14-19, 21.

54. Ferencz and Keyes, *Planethood*, 28, 29.

55. Ferencz and Keyes, *Planethood* 26-28.

56. Ferencz and Keyes, *Planethood*, 31.

57. Creme, *The Reappearance of the Christ*, 168, 169. See also Alexander King and Bertrand Schneider, *The First Global Revelation* (New York: Pantheon Books, 1991).

58. Creme, *The Reappearance of the Christ*, 170, 171.

59. Satin, *New Age Politics*, 188-191.

60. Satin, *New Age Politics*, 192, 193.

61. Keyes, *Earth at Omega*, 114, 115.

62. Creme, *The Reappearance of the Christ*, 172, 173; Leonard Orr and Sondra Ray, *Rebirthing in the New Age* (Berkeley, CA: Celestial Arts, 1983), 220.

63. Toffler, *The Third Wave*, 417, 421.

64. Toffler, *The Third Wave*, 427-431.

65. Toffler, *The Third Wave*, 431-434.

66. Keys, *Earth at Omega*, 133-138; Melton, *New Age Almanac*, 426; Groothuis, *Unmasking the New Age*, 118.

67. Melton, *New Age Almanac*, 422. See Capra and Spretnak, *Green Politics*, 3-81; Capra and Spretnak, "Who Are the Greens?" 34-94; Ronald

J. Sider, "Green Politics: Biblical or Buddhist?" *SCP Newsletter* 11, no. 3 (1985): 7-11.

68. Melton, *New Age Almanac*, 422, 423; Capra and Spretnak, *Green Politics*, 193-236; Capra and Spretnak, "Who Are the Greens?" 40.

69. Groothuis, "Politics: Building an International Platform," 95.

70. Melton, *New Age Almanac*, 423; Richard Blow, "Moronic Convergence," *New Republic* January 25, 1988, p. 27.

71. Miller, *A Crash Course on the New Age Movement*, 125, 126.

72. Toffler, *The Third Wave*, 392,-415.

73. Keys, *Earth at Omega*, 128, 129.

74. Satin, *New Options for America*, 182-185.

75. Ferencz and Keyes, *Planethood*, xi, 6.

76. Ferencz and Keyes, *Planethood*, xix, 34.

77. Satin, *New Age Politics*, 159.

78. Satin, *New Age Politics*, 159.

79. Capra, *The Turning Point*, 188, 189, 195-197.

80. Ferguson, *Aquarian Conspiracy*, 325.

81. Ferguson, *Aquarian Conspiracy*, 337, 340; Jonathan Adolph, "What is New Age?" *The Guide to New Age Living* (1988): 6.

82. Satin, *New Age Politics*, 159.

83. Ferguson, *Aquarian Conspiracy*, 343-345.

84. Capra, *The Turning Point*, 222-229; Satin, *New Age Politics*, 159. See also Carl Raschke, "New Age Economics," in *Not Necessarily New Age* ed. Robert Basil (Buffalo: Prometheus Books, 1988), 334.

85. Melton, *New Age Almanac*, 378.

86. Theodore Roszak, *Person/Planet* (New York: Anchor Books, 1979), 33.

87. Toffler, *The Third Wave*, 194-196; Satin, *New Age Politics*, 162, 163; Ferguson, *Aquarian Conspiracy*, 330.

88. Capra and Spretnak, *Green Politics*, 85, 86.

89. Satin, *New Age Politics*, 165, 166.

90. Ferguson, *Aquarian Conspiracy*, 331-338.

91. Ferguson, *Aquarian Conspiracy*, 350-352; Robert Burrows, "Corporate Management Cautioned on the New Age," *Eternity* February 1988, p. 33.

92. Annetta Miller, "Corporate Mind Control, " *Newsweek* May 4, 1987, p. 38; Burrows, "Corporate Management Cautioned on New Age," 33; Ron Zemke, "What's New in the New Age," *Training Magazine* (September 1987): 28, 29.

93. Burrows, "Corporate Management Cautioned on New Age," 33; Steve Rabey, "Karma for Cash: A 'New Age' for Workers?" *Christianity Today* June 17, 1988, p. 71; J. Yutaka Amano, "Bad for Business," *Eternity* March, 1986, pp. 55-57; Glenn A. Rupert, "Employing the New Age:

Training Seminars," in *Perspectives on the New Age* eds. James R. Lewis and J. Gordon Melton (Albany, NY: State University of New York Press, 1992), 127, 135.

94. Miller, "Corporate Mind Control, " 38; Rabey, "Karma for Cash: A New Age for Workers," 71, 74; Richard Watring, "New Age Training in Business: Mind Control in Upper Management?" *Eternity* February, 1988, p. 30.

95. John Naisbitt and Patricia Aburdene, *Megatrends 2000* (New York: Wm. Morrow Co., 1990), 14, 15, 298-301.

96. Toffler, *The Third Wave*, 139.

97. Toffler, *The Third Wave*, 194.

98. Alvin Toffler, *Powershift* (New York: Bantam Books, 1990); Alvin Toffler, "Powershift," *Newsweek* October 15, 1990, p. 86; Toffler, *The Third Wave*, 181-185.

99. Toffler, "Powershift," 86, 87; Toffler, *The Third Wave*, 187.

Chapter 9: The New Age Turns Inward: Salvation Through Psychology

1. Jacob Needleman, *The New Religions* (New York: Dulton, 1977), 18, 19. See Brock Kilbourne and James T. Richardson, "Psychotherapy and New Religions in a Pluralistic Society," *American Psychologist* (March 1984): 237-251; Martin and Deidre Bobgan, *The Psychological Way/The Spiritual Way* (Minneapolis: Bethany House, 1979).

2. Kenneth Cinnamon and Dave Farson, *Cults and Cons* (Chicago: Nelson-Hall, 1979), xiv, xv.

3. Jacob Needleman, "Young America Turns Eastward," in *Religion for a New Generation* eds. Jacob Needleman, A. K. Bierman, and J. H. Gould (New York: Dutton, 1970), 8-15; Needleman, *The New Religions*, 10-13, 18-19. See also Philip Rieff, *The Triumph of the Therapeutic* (New York: Harper and Row, 1966); Richard Kyle, *The Religious Fringe* (Downers Grove, IL: InterVarsity Press, 1993), 201.

4. Needleman, *The New Religions*, 10-13, 18-19; Needleman, "Young America Turns Eastward," 8-15. See also William C. Henderson, *Awakening: Ways to Psycho-Spiritual Growth* (Englewood Cliffs, NJ: Prentice Hall, 1975), 110-202; Kyle, *The Religious Fringe*, 201.

5. Peter Berger, Brigitte Berger, and Hansfried Kellner, *The Homeless Mind* (New York: Random House, 1974), 77, 78; Douglas Groothuis, *Unmasking the New Age* (Downers Grove, IL: InterVarsity Press, 1986), 71, 72; Harvey Cox, *Turning East* (New York: Simon and Schuster, 1977), 97, 98; Harvey Cox, "Eastern Cults and Western Culture: Why Young Americans Are Buying Oriental Religions," *Psychology Today* July 1977, p. 39.

6. Groothuis, *Unmasking the New Age*, 72.

7. Ronald Enroth, *The Lure of the Cults* (Chappaqua, NY: Christian Herald Books, 1979), 29; Kyle, *The Religious Fringe*, 299; Kenneth Woodward *et el*, "Getting Your Head Together," *Newsweek* September 6, 1976, pp. 56, 60, 61. See also Alan Gartner and Frank Reissman, eds. *The Self-Help Revolution* (New York: Human Sciences Press, 1984); Kilbourne and Richardson, "Psychotherapy and New Religions in a Pluralistic Society," 237-51.

8. Flo Conway and Jim Siegelman, *Snapping* (New York: Delta, 1978), 19; Cinnamon and Farson, *Cults and Cons*, 40; Enroth, *Lure of the Cults*, 29, 30; Edwin Schur, *The Awareness Trap* (New York: McGraw-Hill, 1976), 43. See also Daniel Yankelovich, "New Rules in American Life," *Psychology Today* April 1981, pp. 35-91; Daniel Yankelovich, *New Rules* (New York: Bantam Books, 1982).

9. John Newport, *Christ and the New Consciousness* (Nashville: Broadman, 1978), 7-11; Groothuis, *Unmasking the New Age*, 15, 16; James W. Sire, *The Universe Next Door* (Downers Grove, IL: InterVarsity Press, 1976), 151-196.

10. Woodward, "Getting Your Head Together," 56, 57.

11. Harriet Mosatche, *Searching* (New York: Stravon Educational Press, 1983), 13. See also Cinnamon and Farson, *Cults and Cons*, xvi.

12. Newport, *Christ and the New Consciousness*, 7-11; Groothuis, *Unmasking the New Age*, 15, 16.

13. Kyle, *The Religious Fringe*, 301.

14. John Allan, *Shopping for a God* (Leicester, UK: InterVarsity Press, 1986), 96; Woodward, "Getting Your Head Together," 62; Frances Adeney, "The Flowering of the Human Potential Movement," *SCP Journal* 5, no 1 (Winter 1981-82): 15, 16.

15. Adeney, "The Flowering of the Human Potential Movement," 10, 11. See Sigmund Freud, *An Outline of Psychoanalysis* (New York: Norton, 1949); Sigmund Freud, *Group Psychology and the Analysis of the Ego* (New York: Liveright Publishing, 1951); Sigmund Freud, *Delusion and Dream* (Boston: Beacon Press, 1956); Sigmund Freud, *On Creativity and the Unconscious* (New York: Harper, 1958); Sigmund Freud, *Freud: On War, Sex and Neurosis* (New York: Arts and Science Press, 1947).

16. Adeney, "The Flowering of the Human Potential Movement," 11; Groothuis, *Unmasking the New Age*, 73, 74. See also Carl G. Jung, *Psychology and Religion* (New Haven, CN: Yale University Press, 1938); C. G. Jung, *Modern Man in Search of a Soul* (New York: Harcourt, Brace, 1933); C. G. Jung, *The Undiscovered Self* (Boston: Little, Brown, 1957).

17. Groothuis, *Unmasking the New Age*, 75; Adeney, "The Flowering of the Human Potential Movement," 11, 12. See also B. F. Skinner, *About Behaviorism* (New York: Alfred Knopf, 1974); B. F. Skinner, *The Behavior of Organisms* (New York: Appleton-Century-Crofts, 1938); B. F. Skinner, *Science and Human Behavior* (New York: Free Press, 1953); B. F. Skinner,

Beyond Freedom and Dignity (New York: Alfred Knopf, 1971); John B. Watson, *Behaviorism* (New York: Norton, 1925).

18. Fritjof Capra, *The Turning Point* (New York: Bantam, 1982), 164-187.

19. Frank G. Goble, *The Third Force* (New York: Grossman, 1970), 16.

20. Abraham H. Maslow, *Toward A Psychology of Being* (Princeton, NJ: Van Nostrand, 1962).

21. Abraham H. Maslow, *The Farther Reaches of Human Nature* (New York: Penguin Books, 1972), 259-269; Maslow, *Toward a Psychology of Being*, 82-86; Globe, *The Third Force*, 50.

22. Maslow, *The Farther Reaches of Human Nature*, 261, 264.

23. Paul C. Vitz, *Psychology As Religion* (Grand Rapids: Eerdmans, 1977), 25; Groothuis, *Unmasking the New Age*, 78; Adeney, "The Flowering of the Human Potential Movement," 12.

24. Erich Fromm, D. T. Suzaki, and Richard De Martino, *Zen Buddhism and Western Psychoanalysis* (New York: Harper and Row, 1960), 141.

25. Erich Fromm, *Psychoanalysis and Religion* (New Haven, CN: Yale University Press, 1950), 37.

26. Groothuis, *Unmasking the New Age*, 77, 78; William Kirk Kilpatrick, "Therapy for the Masses," *Christianity Today* November 8, 1985, pp. 21-23. See also Carl R. Rogers, *On Becoming a Person* (Boston: Houghton Mifflin Co., 1961).

27. Adeney, "The Flowering of the Human Potential Movement," 13.

28. David Toolan, *Facing West From California's Shores* (New York: Crossroad, 1987), 37.

29. Anthony Sutich, "Some Considerations Regarding Transpersonal Psychology," *The Journal of Transpersonal Psychology* 1 no. 1 (1969): 11-20; Toolan, *Facing West From California's Shores*, 37, 38.

30. Toolan, *Facing West From California's Shores*, 37, 38.

31. Frances S. Adeney, "Transpersonal Psychology: Psychology and Salvation Meet," in *The New Age Rage* ed. Karen Hoyt (Old Tappan, NJ: Fleming H. Revell, 1987), 109, 110; Ken Wilber, *Up From Eden* (Garden City, NY: Anchor Press, 1981), 1-7.

32. Adeney, "Transpersonal Psychology: Psychology and Salvation Meet," 109.

33. Groothuis, *Unmasking the New Age*, 80, 81; Adeney, "Transpersonal Psychology: Psychology and Salvation Meet," 109, 110; Adeney, "The Flowering of the Human Potential Movement," 16; Ken Wilber, *The Atman Project* (Wheaton, IL: Theosophical Publishing House, 1980), 112-150; Ken Wilber, *A Sociable God* (Boulder, CO: Shambhala, 1983), 2-5; Ken Wilber, *No Boundary* (Los Angeles: Center Publications, 1979), 141-160.

34.   Adeney, "Transpersonal Psychology: Psychology and Salvation Meet," 112, 113; Groothuis, *Unmasking the New Age*, 80, 81; Adeney, "The Flowering of the Human Potential Movement," 16.

35.   Wilber, *The Atman Project*, 4, 5, 15, 19, 28, 34, 50, 72, 73, 161; Wilber, *No Boundary*, 123-160; Wilber, *A Sociable God*, 19-33; Adeney, "Transpersonal Psychology: Psychology and Salvation Meet," 122, 123.

36.   Kyle, *The Religious Fringe*, 289, 290.

37.   Roy Wallis, "The Dynamics of Change in the Human Potential Movement," in *Religious Movements* ed. Rodney Stark (New York: Paragon House, 1985), 132; John H. Marx and Joseph P. Seldin, "Crossroads of Crisis I. Therapeutic Sources and Quasi-Therapeutic Functions of Post-Industrial Communes," *Journal of Health and Social Behavior* 14, no. 1 (1973): 46, 47.

38.   Wallis, "The Dynamics of Change in the Human Potential Movement," 133.

39.   Carl A. Raschke, "The Human Potential Movement," *Theology Today* 33, no. 3 (1976): 253.

40.   Barbara Hargrove, *The Sociology of Religion* (Arlington Heights, IL: AHM Publishing, 1979), 275. See also Leonard Orr and Sondra Ray, *Rebirthing in the New Age* (Berkeley, CA: Celestial Arts, 1983), 52-142.

41.   Adeney, "The Flowering of the Human Potential Movement," 16; Henderson, *Awakening*, 162-177.

42.   Raschke, "The Human Potential Movement," 253-254. See also William C. Henderson, *Awakening: Ways to Psycho-Spiritual Growth* (Englewood Cliffs, NJ: Prentice Hall, 1975); Paul C. Vitz, *Psychology as Religion* (Grand Rapids: Eerdmans, 1977), 74-80.

43.   Donald Stone, "The Human Potential Movement," in *The New Religious Consciousness* eds. Charles Glock and Robert Bellah (Berkeley, CA: University of California Press, 1976), 93, 94; Wallis, "The Dynamics of Change," 134, 135. See Leslie J. Kaslof, *Wholistic Dimensions in Healing* (Garden City, NY: Doubleday, 1978), 236-244; Philip Zimbardo, "Mind Control in 1984," *Psychology Today* January 1984, pp. 68-72; Mark Teich and Giselle Dodeles, "Mind Control," *Omni* (October 1987): 54-59.

44.   Toolan, *Facing West From California's Shores*, 4, 5; Jeffrey Klein, "Esalen Slides off the Cliff," *Mother Jones* (December 1979):26.

45.   J. Gordon Melton *et al*, *New Age Almanac* (Detroit: Visible Ink Press, 1991), 205.

46.   Toolan, *Facing West From California's Shores*, 16. See Alice Kahn, "Esalen at 25," *Los Angeles Times Magazine* December 6, 1987, pp. 16-22, 40-43; Klein, "Esalen Slides off the Cliff," 26.

47.   Melton, *New Age Almanac*, 205.

48.   Raschke, "Human Potential Movement," 253-254; Donald Meyer, *Positive Thinkers*, 2nd ed. (New York: Pantheon Books, 1980); Vitz, *Psychology as Religion*, 69-74.

49. Catherine Albanese, *America: Religion and Religions* (Belmont, CA: Wadsworth, 1981), 325; Raschke, "Human Potential Movement," 255; Kyle, *The Religious Fringe*, 291; John T. Teahan, "Warren Felt Evans and Mental Healing: Romantic Idealism and Practical Mysticism in Nineteenth-Century America," *Church History* 48, no. 1 (March 1979): 63-80.

50. Albanese, *America*, 325, 326; Kyle, *The Religious Fringe*, 291.

51. Woodward, "Getting Your Head Together," 56, 57; Stone, "The Human Potential Movement," 93; Cinnamon and Farson, *Cults and Cons*, 41-50; Yankelovich, "New Rules in American Life," 36-43.

52. Peter Marin, "The New Narcissism," *Harper's* October 1975, p. 48; Woodward, "Getting Your Head Together," 57; Albert C. Outler, "Recovery of the Sacred," *Christianity Today* January 23, 1981, p. 23; Christopher Lasch, "The Narcissistic Personality of Our Time," *Partisan Review* 1 (1977); Joseph H. Fichter, "The Trend to Spiritual Narcissism," *Commonweal* 105, no. 6 (1978): 169-173; Christopher Lasch, *The Culture of Narcissism* (New York: Norton, 1978).

53. Alvin Toffler, *The Third Wave* (New York: Bantam Books, 1980), 366.

54. Woodward, "Getting Your Head Together," 56.

55. Woodward, "Getting Your Head Together," 56, 57; Raschke, "The Human Potential Movement," 253, 254; Wallis, "The Dynamics of Change in the Human Potential Movement," 134, 125.

56. Allan, *Shopping for a God*, 97, 98; Woodward, "Getting Your Head Together," 62. See Carl A. Raschke, *The Interruption of Eternity* (Chicago: Nelson-Hall, 1980).

57. Allan, *Shopping for a God*, 97, 98; Kyle, *The Religious Fringe*, 302, 303; Vitz, *Psychology as Religion*, 60-65. See Gary Zukav, *The Seat of the Soul* (New York: Simon and Schuster, 1989).

58. Marilyn Ferguson, *The Aquarian Conspiracy* (Los Angeles: J. P. Tarcher, 1980), 87, 89.

Chapter 10: Health and Healing in the New Age

1. Robert Bezilla ed., *Religion in America 1992-1992* (Princeton, NJ: The Princeton Religion Research Center, 1993), 32. See Sharon Fish, "Is There a Doctor in the Church?" *Eternity* August 1979, pp. 15-20.

2. Marilyn Ferguson, *The Aquarian Conspiracy* (Los Angeles: Tarcher, 1980), 257, 258.

3. Shirley MacLaine, *Dancing in the Light* (New York: Bantam Books, 1985), 7, 8.

4. Jill Ireland, *Life Wish* (Boston: Little, Brown and Co., 1987), 77.

5. Catherine L. Albanese, "The Magical Staff: Quantum Healing in the New Age," in *Perspectives on the New Age* eds. James R. Lewis and J. Gordon Melton (Albany, NY: State University of New York Press, 1992), 75; J. Gordon Melton *et al*, *New Age Almanac* (Detroit: Visible Ink Press,

1991), 169; Jeffrey A. Trachtenberg and Edward Gilteman, "Mainstream Metaphysics," *Forbes Magazine* (June 1, 1987): 157.

6. Robert C. Fuller, *Alternative Medicine and American Religious Life* (New York: Oxford University Press, 1989), 5.

7. Fuller, *Alternative Medicine*, 7.

8. Fuller, *Alternative Medicine*, 4,7.

9. Robert M. Giller, "Introduction to Wholistic Healing Groups and Centers," in *Wholistic Dimensions in Healing* ed. Leslie J. Kaslof (Garden City, NY: Doubleday, 1978), 24.

10. Melton, *New Age Almanac*, 169.

11. Melton, *New Age Almanac*, 169, 174.

12. Melton, *New Age Almanac*, 169, 174.

13. Fuller, *Alternative Medicine*, 91.

14. John Naisbitt, *Megatrends* (New York: Warner Books, 1982), 131.

15. Naisbitt, *Megatrends*, 132, 133; Paul C. Reisser, "Holistic Health Update," *Spiritual Counterfeits Project Newsletter* 9, no. 4 (1983):4.

16. J. Gordon Melton, "How New Is New? The Flowering of the 'New' Religious Consciousness since 1965," in *The Future of New Religious Movements* eds. David G. Bromley and Phillip E. Hammond (Macon, GA: Mercer University Press, 1987), 51, 52; J. Gordon Melton, "The Flowering of the New Religious Consciousness," in *Why Cults Succeed Where the Church Fails* eds. Ronald M. Enroth and J. Gordon Melton (Elgin, IL: Brethren Press, 1985), 124; Melton, *New Age Almanac*, 192, 193.

17. Ferguson, *Aquarian Conspiracy*, 244, 245; Kenneth R. Pelletier, *Holistic Medicine* (New York: Dell, 1979), 1-22; Paul C. Reisser, Teri K. Reisser and John Weldon, *New Age Medicine* (Downers Grove, IL: InterVarsity, 1987), 9, 10.

18. Ferguson, *Aquarian Conspiracy*, 242.

19. Fuller, *Alternative Medicine*, 91; Reisser, "Holistic Health Update," 4.

20. Reisser *et al*, *New Age Medicine*, 9; Kyle, *The Religious Fringe* (Downers Grove, IL: InterVarsity Press, 1993), 293; Douglas Groothuis, *Unmasking the New Age* (Downers Grove, IL: InterVarsity Press, 1986), 57.

21. William McLoughlin, *Revivals, Awakenings, and Reform* (Chicago: University of Chicago Press, 1978); Fuller, *Alternative Medicine* , 19, 20.

22. Albanese, "The Magical Staff," 71; Fuller, *Alternative Medicine*, 51; Albanese, "Physic and Metaphysic in Nineteenth-Century America: Medical Sectarians and Religious Healing," *Church History* 55, no. 4 (19856): 493; Robert C. Fuller, *Mesmerism and the American Cure of Souls* (Philadelphia: University of Pennsylvania Press, 1982).

23. Fuller, *Alternative Medicine*, 9; Stephen Nissenbaum, *Sex, Diet, and Debility in Jacksonian America* (Chicago: Dorsey Press, 1980); Alice Felt Tyler, *Freedom's Ferment* (New York: Harper and Row, 1962), 47-165;

Russell Blaine Nye, *Society and Culture in America, 1830-1860* (New York: Harper and Row, 1974), 338-356.

24. Fuller, *Alternative Medicine*, 17, 22, 26, 30; Nissenbaum, *Sex, Diet, and Debility*, 5-9; Nye, *Society and Culture*, 345, 346, 351-353; Catherine Albanese, *Nature Religion in America* (Chicago: University of Chicago Press, 1990), 133-136.

25. Fuller, *Alternative Medicine*, 59. See also Charles S. Braden, *Spirits in Rebellion: The Rise and Development of New Thought* (Dallas: Southern Methodist University Press, 1963), 9-25; J. Stillson Judah, *The History and Philosophy of Metaphysical Movements in America* (Philadelphia: Westminster Press, 1957), 176-193; Albanese, "Physic and Metaphysic in Nineteenth-Century America," 497; Horatio W. Dresser, *A History of the New Thought Movement* (New York: Thomas Y. Crowell, 1919); John F. Teahan, "Warren Felt Evans and Mental Healing: Romantic Idealism and Practical Mysticism in Nineteenth-Century America," *Church History* 48, no. 1 (1979): 63-80.

26. Fuller, *Alternative Medicine*, 61; Ruth Tucker, *Another Gospel* (Grand Rapids: Zondervan, 1989), 171, 172; Richard Kyle, "Church of Christ, Scientist," in *Encyclopedia USA* ed. Archie P. McDonald (Gulf Breeze, FL: Academic International Press, 1989), 95; Judah, *History and Philosophy of Metaphysical Movements*, 283. See Stephen Gottshcalk, *The Emergence of Christian Science in American Religious Life* (Berkeley, CA: University of California Press, 1973).

27. Julius Dintenfass, "Chiropractic Today," in *Wholistic Dimensions in Healing*, 64, 65; J. Dudley, "Osteopathy," in *Wholistic Dimensions in Healing*, 55, 56; Fuller, *Alternative Medicine*, 66-68.

28. Fuller, *Alternative Medicine*, 72, 73; Dintenfass, "Chiropractic Today," 64, 65; Albanese, "Physic and Metaphysic in Nineteenth-Century America," 495, 496.

29. Fuller, *Alternative Medicine*, 84-87; Dudley, "Osteopathy," 55, 56.

30. Albanese, "The Magical Staff," 77.

31. Most of these books are listed in Melton, *New Age Almanac*, 172. See Jan Christian Smuts, *Holism and Evolution* (New York: Macmillan, 1926); Rene Dubos, *Man, Medicine, and Environment* (London: Pall Mall Press, 1968); Ashley Montagu, *Touching: The Human Significance of Skin* (New York: Columbia University Press, 1971); Rick Carlson ed. *The Frontiers of Science and Medicine* (London: Wildwood House, 1975); Kenneth R. Pelletier, *Holistic Medicine* (New York: Delta, 1979).

32. Melton, *New Age Almanac*, 172, 173.

33. Kaslof, *Wholistic Dimensions in Healing*.

34. Melton, *New Age Almanac*, 173, 174.

35. Reisser, *et al*, *New Age Medicine*, 11.

36. Rick Carlson, "Holistic Health: Concept, Movement, Modality," *Holistic Health Review* (Fall 1977): 5; Brooks Alexander, "Holistic Health from the Inside," *SCP Journal* (August 1978): 7.

37. William James, *The Varieties of Religious Experience* (New York: Collier Books, 1961), 393; Alexander, "Holistic Health from the Inside," 8.

38. Kenneth R. Pelletier, *Mind as Healer, Mind as Slayer* (New York: Delta, 1977), 301.

39. Pelletier, *Holistic Medicine*, 93, 94; Fuller, *Alternative Medicine*, 93, 94.

40. Richard B. Mides, "What Is Holistic Health?" *Holistic Health Review* (Fall 1977): 4; Alexander, "Holistic Health from the Inside," 8, 9.

41. Mary Belknap, Robert Blau, and Rosaline Grossman, eds., *Case Studies and Methods in Humanistic Medicine* (San Francisco: Institute for the Study of Humanistic Medicine, 1973), 18; Fuller, *Alternative Medicine*, 92.

42. Paul Reisser, "Holistic Health: Marcus Welby Enters the New Age," in *The New Age Rage* ed. Karen Hoyt (Old Tappan, NJ: Fleming Revell, 1987), 58-61; Russell Chandler, *Understanding the New Age* (Dallas: Word Publishing, 1988), 184, 185; Reisser, "Holistic Health Update," 3.

43. Reisser, "Holistic Health," 58-61; Reisser, *et al, New Age Medicine*, 48, 49.

44. Fuller, *Alternative Medicine*, 38-65; Reisser, "Holistic Health," 61.

45. Reisser, "Holistic Health," 14-31; Groothuis, *Unmasking the New Age*, 58-64.

46. Reisser, "Holistic Health," 15, 16.

47. Fritjof Capra, *The Turning Point* (New York: Bantam Books, 1982), 123.

48. Pelletier, *Holistic Medicine,* 23, 31, 32.

49. George Leonard, "The Holistic Health Revolution," *The Journal of Wholistic Health* (1977): 81.

50. Capra, *The Turning Point*, 134.

51. Ferguson, *Aquarian Conspiracy*, 247.

52. Ferguson, *Aquarian Conspiracy*, 247, 248; Reisser, *et al, New Age Medicine*, 17.

53. Capra, *The Turning Point*, 158.

54. Pelletier, *Holistic Medicine*, 64, 93; Reisser, *et al, New Age Medicine*, 19, 20.

55. Reisser, *et al, New Age Medicine*, 20-26.

56. Reisser, *et al, New Age Medicine*, 26, 27.

57. James Fadiman, "The Prime Cause of Healing," *Journal of Holistic Health* (1977): 13, 14; Reisser, *et al, New Age Medicine*, 28, 36.

58. Larry Dossey, *Space, Time and Medicine* (Boston: Shambhala, 1982), 143.

262 The New Age Movement in American Culture

76. Melton, *New Age Almanac*, 215, 216; Bernard Jensen, "Iridology: Its Origin, Development, and Meaning," in *Wholistic Dimensions in Healing*, 165, 166; Reisser, *et al*, *New Age Medicine* 22; Chandler, *Understanding the New Age*, 166; E. M. Oakley, "Iridology," *New Realities* (November/December 1984): 42-46.

77. Elmer Green, "Biofeedback," in *Wholistic Dimensions in Healing*, 169-171; Reisser, *et al*, *New Age Medicine*, 21; Dossey, *Space, Time and Medicine*, 19, 20; Pelletier, *Mind as Healer*, 264-298.

78. Olga N. Worrall, "Unconventional Healing," in *Wholistic Dimensions in Healing*, 180, 181; Miller, "Healing in the New Age Groups," 44, 45.

79. Fuller, *Alternative Medicine*, 103; Miller, "Healing in the New Age," 44, 45; Michael Brown, "Getting Serious About the Occult," *Atlantic Monthly* (October 1978), p. 100.

80. Reisser, *et al*, *New Age Medicine*, 25, 26; Fuller, *Alternative Medicine*, 103; Miller, "Healing in the New Age Groups," 44, 45; Elliot Miller, *A Crash Course on the New Age Movement* (Grand Rapids: Baker Book House, 1989), 93; Dolores Krieger, "The Potential Use of Therapeutic Touch," in *Wholistic Dimensions in Healing*, 182, 183.

81. Reisser, *et al*, *New Age Medicine*, 26, 108-112; Martin Gardner, *The New Age: Notes of a Fringe Watcher* (Buffalo: Prometheus, 1988), 167-169.

82. Fuller, *Alternative Medicine*, 106; Reisser, *et al*, *New Age Medicine*, 112-121. See Jess Stearn, *Edgar Cayce: The Sleeping Prophet* (New York: New American Library, 1969); Richard Woods, *The Occult Revolution* (New York: Herder and Herder, 1971), 161ff.

83. Worrall, "Unconventional Healing," 180, 181; Reisser, *et al*, *New Age Medicine*, 101-103; Alexander, "Holistic Health from the Inside," 12, 13.

84. Quotes from Melton, *New Age Almanac*, 225, 227. See also Katsusuke Serizawa, "Massage," in *Wholistic Dimensions in Healing*, 206-208.

85. Ida P. Rolf, "Rolfing," in *Wholistic Dimensions in Healing*, 225-227; Reisser, *et al*, *New Age Medicine*, 23; Melton, *New Age Almanac*, 247; Kenneth L. Woodward, "Getting Your Head Together," *Newsweek*, September 6, 1976, p. 60.

86. Reisser, *et al*, *New Age Medicine*, 23; Melton, *New Age Almanac*, 243, 244.

87. Reisser, *et al*, *New Age Medicine*, 23, 24; Melton, *New Age Almanac*, 194.

Chapter 11: The "Pop" New Age: Occult Practices

1. Nina Easton, "Shirley MacLaine's Mysticism for the Masses," *Los Angeles Times Magazine* (September 6, 1987), pp. 7, 9; Otto Friedrich, "New Age Harmonies," *Time* (December 7, 1987), pp. 61-69; Phyllis Battelle, "Shirley MacLaine: An interview that will amaze you," *Ladies Home Journal* (June 1983), pp. 24-33; Stephen Fuchs, "The New Age

59. Capra, *The Turning Point*, 339; Chandler, *Understanding the New Age*, 164; Reisser, *et al, New Age Medicine*, 34; Reisser, "Holistic Health," 3.

60. Chandler, *Understanding the New Age*, 164, 165; Reisser, *et al, New Age Medicine*, 28, 29; Reisser, "Holistic Health," 3.

61. Pelletier, *Holistic Medicine*, 189. Leonard Orr and Sondra Ray go much further in their projection. See Leonard Orr and Sondra Ray, *Rebirthing in the New Age* (Berkeley, CA: Celestial Arts, 1983), 150-170.

62. Reisser, *et al, New Age Medicine*, 30; Groothuis, *Unmasking the New Age*, 63, 64.

63. Dossey, *Space, Time and Medicine*, 154-158.

64. Andrea Grace Diem and James R. Lewis, "Imagining India: The Influence of Hinduism on the New Age Movement," in *Perspectives on the New Age* eds. James R. Lewis and J. Gordon Melton (Albany, NY: State University of New York Press, 1992), 49-52; Fritjof Capra, *The Tao of Physics* (Boston: Shambhala, 1991).

65. Reisser, *et al, New Age Medicine*, 30, 31.

66. Mark Satin, *New Age Politics* (New York: Delta Book, 1978), 249, 250.

67. Ferguson, *Aquarian Conspiracy*, 259, 260.

68. Capra, *The Turning Point*, 333, 334. See also Kenneth R. Pelletier, *Healthy People in Unhealthy Places* (New York: Delta, 1984), 122-132.

69. Harris L. Coulter, "Homeopathy," in *Wholistic Dimensions in Healing*, 47, 48; Reisser, *et al, New Age Medicine*, 21, 22; Melton, *New Age Almanac*, 197, 215; Fuller, *Alternative Medicine*, 22-26, 67; Dintenfass, "Chiropractic Today," 64, 65.

70. Melton, *New Age Almanac*, 229, 236.

71. Quoted in Joseph A. Boucher, "Naturopathic Medicine: A Separate and Distinct Healing Profession," in *Wholistic Dimensions in Healing*, 80, 81.

72. Boucher, "Naturopathic Medicine," 80, 81; Melton, *New Age Almanac*, 229.

73. George J. Goodheart and Walter H. Schmitt, "Applied Kinesiology," in *Wholistic Dimensions in Healing*, 77, 78; Reisser, *et al, New Age Medicine*, 80-83; Melton, *New Age Almanac*, 178, 179.

74. Richard O. Brennan, "Preventive Nutrition and Health Maintenance," in *Wholistic Dimensions in Healing*, 95-97; Melton, *New Age Almanac*, 213, 214, 264; John F. Miller, "Healing in the New Age Groups," *The Journal of Religion and Physical Research* 7, no. 1 (1984): 40.

75. David E. Bresler, Richard J. Kroening, and Michael P. Volen, "Acupuncture in America," in *Wholistic Dimensions in Healing*, 132-134; Melton, *New Age Almanac*, 194-196; Miller, "Healing in the New Age Groups," 42.

Movement," *Aeropagus* 4, no. 3 (1991): 7. See Shirley MacLaine, *Out on a Limb* (New York: Bantam Books, 1984); Shirley MacLaine, *Dancing in the Light* (New York: Bantam Books, 1986); Shirley MacLaine, *It's All in the Playing* (New York: Bantam Books, 1988).

2. Jonathan Adolph, "What is New Age?" *The Guide to New Age Living* (1988): 6.

3. Some examples include the following: David Spangler, *Revelation: The Birth of a New Age* (San Francisco: Rainbow Bridge, 1978); David Spangler, *Towards a Planetary Vision* (The Park, Scotland: Findhorn Publications, 1977); David Spangler, *Emergence* (New York: Delta, 1984); Marilyn Ferguson, *The Aquarian Conspiracy* (Los Angeles: Tarcher, 1980); George Trevelyan, *A Vision of the Aquarian Age* (Walpole, NH: Stillpoint Publishing, 1984); Fritjof Capra, *The Turning Point* (New York: Bantam Books, 1982); Alvin Toffler, *The Third Wave* (New York: Bantam Books, 1980); John Naisbitt, *Megatrends* (New York: Warner, 1982); Mark Satin, *New Age Politics* (New York: Delta Books, 1978). On the other hand, Benjamin Creme gives considerable attention to occult phenomena. See Benjamin Creme, *The Reappearance of the Christ and the Masters of Wisdom* (North Hollywood, CA: Tara Center, 1980).

4. Jeffrey A. Trachtenberg, "Mainstream Metaphysics," *Forbes Magazine* (June 1, 1987, pp. 156-158; Art Levine, "Mystics on Main Street," *U.S. News and World Report* February 9, 1987, 67-69; "Update," *Aeropagus* 2, no. 1 (1989): 48.

5. Levine, "Mystics on Main Street," 67, 68; Leon Jaroff, "Fighting Against Flimflam," *Time* June 13, 1988, pp. 70-72; Richard Blow, "Moronic Convergence," *The New Republic* January 25, 1988, pp. 24-27.

6. Ted Peters, *The Cosmic Self* (San Francisco: Harper San Francisco, 1991), 8; Catherine L. Albanese, *America: Religions and Religion* 2nd ed. (Belmont, CA: Wadsworth, 1992), 361.

7. Vishal Mangalwadi, *When the New Age Gets Old* (Downers Grove, IL: InterVarsity Press, 1992), 22, 23.

8. Suzanne Riordan, "Channeling: A New Revelation?" in *Perspectives on the New Age* eds. James R. Lewis and J. Gordon Melton (Albany, NY: State University of New York Press, 1992), 105.

9. Albanese, *America* (2nd ed.), 362-367.

10. Ferguson, *Aquarian Conspiracy*, 85-90; Levine, "Mystics on Main Street," 69.

11. Jon Klimo, "The Psychology of Channeling," *New Age Journal* (November/December 1987): 33.

12. Peters, *Cosmic Self*, 28; Robert J. L. Burrows, "Americans Get Religion in the New Age," *Christianity Today* May 16, 1986, p. 20; Elliot Miller, "Channeling: Spiritistic Revelations for the New Age," Pt. 1 *Christian Research Journal* 10, no. 2 (1987): 9.

13. Peters, *Cosmic Self*, 28; Katherine Lowry, "Channelers," *Omni* (October 1987): 48.

14. James R. Lewis and J. Gordon Melton, "Introduction," in *Perspectives on the New Age*, xii; Brooks Alexander, "Twilight Zone," *Christianity Today* September 18, 1987, pp. 24, 25.

15. Martin Gardner, *The New Age: Notes of a Fringe Watcher* (Buffalo: Prometheus Books, 1988), 203-207; Martin Gardner, "Isness is Her Business: Shirley MacLaine," in *Not Necessarily New Age* ed. Robert Basil (Buffalo: Prometheus Books, 1988), 186, 187. See MacLaine, *Out on a Limb*; MacLaine, *It's All in the Playing*; MacLaine, *Dancing in the Light*.

16. Peters, *Cosmic Self*, 33; Miller, "Channeling," pt. 1, 14.

17. Henry Gordon, *Channeling into the New Age* (Buffalo: Prometheus Books, 1988), 94; Lowry, "Channelers," 45, 50.

18. Elliot Miller, *A Crash Course on the New Age Movement* (Grand Rapids: Baker Book House, 1989), 161, 162; Gordon, *Channeling into the New Age*, 94.

19. Gardner, *The New Age*, 208; Gardner, "Isness Is Her Business," 201.

20. J. Gordon Melton, *et al*, *New Age Almanac* (Detroit: Visible Ink Press, 1991), 45, 46; Klimo, "Channeling," 34; Marvin Olasky, "The Return of Spiritism," *Christianity Today* December 14, 1992, pp. 20-24.

21. Mangalwadi, *When the New Age Gets Old*, 64-66.

22. Mangalwadi, *When the New Age Gets Old*, 66.

23. Jon Klimo, *Channeling* (Los Angeles: Tarcher, 1987), 105-107; Melton, *New Age Almanac*, 48, 49; Miller, "Channeling" Pt. 1, 10.

24. Melton, *New Age Almanac*, 49; Peters, *Cosmic Self*, 29; Miller, *A Crash Course on the New Age Movement*, 146.

25. Klimo, *Channeling*, 121, 122; Melton, *New Age Almanac*, 48, 49; Miller, "Channeling," Pt. 1, 11.

26. Melton, *New Age Almanac*, 49; Peters, *Cosmic Self*, 29; Klimo, *Channeling*, 113-116; Richard Woods, *The Occult Revolution* (New York: Herder and Herder, 1971), 161-164; Klimo, "Channeling," 38.

27. Melton, *New Age Almanac*, 50, 51; Peters, *Cosmic Self*, 29; Klimo, "Psychology of Channeling," 34, 35; Miller, "Channeling," pt. 1, 11.

28. Klimo, "Channeling," 36; Klimo, *Channeling*, 27, 28. Quote from Melton, *New Age Almanac*, 53; Riordan, "Channeling," 110.

29. Lowry, "Channelers," 50; Miller, *A Crash Course on the New Age Movement*, 155, 156; Gardner, "Isness Is Her Business," 196.

30. Steven Lee Weinberg, ed. *Ramtha* (Eastsound, WA: Sovereignty, 1986), 5-21; Miller, "Channeling," 12; Melton, *New Age Almanac*, 65; George Hackett, "Ramtha, a Voice From Beyond," *Newsweek* December 16, 1986, p. 42. Quote from Klimo, "Psychology of Channeling," 36.

31. Melton, *New Age Almanac*, 66; Peters, *Cosmic Self*, 33; Miller, *A Crash Course in the New Age Movement*, 150, 151; Klimo, *Channeling*, 42-44. In *Dancing in the Light* (1985), Shirley MacLaine spoke of Ramtha.

32. Gardner, "Isness Is Her Business," 197; Miller, *A Crash Course on the New Age Movement*, 152; Gordon, *Channeling into the New Age*, 97, 98.

33. Klimo, "Psychology of Channeling," 38; Klimo, *Channeling*, 47-49; Miller, "Channeling," pt. 1, 12, 13; Gordon, *Channeling into the New Age*, 102, 103. In *It's All in the Playing*, Shirley MacLaine writes approvingly of Pursel and Lazaris.

34. Klimo, "Psychology of Channeling," 37; Miller, "Channeling," pt. 1; Melton, *New Age Almanac*, 96, 97; Klimo, *Channeling*, 45, 46; MacLaine, *Out on a Limb*; MacLaine, *Dancing in the Light*; MacLaine, *It's all In The Playing*.

35. Rirodan, "Channeling," 110, 111; Miller, *A Crash Course on the New Age Movement*, 169-176.

36. Riordan, "Channeling," 111.

37. Riordan, "Channeling," 111, 112; Melton, *The New Age Almanac*, 51.

38. Elliot Miller, "Channeling" pt. 2 *Christian Research Journal* 10, no. 3 (1988): 18, 19; Miller, *A Crash Course on the New Age Movement*, 169, 170; Riordan, "Channeling," 114-116.

39. Quotes from Miller, "Channeling," pt. 2, 19, 20 and Miller, *A Crash Course on the New Age Movement*, 170-174. See also Russell Chandler, *Understanding the New Age* (Dallas: Word Publishing, 1988), 83; Klimo, *Channeling*, 347.

40. Melton, *New Age Almanac*, 50; Klimo, *Channeling*, 178, 179.

41. Miller, "Channeling," pt. 1, 11; Melton, *New Age Almanac*, 51.

42. Miller, *A Crash Course on the New Age Movement*, 148, 149.

43. Riordan, "Channeling," 105.

44. Klimo, "The Psychology of Channeling," 67. See also Klimo, *Channeling*, 205-299.

45. Peters, *Cosmic Self*, 34.

46. Miller, "Channeling," pt. 2, 18; Miller, *A Crash Course on the New Age Movement*, 168.

47. Chandler, *Understanding the New Age*, 84.

48. Chandler, *Understanding the New Age*, 103; Martha Smilgis, "Rock Power for Health and Wealth," *Time* January 19, 1987, p. 6.

49. The front cover illustrates the feature article: Friedrich, "New Age Harmonies," p. 62-72. Melton, *New Age Almanac*, 287; Gordon, *Channeling into the New Age*, 35.

50. Peters, *Cosmic Self*, 26. For more on crystals see R. Bonewitz, *Cosmic Crystals* (Wellingborough, UK: Turnstone Press, 1983); Korrea Deaver, *Rock Crystals:The Magic Stone* (York Beach, ME: Samuel Weiser,

1985); Daya Sarai Chocron, *Healing With Crystals and Gemstones* (York Beach, ME: Samuel Weiser, 1983).

51. Melton, *New Age Almanac*, 285, 286; W. B. Crow, *A History of Magic, Witchcraft and Occultism* (North Hollywood, CA: Wilshire Book Co., 1968), 71; Bernard Bromage, *The Occult Arts of Ancient Egypt* (New York: Samuel Weiser, Inc., 1971), 88-115; Gordon, *Channeling*, 35; W. Crow, *Precious Stones: Their Occult Power and Hidden Significance* (York Beach, ME: Samuel Weiser, 1968).

52. Melton, *New Age Almanac*, 286, 287. See Edgar Cayce, *Scientific Properties and Occult Aspects of 22 Gems, Stones and Metals* (Virginia Beach, VA: ARE Press).

53. Robert Fuller, *Alternative Medicine and Religious Life* (New York: Oxford University Press, 1989), 112, 113; Peters, *Cosmic Self*, 25.

54. Peters, *Cosmic Self*, 25, 26.

55. Chocron, *Healing With Crystals*, 34; Miller, *A Crash Course on the New Age Movement*, 189; Peters, *Cocmic Self*, 26.

56. Miller, *A Crash Course on the New Age Movement*, 189.

57. Melton, *New Age Almanac*, 287, 288; Miller, *A Crash Course on the New Age Movement*, 189.

58. Ruth Tucker, *Another Gospel* (Grand Rapids: Zondervan, 1989), 345, 346; Peters, *Cosmic Self*, 40; Fuchs, "The New Age Movement," 7.

59. Mangalwadi, *When the New Age Gets Old*, 33, 40; Fuchs, "The New Age Movement," 7, 8; Melton, *New Age Almanac*, 271. See also Michael Gauquelin, *Astrology and Science* (London: Mayflower Books, 1972); J. A. West and J. G. Toonder, *The Case for Astrology* (Harmondsworth, UK: Penguin Books, 1973).

60. Fuchs, "The New Age Movement," 8.

61. Mangalwadi, *When the New Age Gets Old*, 33.

62. Quote from Fuchs, "The New Age Movement," 8; Mangalwadi, *When the New Age Gets Old*, 33, 34.

63. Claude Fischler, "Astrology and French Society," in *On the Margin of the Visible* ed. Edward A. Tiryakian (New York: John Wiley, 1974), 283-284.

64. Fischler, "Astrology and French Society," 284; Keith Thomas, *Religion and the Decline of Magic* (New York: Charles Scribner's, 1971), 283-285; Irving Hexham and Karla Poewe, *Understanding Cults and New Religions* (Grand Rapids: Eerdmans, 1986), 79.

65. Peters, *Cosmic Self*, 40, 41; Melton, *New Age Almanac*, 274, 275.

66. Peters, *Cosmic Self*, 39.

67. Melton, *New Age Almanac*, 277.

68. Robert Bezilla ed., *Religion in America 1992-1993* (Princeton, NJ: Princeton Religion Research Center, 1993), 32; Tucker, *Another Gospel*, 343.

69. See Donald T. Regan, *For the Record: From Wall Street to Washington* (New York: Harcourt, Brace, Jovanovich, 1988), 3, 74; Barrett Seaman, "Good Heavens!" *Time* May 16, 1988, pp. 24, 25; Laurence Zuckerman, "The First Lady's Astrologer," *Time* May 16, 1988, p. 41; Lance Morrow, "The Five-and-Dime Charms of Astrology," *Time* May 16, 1988, p. 100.

70. Melton, *New Age Almanac*, 276, 277.

71. Melton, *New Age Almanac*, 272, 277; Tucker, *Another Gospel*, 347. See Steven Forrest, *A Practical Guide to the New Predictive Astrology* (New York: Bantam Books, 1986).

72. Schoshanah Feher, "Who Holds the Cards? Women and New Age Astrology," in *Perspectives on the New Age*, 180, 181.

73. David M. Jacobs, "UFOs and Scientific Legitimacy," in *The Occult in America* eds. Howard Kerr and Charles Crow (Urbana, IL: University of Illinois Press, 1983), 219, 228, 229; William M. Alnor, "UFO Cults are Flourishing in New Age Circles," *Christian Research Journal* 13, no. 1 (1990): 5, 6; "UFO believers demand end to cosmic cover-up," *Wichita Eagle* July 6, 1993, p. 10A.

74. Robert W. Balch and David Taylor, "Salvation in a UFO," *Psychology Today*, October 1976, pp. 58-66, 106; Robert W. Balch and David Taylor, "Seekers and Saucers: The Role of the Cultic Milieu in Joining a UFO Cult," *American Behavioral Scientist* 20, no. 6 (1977): 839-860; Jacobs, "UFOs and Scientific Legitimacy," 219, 228-229.

75. Gordon Melton, *The Encyclopedia of American Religions*, 2 vols. (Wilmington, NC: McGrath, 1978): 2: 199; Chandler, *Understanding the New Age*, 92, 93; Ted Peters, *UFOs--God's Chariots: Flying Saucers in Politics, Science and Religion* (Atlanta: John Knox Press, 1977).

76. David Spangler, *Links with Space* (Marina de Rey, CA: De Vorss), 1971.

77. Benjamin Creme, *The Reappearance of the Christ and the Masters of Wisdom* (Los Angeles: Tara Center, 1980), 205, 206.

78. See MacLaine, *Out on a Limb*; MacLaine, *It's All in the Playing*; Whitley Streiber, *Communion* (New York: Wm. Morrow, 1987); Whitley Streiber, *Transformation* (New York: Wm. Morrow, 1988).

79. Bill Lawren, "UFO Poll," *Omni* (October 1987): 144.

80. Melton, *New Age Almanac*, 136; Peters, *Cosmic Self*, 36, 37; Strieber, *Communion*, 100, 224.

81. Ruth Montgomery, *Aliens Among Us* (New York: Ballantine, 1986), 129, 137; Peters, *Cosmic Self*, 36.

82. Michael Harner, *The Way of the Shaman* (San Francisco: Harper San Francisco, 1990), xvii. See also Michael Ripinsky-Naxon, *The Nature of Shamanism: Substance and Function of a Religious Metaphor* (Albany, NY: State University of New York Press, 1993).

83. Harner, *The Way of the Shaman*, 20.

84. Hexham and Poewe, *Understanding Cults and New Religions*, 131, 132.

85. James R. Lewis and J. Gordon Melton, "Introduction," in *Perspectives on the New Age*, xii; Chandler, *Understanding the New Age*, 117.

86. See Elizabeth Clare Prophet, *The Lost Years of Jesus* (Livingston, MT: Summit University Press, 1987); Creme, *The Reappearance of the Christ*, 46-89; David Spangler, *Reflections on the Christ* (Forres, Scotland: Findhorn Publications, 1978); Douglas Groothuis, "The Shamanized Jesus," *Christianity Today* April 29, 1991, pp. 20-23; Don Rhodes, *The Counterfeit Christ of the New Age Movement* (Grand Rapids: Baker Book House, 1990); Douglas Groothuis, *Revealing the New Age Jesus* (Downers Grove, IL: InterVarsity Press, 1991).

87. Chandler, *Understanding the New Age*, 115; Melton, *New Age Almanac*, 248. See also Jon Magnuson, "Affirming Native Spirituality: A Call to Justice," *The Christian Century* December 9, 1987, pp. 1114-1117; Jon W. Magnuson, "Echoes of a Shaman's Song," *The Christian Century* April 29, 1987, pp. 406-408; Catherine L. Albanese, *Nature Religion in America* (Chicago: University of Chicago Press, 1990), 153 ff.

88. James R. Lewis, "Approaches to the Study of the New Age Movement," in *Perspectives on the New Age*, 6, 7; Harner, *The Way of the Shaman*, 43, 44.

89. Melton, *New Age Almanac*, 248; Hexham and Poewe, *Understanding Cults and New Religions*, 131, 132.

90. Robert S. Ellwood and Harry B. Partin, *Religious and Spiritual Groups in Modern America* 2nd ed. (Englewood Cliffs, NJ: Prentice Hall, 1988), 13.

91. Brooks Alexander, "A Generation of Wizards: Shamanism and Contemporary Culture," *Spiritual Counterfeits Profit Special Collection Journal* 6, no. 1 (Winter 1984): 28; Chandler, *Understanding the New Age*, 116.

Chapter 12: Evaluating the New Age

1. Randall Balmer, "Death of New Age a new era for U.S.," *Wichita Eagle*, June 3, 1991, p. 11A; "Americans still want old-time religion," *Wichtia Eagle*, April 11, 1991, p. 5A; Douglas Groothuis, *Confronting the New Age* (Downers Grove, IL: InterVarsity Press), 1988, 201.

2. Balmer, "Death of New Age a new era for U.S.," p. 11A.

3. Christopher Lasch, "Soul of a New Age," *OMNI* October 1987, pp. 80, 82; Groothuis, *Confronting the New Age*, 202, 203.

4. J. Gordon Melton, "A History of the New Age Movement," in *Not Necessarily the New Age* ed. Robert Basil (Buffalo: Prometheus Books, 1988), 50, 51; J. Gordon Melton, *Encyclopedic Handbook of Cults in America* (New York: Garland Publishing, 1986), 116.

5. Melton, "A History of the New Age Movement," 51, 52.

6. The perception of the New Age as a shift in American culture can be found in several sources. Some examples include Elliot Miller, *A Crash Course on the New Age Movement* (Grand Rapids: Baker Book House, 1989); Douglas Groothuis, *Unmasking the New Age* (Downers Grove, IL: InterVarsity Press, 1986); Groothuis, *Confronting the New Age*; Robert J. L. Burrows, "Americans Get Religion in the New Age," *Christianity Today* May 16, 1986, pp. 17-23; Brooks Alexander, "Compromise and Vulnerability," *Spiritual Counterfeits Project Newsletter* 15, no. 1 (1990): 6-8; Robert M. Bowman, Jr., "Cult Update: Trends in New Religions," *Christian Research Journal* 10, no. 2 (1987): 16-22.

7. Jeffrey A. Trachtenberg, "Mainstream Metaphysics," *Forbes Magazine* (June 1, 1987) pp. 156-158; Art Levine, "Mystics on Main Street," *U.S. News and World Report* February 9, 1987, pp. 67-69; Donald G. Bloesch, "Lost in the Mystical Myths," *Christianity Today* August 19, 1991, pp. 22, 23.

8. Jeremy P. Tarcher, "Here's to the End of New Age Publishing," *Publishers Weekly* November 8, 1989, p. 36; Russell Chandler, *Racing Toward 2001* (Grand Rapids: Zondervan, 1992), 200, 201.

9. Robert Bezilla ed., *Religion in America 1992-1993* (Princeton, NJ: Princeton Religion Research Center, 1993), 32, 33.

10. Kenneth L. Woodward, "A Time to Seek," *Newsweek* December 17, 1990, p. 56; John Wimber, "Facing the 90s," *Equipping the Saints* (Summer 1989): 21, 22; Chandler, *Racing Toward 2000*, 196.

11. Chandler, *Racing Toward 2001*, 194-196; George Barna, *The Frog in the Kettle* (Ventura, CA: Regal Books, 1990), 141.

12. Chandler, *Racing Toward 2001*, 192-194; Barna, *Frog in the Kettle*, 131; Russell Chandler, "The Challenge is Acute; the Fields Ripe," *Evangelical Beacon* January 8, 1990.

13. Diogenes Allen, "The End of the Modern World: A New Openness for Faith," *The Princeton Seminary Bulletin* 11, no. 1 (1990): 11-31; Martin Marty, "An Old New Age in Publishing," *The Christian Century* November 18, 1987, p. 1019; Os Guinness, *The American Hour* (New York: Free Press, 1993), 70, 129.

14. Alexander, "Compromise and Vulnerability," 6-8; Chandler, *Racing Toward 2001*, 205; Bloesch, "Lost in the Mystical Myths," 22, 23; Miller, *A Crash Course on the New Age Movement*, 184, 185.

15. Constance Cumbey, *The Hidden Dangers of the Rainbow* rev. ed. (Lafayette, LA: Huntington House, 1983), 7.

16. Cumbey, *Hidden Dangers of the Rainbow*, 16, 58.

17. For some arguments against the Cumbey thesis see Miller, *A Crash Course on the New Age Movement*, 193-196; Ted Peters, *The Cosmic Self* (San Francisco: Harper San Francisco, 1991), 96-101; Chandler, *Understanding the New Age*, 227-234.

18. Constance E. Cumbey, *A Planned Deception* (Centerline, MI: Pointe Publishers, 1985).

19. Texe Marrs, *Dark Secrets of the New Age* (Westchester, IL: Crossway Books, 1987), 262. Other books taking a similar approach to the New Age include Caryl Matrisciana, *Gods of the New Age* (Eugene, OR: Harvest House, 1985); Paul de Parrie and Mary Pride, *Unholy Sacrifices of the New Age* (Westchester, IL: Crossway Books, 1988); Randall N. Baer, *Inside the New Age Nightmare* (Lafayette, LA: Huntington House, 1989); Elissa Lindsey McClain, *Rest from the Quest* (Shreveport, LA: Huntington House, 1984).

20. Dave Hunt and T. A. McMahon, *The Seduction of Christianity* (Eugene, OR: Harvest House, 1985); Dave Hunt, *Peace, Prosperity and the Coming Holocaust* (Eugene, OR: Harvest House, 1983); Dave Hunt and T. S. McMahon, *America: The Sorcerer's New Apprentice* (Eugene, OR: Harvest House, 1988). See also Chandler, *Understanding the New Age*, 228-230; Miller, *A Crash Course on the New Age Movement*, 187, 188. See "Under Fire," *Christianity Today* September 18, 1987, pp. 17-21.

21. See Karen Hoyt, ed., *The New Age Rage* (Old Tappan, NJ: Fleming Revell, 1987); Miller, *A Crash Course on the New Age Movement*; Groothuis, *Unmasking the New Age*; Groothuis, *Confronting the New Age*; Chandler, *Understanding the New Age*.

22. J. Gordon Melton *et al*, *New Age Almanac* (Detroit: Visible Ink Press, 1991); 313, 314. For a critique of the evangelical writings on the New Age see Irving Hexham, "The Evangelical Response to the New Age," in *Perspectives on the New Age* eds. James R. Lewis and J. Gordon Melton (Albany, NY: State University of New York Press, 1992), 152-163.

23. See Bede Griffiths, *The Marriage of East and West* (Springfield, IL: Templegate Publishers, 1982); Bede Griffiths, *The Golden String* (Glasgow: Collins, 1954); Bede Griffiths, "Sacred Simplicity: The Style of the Sage," in *Dialogues with Scientists and Sages* ed. Reneé Weber (London: Routledge and Kegan Paul, 1986); Peters, *Cosmic Self*, 108-114.

24. Matthew Fox, *Original Blessing* (Santa Fe, NM: Bear and Co., 1983), 90, 300; Matthew Fox, *The Coming of the Cosmic Christ* (San Francisco: Harper and Row, 1988); Peters, *Cosmic Self*, 120-123; Melton, *New Age Almanac*, 324, 325. Doug LeBlanc, "A Comeback for Matthew Fox?" *Christianity Today* June 20, 1994, p. 64.

25. Morton T. Kelsey, *The Christian and the Supernatural* (Minneapolis: Augsburg, 1976), 93, 133; Ruth Tucker, *Another Gospel* (Grand Rapids: Zondervan, 1989), 354.

26. Rodney R. Romney, *Journey to Inner Space: Finding God-in-Us* (Nashville: Abingdon, 1980), 26, 29, 31. Cited in Tucker, *Another Gospel*, 353.

27. Agnes Sanford, *The Healing Gifts of the Spirit* (New York: J. B. Lippincott, 1966), 165; Tucker, *Another Gospel*, 354.

28. Bezilla, *Religion in America 1992-1993*, 34.

29. Peters, *Cosmic Self*, 169.

30. Ted Peters, "Discerning the Spirits of the New Age," *The Christian Century* September 7, 1988, p. 765.

31. Fritjof Capra, *The Turning Point* (New York: Bantam Books, 1982), 31.

32. Ronald J. Sider, "Green Politics: Biblical or Buddhist? *Spiritual Counterfeits Project Newsletter* 11, no. 3 (1985): 11.

33. In the introduction to *The New Age Rage*, Karen Hoyt presents ten positive aspects of the New Age. On these points, she says that Christianity can have some agreement with the New Age. Some of the ideas in this and several succeeding paragraphs have been drawn from these ten points.

34. Peters, "Discerning the Spirits of the New Age," 765, 766; Chandler, *Understanding the New Age*, 225.

35. Melton, *Cults in America*, 107; Chandler, *Understanding the New Age*, 226.

36. For a discussion on the logic of interrelegious dialogue see Paul J. Griffiths, *An Apology for Apologetics* (Maryknoll, NY: Orbis Books, 1991).

37. Brooks Alexander and Robert Burrows, "New Age and Biblical World-Views," in *The New Age Rage*, 248, 249; Groothuis, *Unmasking the New Age*, 18-21.

38. Peters, "Discerning the Spirits of the New Age," 766; Alexander and Burrows, "New Age and Biblical World Views," 248; Peters, *Cosmic Self*, 191. See Soren Kierkegaard, *Philosophical Fragments* (Princeton, NJ: Princeton University Press, 1962).

39. Alexander and Burrows, "New Age and Biblical World Views," 248, 249; Groothuis, *Unmasking the New Age*, 20-22; John W. Cooper, "Testing the Spirit of the Age of Aquarius: The New Age Movement," *Calvin Theological Journal* 22, no. 2 (1987): 297, 298.

40. Alexander and Burrows, "New Age and Biblical World Views," 249, 250; Groothuis, *Unmasking the New Age* 23-27.

41. Alexander and Burrows, "New Age and Biblical World Views," 251, 252; Peters, "Discerning and Spirits of the New Age," 766; Peters, *Cosmic Self*, 175, 176.

42. Peters, "Discerning the Spirits of the New Age," 766; Alexander and Burrows, "New Age and Biblical World Views," 251, 252.

43. Art Lindsley, "The Way to New Life: Transformation or Renewal," in *The New Age Rage*, 228; Melton, *Cults in America*, 113.

44. Marilyn Ferguson, *The Aquarian Conspiracy* (Los Angeles: J. P. Tarcher, 1980), 100.

45. Lindsley, "The Way to New Life," 229-231.

46. Lindsley, "The Way to New Life," 229, 230; Richard H. Bube, "Science and Pseudoscience," *The Reformed Journal* (November 1982): 11.

47. Vishal Mangalwadi, *When the New Age Gets Old* (Downers Grove: InterVarsity Press, 1992), 17.

48. Peters, *Cosmic Self*, 188; Benjamin Creme, *The Reappearance of the Christ and the Masters of Wisdom* (Los Angeles: Tara Center, 1980), 71-83.

49. Andrea Grace Diem and James R. Lewis, "Imagining India: The Influence of Hinduism on the New Age Movement," in *Perspectives on the New Age*, 49-52; Karla Poewe-Hexham and Irving Hexham, "The Evidence for Atlantis," *Christian Research Journal* 12, no. 1 (1989): 16-19.

50. Diem and Lewis, "Imagining India," 56.

51. Peters, *Cosmic Self*, 188, 189; Chandler, *Understanding the New Age*, 252.

52. Ferguson, *Aquarian Conspiracy*, 156; Chandler, *Understanding the New Age*, 101, 251. See Ravi Dykema, "The Mythical Monkey Miracle," *Nexus* (Fall 1986); Maureen O'Hara, "Of Myths and Monkeys: A Critical Look at Critical Mass," *Nexus* (Fall 1986).

53. Chandler, *Understanding the New Age*, 252.

54. Fritjof Capra, *The Tao of Physics* rev. ed. (Boston: Shambhala, 1991), 68; Michael Wiebe, "Science and the New Age," *Rivendell Times* September 1, 1987.

55. Chandler, *Understanding the New Age*, 250.

56. Ferguson, *Aquarian Conspiracy*, 169.

57. M. Scott Peck, *The Road Less Traveled* (New York: Touchstone Book, 1978), 263-268.

58. Chandler, *Understanding the New Age*, 241, 248. See also Mark Noll *et al* eds., *Eerdmans Handbook to Christianity in America* (Grand Rapids: Eerdmans, 1983), 473; Bruce Barron, *The Health and Wealth Gospel* (Downers Grove, IL: InterVarsity, 1987); D. R. McConnell, *A Different Gospel* (Peabody, MA: Hendrickson Publishers, 1988).

59. Ferguson, *Aquarian Conspiracy*, 262n.; Chandler, *Understanding the New Age*, 238.

60. Paul C. Reisser, "Holistic Health Update," *Spiritual Counterfeits Project Newsletter* 9, no 4 (1983): 4; Paul C. Reisser, Tere K. Reisser and John Weldon, *New Age Medicine* (Downers Grove, IL: InterVarsity Press, 1987), 26, 37, 44, 52-62, 80-85, 138-141.

61. Reisser, *et al*, *New Age Medicine*, 108-113; Stephen H. Allison and Newton Malony, "Filipino Psychic Surgery: Myth, Magic, or Miracle," *Journal of Religion and Health* 20 (Spring 1981): 57.

62. Chandler, *Understanding the New Age*, 239, 240. See Lawrence E. Jerome, *Astrology Disproved* (Buffalo: Prometheus Books, 1977).

63. Jon Klimo, "The Psychology of Channeling," *New Age Journal* (November/December 1987): 67; Chandler, *Understanding the New Age*,

239, 240; Jon Klimo, *Channeling* (Los Angeles: J. P. Tarcher, 1987), 205-299.

64. Hexham, "The Evangelical Response to the New Age," 163.

65. Alexander, "Compromise and Vulnerability," 8. See Ron Zemke, "What's New in the New Age?" *Training Magazine* September 1987, p. 29.

66. Alvin Toffler, *Powershift* (New York: Bantam, 1990), xix.

67. Lance Morrow, "Old Paradigm, New Paradigm," *Time* January 14, 1991, p. 65.

68. Allen, "The End of the Modern World," 12. See Norman L. Geisler, "The New Age Movement," *Bibliotheca Sacra* 144, no. 573 (1987): 79-82.

69. Tim Stafford, "The Kingdom of the Cult Watchers," *Christianity Today* October 7, 1991, p. 20.

70. Quoted in George W. Cornell, "Paganism Seen Ruin of Western Civilization," *Los Angeles Times* July 11, 1987, pt. 2, p. 6; Chandler, *Understanding the New Age*, 279.

71. Groothuis, *Unmasking the New Age*, 163, 164; Chandler, *Understanding the New Age*, 279-291. See Maxine Negri, "Age-old Problems of the New Age Movement," *Humanist* (March/April 1988): 25; Robert Wuthnow and Charles Y. Glock, "God in the Gut," *Psychology Today* November 1974, pp. 131-136.

72. See Mark A. Noll, Nathan O. Hatch and George M. Marsden, *The Search for Christian America* (Colorado Springs, CO: Helmers and Howard, 1989).

73. Robert J. L. Burrows, "Americans Get Religion in the New Age," *Christianity Today* May 16, 1986, p. 23.

74. Chandler, *Understanding the New Age*, 261; Burrows, "Americans Get Religion in the New Age," 23.

75. For a critique of the decline of doctrine and the growth of subjectivity in the evangelical church see David F. Wells, *No Place for Truth or Whatever Happened to Evangelical Theology?* (Grand Rapids: Eerdmans, 1993); Mark A. Noll, *The Scandal of the Evangelical Mind* (Grand Rapids: Eerdmans, 1994).

SELECTED BIBLIOGRAPHY

This brief bibliography is not a comprehensive list of the sources cited in this study. Instead, here I list books and articles that will be helpful to the individual interested in further reading on the New Age and the historical context in which it developed. For more detailed information regarding the sources utilized, see the appropriate endnotes.

New Age Sources

Adolph, Jonathan. "What is New Age?" *The Guide to New Age Living* (1988): 5-14, 120.

Anderson, William. *Green Men* (London: Harper Collins, 1990).

Bailey, Alice. *The Reappearance of the Christ* (New York: Lucis Publishing Co., 1979).

Benson, Herbert and William Proctor. "Your Maximum Mind," *New Age Journal* (November/December, 1987): 19-23, 75-77.

Capra, Fritjof. *The Tao of Physics* (Boston: Shambhala, 1991).

_____. *The Turning Point* (New York: Bantam Books, 1982).

Capra, Fritjof and Charlene Spretnak. *Green Politics* (New York: Dutton, 1984).

Creme, Benjamin. *Messages from Maitreya the Christ* (London: Tara Center, 1980).

_____. *The Reappearance of the Christ and the Masters of Wisdom* (Los Angeles: Tara Press, 1980).

Dass, Baba Ram. *Be Here and Now* (Christobal, NM: Lama Foundation, 1972).

Dass, Baba Ram and Stephen Levine. *Grist for the Mill* (Castro Valley, CA: Unity Press, 1977).

Davies, Paul. *God and the New Physics* (New York: Simon and Schuster, 1983).

Dossey, Larry. *Space, Time and Medicine* (Boston: Shambhala, 1982).

Ferencz, Benjamin and Ken Keyes, Jr. *Planethood* (Coos Bay, OR:Love Lane Books, 1991).

Ferguson, Marilyn. *The Aquarian Conspiracy* (Los Angeles: J. P. Tarcher, 1980).

Grim, Harold. "Deep Ecology vs. Environmentalism," *Utne Reader* (October/November 1985).

Kaslof, Leslie, ed. *Wholistic Dimensions in Healing* (Garden City, NY: Doubleday, 1978).

Keys, Donald. *Earth at Omega* (Boston: Branden Press, 1985).

Klimo, Jon. *Channeling* (Los Angeles: J. P. Tarcher, 1987).

_____. "The Psychology of Channeling," *New Age Journal* (November/December 1987): 32-40, 62-67.

MacLaine, Shirley. *Dancing in the Light* (New York: Bantam Books, 1985).

_____. *Going Within* (New York: Bantam Books, 1990).

_____. *It's All in the Playing* (New York: Bantam Books, 1987).

_____. *Out on a Limb* (New York: Bantam Books, 1983).

Muller, Robert. *New Genesis* (Garden City, NY: Doubleday, 1982).

Naisbitt, John and Patricia Aburdene. *Megatrends 2000* (New York: Wm. Morrow Co., 1990).

Orr, Leonard and Sondra Ray. *Rebirthing in the New Age* (Berkeley, CA: Celestial Arts, 1983).

Peck, M. Scott. "A New American Revolution," *New Age Journal* (May/June 1987): 33-37, 50-55.

Pelletier, Kenneth R. *Holistic Medicine* (New York: Dell, 1979).

_____. *Mind as Healer, Mind as Slayer* (New York: Delta, 1977).

Russell, Peter. *The Global Brain* (Los Angeles: J. P. Tarcher, 1983).

Satin, Mark. *New Age Politics* (New York: Delta Books, 1978).

_____. *New Options for America* (Fresno, CA: California State University Press, 1991).

Spangler, David. *Emergence: The Rebirth of the Sacred* (New York: Delta, 1984).

_____. *Reflections on the Christ* (Forres, Scotland: Findhorn Publications, 1978).

_____. *Revelation: The Birth of a New Age* (San Francisco: The Rainbow Bridge, 1976).

Sutich, Anthony. "Some Considerations Regarding Transpersonal Psychology," *The Journal of Transpersonal Psychology* no. 1 (1969): 11-20.

Talbot, Michael. *Beyond the Quantum* (New York: Bantam Books, 1985).

_____. *Mysticism and the New Physics* (New York: Bantam Books, 1981).

Toffler, Alvin. *Powershift* (New York: Bantam Books, 1990).

_____. "Powershift," *Newsweek*, October 15, 1990, pp. 86-92.

_____. *The Third Wave* (New York: Bantam Books, 1980).

Toolan, David. *Facing West From California's Shores* (New York: Crossroad, 1987).

Trevelyan, George. *Vision of the Aquarian Age* (Walpole, NH: Stillpoint Publishing, 1984).

Wilber, Ken. *A Sociable God* (Boulder, CO: Shambhala, 1983).

_____. *The Atman Project* (Wheaton, IL: Theosophical Publishing House, 1980).

_____. *Up From Eden* (Garden City, NY: Anchor Press, 1981).

_____, ed. *Holographic Paradigm* (Boulder, CO: Shambhala, 1982).

Wolf, Fred Alan. *Taking the Quantum Leap* (San Francisco: Harper and Row, 1981).

Zukav, Gary. *The Dancing Wu Le Masters* (New York: Morrow, 1979).

_____. *The Seat of the Soul* (New York: Simon and Schuster, 1989).

Other Sources

Adeney, Frances. "The Flowering of the Human Potential Movement," *SCP Journal 5*, no. 1 (Winter 1981-82): 7-18.

Albanese, Catherine. *America: Religions and Religion* 2nd ed. (Belmont, CA: Wadsworth, 1992).

_____. "Religion and the American Experience: A Century After," *Church History 57*, no. 3 (1988): 337-351.

Allan, John. *Shopping for a God* (Leicester, UK: InterVarsity Press, 1986).

Barol, Bill. "The End of the World (Again)," *Newsweek*, August 17, 1987, pp. 70, 71.

Basil, Robert, ed. *Not Necessarily the New Age* (Buffalo: Prometheus, 1988).

Bednarowski, Mary Farrell. *New Religions and the Theological Imagination in America* (Bloomington, IN: Indiana University Press, 1989).

Blow, Richard. "Moronic Convergence," *New Republic*, January 25, 1988, pp. 24-27.

Burrows, Robert J. L. "Americans Get Religion in the New Age," *Christianity Today*, May 16, 1986, pp. 17-23.

_____. "Corporate Management Cautioned on New Age," *Eternity*, February 1988, pp. 33, 34.

_____. "New Age Movement: Self-Deification in a Secular Culture," *SCP Newsletter 10*, no. 5 (1984-85): 1, 4-8.

Chandler, Russell. *Understanding the New Age* (Dallas: Word Publishing, 1988).

Connor, Tod. "Is the Earth Alive?" *Christianity Today*, January 11, 1993, pp. 22-25.

Cooper, John W. "Testing the Spirit of the Age of Aquarius: The New Age Movement," *Calvin Theological Journal 22*, no. 2 (1987): 295-303.

Ellwood, Robert S. and Harry B. Partin. *Religious and Spiritual Groups in Modern America* 2nd ed. (Englewood Cliffs, NJ: Prentice Hall, 1988).

Friedrich, Otto. "New Age Harmonies," *Time*, December 7, 1987, pp. 62-72.

Fuchs, Stephen. "The New Age Movement," *Areopagus* 4, no. 3 (1991): 6-8.

Fuller, Robert C. *Alternative Medicine and American Religious Life* (New York: Oxford University Press, 1989).

Gardner, Martin. *The New Age: Notes of a Fringe Watcher*. (Buffalo: Prometheus Books, 1988).

Groothuis, Douglas. *Confronting the New Age* (Downers Grove, IL: InterVarsity Press, 1988).

_____.*Unmasking the New Age* (Downers Grove, IL: InterVarsity Press, 1986).

Hopkins, Joseph M. "Experts on Nontraditional Religions Try to Pin Down the New Age Movement," *Christianity Today*, May 17, 1985, pp. 68, 69.

Hoyt, Karen, ed. *The New Age Rage* (Old Tappan, NJ: Revell, 1987).

Kyle, Richard. *The Religious Fringe* (Downers Grove, IL: InterVarsity Press, 1993).

_____. "Is There a New Age Coming?" *Christian Leader*, January 17, 1989, pp. 4-8.

Lasch, Christopher. *The Culture of Narcissism* (New York: Norton, 1979).

Lewis, James R. and J. Gordon Melton, eds. *Perspectives on the New Age* (Albany, NY: State University of New York Press, 1992).

Mangalwadi, Vishal. *When the New Age Gets Old* (Downers Grove, IL: InterVarsity Press, 1992).

Melton, Gordon. *Encyclopedic Handbook of Cults in America* (New York: Garland Publishing, 1985).

Melton, Gordon *et al. New Age Almanac* (Detroit: Visible Ink Press, 1991).

Miller, Annette. "Corporate Mind Control," *Newsweek*, May 4, 1987, pp. 38, 39.

Miller, Elliot. *A Crash Course on the New Age Movement* (Grand Rapids: Baker Book House, 1989).

Peters, Ted. *The Cosmic Self* (San Francisco: Harper San Francisco, 1991).

Rabey, Steve. "Karma for Cash: A 'New Age' for Workers?" *Christianity Today*, June 17, 1988, pp. 71, 74.

Reisser, Paul C., Teri K. Reisser and John Weldon. *New Age Medicine* (Downers Grove, IL: InterVarsity Press, 1987).

Rhodes, Ron. *The Counterfeit Christ and the New Age Movement* (Grand Rapids: Baker Book House, 1990).

Streiber, Whitley. "UFO Cults are Flourishing in New Age Circles," *Christian Research Journal* 13, no. 1 (1990): 5,6.

Tucker, Ruth. *Another Gospel* (Grand Rapids: Zondervan, 1989).

Watring, Richard. "New Age Training in Business: Mind Control in Upper Management?" *Eternity*, February 1988, pp. 30-32.

INDEX